GOD IS

From Question to Proof to Embracing the Truth

Joseph H. Casey, S. J.

University Press of America,®Inc.
Lanham • New York • Oxford

Copyright © 1998
University Press of America,® Inc.
4720 Boston Way
Lanham, Maryland 20706

12 Hid's Copse Rd.
Cummor Hill, Oxford OX2 9JJ

All rights reserved
Printed in the United States of America
British Library Cataloging in Publication Information Available

Library of Congress Cataloging-in-Publication Data

Casey, Joseph H.
God is : from question to proof to embracing the truth / Joseph H. Casey.
p. cm.
Includes bibliographical references.
1. God—Proof. I. Title.
BT102.C37 1998 212'.1—dc21 98-27044 CIP

ISBN 0-7618-1207-5 (pbk: alk. ppr.)

☺™ The paper used in this publication meets the minimum
requirements of American National Standard for Information
Sciences—Permanence of Paper for Printed Library Materials,
ANSI Z39.48—1984

Dedicated

with love

and

prayerful hope for a blessed marriage

to

Julie,

My Godchild

CONTENTS

Dedication	iii
Contents	v
Acknowledgements	xi

Part I

Chapter 1. GOD-QUESTIONS TODAY	1
Can an Intelligent Person Reasonably Acknowledge There Is a God?	
Is Knowing and Relating to God a Basic Part of Human Nature?	1
Psychology and These Questions	4
Psychoanalysis	4
Freud	5
Jung	6
Lepp	9
Developmental Psychology	10
How the Issue Emerges for Believers	11
Emergence of the God Question	12
From "Belief In" to "Belief That"	14
Summary and Conclusion	16
Chapter 2. ATHEISM AND SECULAR HUMANISM	19
Atheism: Origin and Today	20
Descartes and Newton	22
The Apologists	23
The Emergence of Proud Atheism	27

Denis Diderot	28
Baron Paul d'Holbach	29
The System of Nature	31
Summary and Conclusion	34

Chapter 3. THE ROAD TO SECULAR HUMANISM — 35
Beginning of Natural Sciences	36
Advancement through Options	38
Further Options Developed	41
Secular Humanism and the Christian Religion	43
The Role of Philosophy	44
Summary and Conclusion	46

Chapter 4. CONTEMPORARY CONSCIOUSNESS — 49
Characteristics of Our Consciousness	50
Further Characteristics	51
Antitheism	53
Mainstream Consciousness	53
Contemporary Consciousness, Theater, Media	58
Summary and Conclusion	60

Chapter 5. FACING THE QUESTION TOGETHER — 63
A Collaborative Effort	64
Is It Possible to Prove God Is?	66
Fideism and Pseudo-Fideism	67
"Feeling" vs. "Knowing"	69
The Place for Agnosticism	70
Dispositive Arguments	72
Natural Sciences	72
Universal Belief	74
Witness of Great Thinkers and Mystics	75
Summary and Conclusion	77

Part II — 79

Chapter 6. MEANING OF "GOD" AND PERSONAL GOD QUESTION — 79
Meaning of "God"	80
Agreement?	82
Definition of God	83
What Is the Reader's Question?	85
The Non-believer's Question	87
The Believer's Question	87

Summary and Conclusion 89

Chapter 7. WHAT KNOWING IS 91
  Knowing As Form of Awareness 91
  Language and Knowing 94
  Knowing and Reasoning 96
  Not Science but Scientism Is the Problem 98
  Logically Unfounded 98
  Destructive of Knowledge and Fulfillment 99
  Limits of Science 100
  Summary and Conclusion 102

Chapter 8. KIND OF REASONING IN THE GOD QUESTION 105
  Intellectual Conversion 106
  Intellectual Conversion and Knowing Awareness 106
  Aids to Intellectual Conversion 107
  Technical Description of Intellectual Conversion 110
  Attaining of the Virtually Unconditioned 112
  Moral Conversion 115
  Do We Need Moral Conversion? 116
  Bias 117
  Religious Conversion 117
  Summary and Conclusion 121

Part III 123
Chapter 9. CLIMBING THE MOUNTAIN: HALF-WAY 124
  A Quasi-Empirical Argument for the Existence of an Uncaused Being 125
  The Four Plateaus 126
  Guide's Map (First Plateau) 127
  Toward the First Plateau 128
  Review of Climb to the First Plateau 134
  Guide's Map (Second Plateau) 135
  Toward the Second Plateau 135
  Review of Climb to the Second Plateau 139

Chapter 10. CLIMBING THE MOUNTAIN: TO THE TOP 141
  Guide's Map (Third Plateau) 141
  Toward the Third Plateau 142
  Review: Propositions Involved in Climbing to the Third Plateau 147

Guide's Map (Fourth Plateau)	148
Toward the Fourth Plateau	149
Review: Key Propositions of the Entire Climb	155
Conclusion	157

Chapter 11. EXPERIENCE OF GOD AND THE FUNCTION OF REASONING   159

Function of Reasoning	159
Religious Experience of Believers	160
Significant Experiences of Nonbelievers	161
Experience of Knowing	163
Phenomenology of Knowing	163
Experience of Love	165
Other-Centered Love and the Unchosen Absolute	166
Love As Chosen Absolute	166
Unchosen Absolute	168
Freedom to Choose the Chosen Absolute	168
Temporary Dimension in the Chosen Absolute	169
Affirmation of the Absolute and Eternal?	170
Starting Point for Nonbelievers	171
Summary and Conclusion	172

Part IV   173
Chapter 12. NATURALISM: FIRST SUPPOSITION   174

Naturalism Defined	174
Naturalism's First Supposition: The Material Universe Exists *Simply Because* It Exists	177
Situating the Problem	178
Two Challenges for the First Supposition	179
Three Solutions	180
First: Metaphysics and Naturalism	180
Second: Lonergan's Philosophy and Naturalism	183
Third: Rejection of Scientism and Naturalism	185
Summary and Conclusion	188

Chapter 13. NATURALISM: SECOND SUPPOSITION   189

The Material Universe Is Self-Sufficient	189
Refutation of Specific Forms of the Supposition	190
First Specific Form: Immense Happening Machine	190
Second Specific Form: Infinite Series of Causes	192
Mediating Causes	193
Confluent Causes	196

Causes Subordinated But Not in Their Causing	197
Summary and Conclusion	198

Chapter 14. SECOND SUPPOSITION:

PRELUDE TO GENERAL ARGUMENT	201
The Material Universe As a Whole Is Self-Sufficient	201
Result of Imagination and Contemporary Consciousness	202
Indirect Refutation	203
The Heart of the Issue	205
The Solution, Briefly	205
Aristotelian-Thomistic Categories	206
Change and Being in Potency	206
Matter - Form	207
Act - Potency	210
Essence - Existence	210
Summary and Conclusion	211

Chapter 15. THE MATERIAL UNIVERSE CANNOT BE

NONCONTINGENT	213
The Material Universe As a Whole	213
Existence Identical with Essence	214
Material Being Cannot Be Identical in Essence and Existence	216
Material Universe Does Not Include Any Noncontingent Factor	217
Summary and Conclusion	219

Chapter 16. QUASI-EMPIRICAL ARGUMENT,

NATURALISM, RATIONALITY NORMS	221
Solution by Appeal to Rationality Norms	221
Rationality Norms	222
Norm 1	224
Norm 2	225
Norm 3	225
Applying Norms 1, 2, and 3	226
Norm 4	229
Applying Norm 4	231
Is There Really an Uncaused Entity?	232
Summary and Conclusion	233

Chapter 17. FINISHING THE JOURNEY

Chapter 17. FINISHING THE JOURNEY	235
Uncaused Entity Is God	235
Religious Conversion: Embracing the Conclusion	236
Personal Experiences Interpreted As Encounters with God	238

A Personal God: Cause of Love, Cause of Oneself	239
God Really Loves	241
Experiencing the Presence of God	243
The Religious Dimension of the Person	244
Religious Response and Human Fulfillment	247
Prayer	248
Revelation	249
Religious Community	250
Believing Community and Human Needs	251
Reply to the Two Initial Questions	252
Summary and Conclusion	253

APPENDIX I
Glossary 255

APPENDIX II
Uncaused Cause and Uncaused Entity 259

Sources and Enrichment 261

ACKNOWLEDGEMENTS

As for the content of this work I want to acknowledge all that my students at Weston College and Boston College helped me to learn. Ronald K. Tacelli, S.J. I am indebted to for supporting my efforts and for offering critical advice and recommendations.

For preparing the text for printing I am deeply indebted to Harvey D. Egan, S.J. for being on call to solve computer problems. Professor Richard Jensen's assistance was invaluable and his generosity truly appreciated. The Help Center at Boston College has also been a constant competent resource for such neeeds. I am especially indebted to Sandi Wang, Computing Consultant, Information Processing Suppport of the Boston College Information Technology Department whose generous, invaluable assistance made it all possible.

For her services beyond the call of duty as the one responsible for preparing and reformatting the text and for her insightful suggestions I shall be forever grateful to Eileen Keane.

I appreciate the material and financial assistance Boston College provided.

PART I

The initial objective is to stimulate genuine readiness to discuss, "Is there a God?" Contrasting questions set the scene. Nonbelievers ask, "Can an intelligent person reasonably acknowledge there is a God?" Believers ask, "Is knowing and relating to God part of human nature?" Although psychoanalysis cannot answer satisfactorily, developmental psychology can provide believers and nonbelievers a common neutral approach to the radical question: "Is there a God?"

Contemporary consciousness, secular humanism, the Enlightenment, the natural sciences, and scientism all must be confronted before facing the radical question. So must the meaning of "proof," fideism, and related challenges. These obstacles cleared away, "dispositive arguments" should convince nonbelievers that "Is there a God?" deserves serious attention.

CHAPTER 1

GOD-QUESTIONS TODAY

CAN AN INTELLIGENT PERSON REASONABLY
ACKNOWLEDGE THERE IS A GOD?
IS KNOWING AND RELATING TO GOD A BASIC PART OF
HUMAN NATURE?

These two questions frame everything in this work.

Since we live in an age of reason the burden of proof falls on believers in answering the first question. On the other hand, believers themselves pose the second question with its implication that human life is incomplete without God.

Just why these two questions frame the God-question can be illustrated by two contemporary plays, Carol Churchill's *Vinegar Tom* (1976) and Marsha Norman's *Traveler in the Dark* (1984 - later revised). Churchill's play highlights the need for reason in religion and suggests why many sophisticated people would ask the first question; Norman's shows the limitations of life based on reason alone and suggests why many believers ask the second.

Set in the 17th century, the first play depicts the irrationality of religious belief in witches, with the injustice and human suffering it causes. Coincidental misfortunes start a witch-hunt; Packer and Goody, professional "finder(s) of witches," examine the accused women. Somehow "the Most High...has so far preserved the male sex from so great a crime." God "has shown me [Packer] a wonderful way of finding out witches, which is finding the place on the body of the witch made insensitive to pain by the devil. So that if you prick that place with a pin no blood comes out and the witch feels nothing at all."

This procedure leads him to declare Joan a witch, "one for hanging." The fact that Joan screams when he finds a spot where no blood comes out - or "hardly a speck" - is explained by, "How she cries, the old liar, pretending it hurts her."

Again Packer searches for the devil's marks, but can say, "Though a mark is a sure sign of a witch's guilt, having no mark is no sign of innocence, for the devil can take marks off." And, of course, it is made clear "why a greater number of witches [is] found in the fragile feminine sex than in men." Because women are more credulous, more impressionable, that's why. They "are feebler in both body and mind." However, "the main reason is she is more carnal than a man," "an imperfect animal, unable to keep faith."

How we needed to rid religion of such ignorance and lack of reason! The Enlightenment helped to liberate us from this kind of superstition.

The second play mentioned, Marsha Norman's *Traveler in the Dark*, shows what happens to a life based on reason alone, where faith and religion have been eliminated. The same Enlightenment also produced deep loss to human fulfillment. We meet Sam, a famous surgeon, who as a boy was deeply wounded by his mother's death and by his preacher-father's teaching. Sam has abandoned his father's religion and has so committed himself to a life of reason that he keeps his son Stephen from belief in God, even from hearing the fairy tales of childhood. Mavis, the man's devoted nurse and dear friend, has died-

-in spite of his surgical efforts to save her. Sam and his wife and son have come to his father's home for Mavis's funeral. He is so upset that he has suddenly made up his mind to divorce his wife and take Stephen away with him. Strikingly, the ability to love, accept love, and believe in God are all intertwined.

Glorification of the intellect is evident when Glory, Sam's wife, expostulates, "I am so tired of your mind. You would've been so much better off without it."

> Sam: I would have been nothing without it! ... I have spent my life straightening out the lies people have told him. No, Stephen, there is no Santa Claus. No, Stephen, when you die, you do not go to heaven...No, Stephen, love is not forever, and God is not good!... God is not in control. We are. There is no heaven, there is no hell. *We* make the progress, and *we* make the mistakes. Not God. God has nothing to do with this, so there is no point in believing in Him. He's just another fairy tale king, as far as I'm concerned. If you want to believe, believe in yourself. In your power, in your mind, in your life. This life. Because that's all there is.

An even sharper rejection of faith is expressed when Everett, Sam's father, tries to explain why he had placed God and church ahead of his wife and son. Everett claims there was a power in him, as there is in Sam, a power to which he felt called. Both he and Sam are called to save lives. This is too much for Sam.

> Sam: We can't save lives...Day after day I've been real proud of myself 'cause I won one more round. Right? Wrong! Death wins. Death always wins."
>
> Everett: Not in my book.
>
> Sam: I don't believe in your book. I don't, in fact, believe in anything. It has taken me my whole life, Dad, but I have finally arrived. I am free of faith. Glory be. Praise the Lord."

Sam goes off to a corner of the garden, torn with the anguish of conflicting thoughts and desires. Stephen provides the occasion for Sam's "conversion" when he wants to crack open a geode to see what's inside. Sam stops him, "[Mother] said that it was better for it to be safe than for you to know what it was, exactly." Then broken himself, he says softly, "I have nothing for you." After a while Stephen asks, "Where did she (Mavis) go, Dad?...Did you see it go, Dad?...Did you cut her open and it got out?"

> Sam, heart broken, his anger now turned to grief and longing, says, "Yes. I cut her open and it got out."

"What was it like?"
"It was...It was forgiveness."

A healing peace reaches deep inside Sam. Sam approaches Glory to apologize; he acknowledges he needs her, loves her. Having allowed love to enter his heart, he asks forgiveness of his father and says, "I love you, Dad."

The play's title is explained in the final exchange.

Stephen: Dad, what holds the stars up there?
Everett: Sam, what was that other verse of "Twinkle, Twinkle"?

"As your bright and tiny spark
Guides the traveler in the dark,
Though I know not what you are
Twinkle, twinkle, little star."

The reviews of this play were not good. The climate of opinion was not receptive to such a direct confrontation of a life without God.

Vinegar Tom alerts us that religion without reason brings terrible injustice and human suffering. And yet, *Traveler in the Dark* suggests the profound religious dimension within every human heart and points out what damage is caused by a life of reason without belief in God. Watching Sam evokes the contrasting questions, "Isn't there a religious dimension to being human? Isn't life humanly deficient without God?"

PSYCHOLOGY AND THESE QUESTIONS

Because psychology is so highly respected now in facing all aspects of human response, let us see how it copes with our questions. Freud and Jung, its pioneers, are identified with modern concerns about religion. We shall then turn to the branch of developmental psychology devoted to religion.

PSYCHOANALYSIS

Both founding fathers of psychoanalysis, Sigmund Freud and Carl Jung, acknowledge the fact of subjective religious experiences. But, do these experiences correspond to any objective reality? Freud says no. His "no" is based not on psychoanalysis, but on acceptance of scientism. According to scientism only empirical science can inform us about what is real. Since, then, the very idea of God is non-scientific, he holds that religious experiences do not put us in touch with anything outside ourselves. How to explain them? "Subjective - within ourselves - wish-fulfillment - sheer illusion"!

Jung, on the other hand, is open to the question. Remaining true to his métier as a psychologist, he insists that all psychology can tell us is that we do have archetypal God-images. The way is left open for philosophy and theology to investigate whether the God-images mediate the living God or not. He assures us, however, that the individual *does not produce* these archetypes. Furthermore, he recognizes how religious experiences benefit human living.

Freud

Freud's famous work, *The Future of an Illusion,* gives us his position. Religious ideas "are not precipitates of experience or end-results of thinking; they are illusion, fulfillments of the oldest, strongest, and most urgent wishes of mankind." As children we all experience a terrifying sense of helplessness which arouses the need for protection. This protection was provided by the father's love. However, we all likewise experience this helplessness throughout our entire lives. This made it necessary to cling to the existence of a father, yes, but a more powerful father.

Thus the benevolent rule of a divine Providence allays our fear of the dangers of life; the establishment of a moral world-order ensures the fulfillment of the demands of justice, which have so often remained unfulfilled in human civilization; and the prolongation of earthly existence in a future life provides the local and temporal framework in which these wish-fulfillments shall take place.
(*The Future of an Illusion,* 30)

That scientism frames Freud's interpretation of religious experience is evident. "...scientific work is the only road which can lead us to a knowledge of reality outside ourselves." This explains how he can write:

> I have said nothing which other and better men have not said before me in a much more complete, forcible and impressive manner...All I have done - and this is the only thing that is new in my exposition - is to add some psychological foundation to the criticism of my great predecessors...Nothing that I have said here against the truth-value of religions needed the support of psycho-analysis; it had been said by others long before analysis came into existence. If the application of the psycho-analytic

method makes it possible to find a new argument against the truths of religion, *tant pis* for religion. (Ibid. 35, 37)

Freud's correspondence with Oskar Pfister, an evangelical Protestant minister and psychoanalyst, confirms how foundational to Freud's interpretation of religious experience his scientism is. Reacting to the publication of *The Future of an Illusion*, Pfister laments:

> I cannot have things out with you properly on the subject of religion because you completely reject philosophy...Your substitute for religion is basically the idea of the eighteenth century Enlightenment in proud modern guise...Thus there remains between us the great difference that I practice analysis within a plan of life which you indulgently regard as servitude to my calling, while I regard this philosophy of life, not only as a powerful aid to treatment...but also as the logical consequence of a philosophy that goes beyond naturalism and positivism. (*Psychoanalysis and Faith,* The Letters of Sigmund Freud and Oskar Pfister, 1963, 114, 116)

Two years later after numerous exchanges on the subject Freud acknowledges that he approaches the issue from a materialistic perspective.

> You are quite right to point out that analysis leads to no new philosophy of life, but it has no need to, for it rests on the general scientific outlook, with which *the religious outlook is incompatible.* For the point of view of the latter it is immaterial whether Christ, Buddha, or Confucius is regarded as the ideal of human conduct...Its essence is the pious illusion of providence and a moral world-order which are in conflict with reason. (Ibid, 129 Italics added)

For Freud, then, religious experiences correspond to nothing in reality and no intelligent person can acknowledge the existence of God. Assuming God does not exist, he believes he explains the genesis of belief in God.

Jung

What is Jung's answer to the question, "Do these religious experiences correspond to any objective reality?" He refuses, as a psychologist, to say "Yes" or "No." Still, he recognizes a religious dimension in people. Open to philosophy and theology, Jung restricts his concern to actual experience. In his understanding, however, the unconscious consists of more than what the individual represses. There is a collective unconscious.

His background and Freud's have many similarities. "I [Jung] grew up in the heyday of scientific materialism, studied natural science and medicine and became a psychiatrist. My education offered me nothing but arguments against religion on the one hand, and on the other the charisma of faith was denied me. I was thrown back on experience alone." ("To Pastor Walter Bernet," 257)

And that experience definitely included experience "of religious realities." These realities he had to accept without concerning himself about their truth. As a psychologist he found no criterion for judging them except how meaningful they were to him and how they "harmonized with man's best utterances." And here is what is significant for Jung: "I don't know whether the archetype is 'true' or not. I only know that it lives and that I have not made it." (Ibid., 258)

Jung experiences the archtype as an "overwhelming force comparable to nothing I know. In view of the terrors of this confrontation I would never dream of addressing this menacing and fascinating opponent familiarly as 'Thou,' though paradoxically it also has this aspect." (Ibid., 260)

Religious experience, in Jung's view, is absolute. It simply cannot be disputed. To the skeptic who insists he has never had such an experience, his only reply is - "I have." This perhaps brings an end to the discussion. But Jung acknowledges such experience as invaluable. "...one who has it possesses a great treasure, a thing that has become for him a source of life, meaning, and beauty, and that has given a new splendour to the world and to mankind. He has *pistis* and peace." (*Psychology and Religion*, 1958, 105)

Granted such subjective satisfaction, is the experience valid, true? No doubt with Freud in mind, Jung goes on to say, "Where is the criterion by which you could say that such a life is not valid, and that such *pistis* is mere illusion? Is there any better truth about the ultimate things than the one that helps you to live?" For this reason he observes with great care the symbols produced by the unconscious. He finds them convincing because they are "overwhelming." Since it is impossible to know what the ultimate things are, "We must therefore take them as we experience them. And if such experience helps us to make life healthier, more beautiful, more complete and more satisfactory to yourself and to those whom you love, you may safely say: 'This was the grace of God.'" (Ibid.)

Although such statements suggest Jung is ready to treat religious experience as evidence of God's existence, he carefully distinguishes experience and interpretation. Working on analysis of dreams Jung reports that he and his colleagues have seen countless cases developing the same kind of symbolism of quaternity, an age-old, even prehistoric, symbol always associated with the idea of a world-creating deity. Modern subjects of analysis tend to misinterpret the symbol they experience. Assumption that the idea of God is an unscientific hypothesis (or, for believers, a religious education which deprecated the idea of a God within as "mystical") prejudices those in whom this "mystical" idea is forced upon the conscious mind by dreams and visions. (Ibid., 57-59)

Immediately Jung insists that these observations in no way prove the existence of God. "They prove only the existence of an archetypal God-image, which to my mind is the most we can assert about God psychologically." (Ibid., 57, 59)

Jung can say this because he does not presume, as a psychologist, to question the authenticity or validity of philosophy and theology. After disclaiming that his observations constitute proof of God's existence, he immediately points out that the archetype in question is a "very important and influential archetype." He then proceeds to suggest that "its relatively frequent occurrence seems to be a noteworthy fact for any *theologia naturalis* (the branch of philosophy dealing with the God-issue). (Ibid.)

There is more. Dealing with the relationship of our psychic life and belief in God, Jung speaks disparagingly of atheism. "The philosophy of the Upanishads corresponds to a psychology that long ago recognized the relativity of the gods. This is not to be confused with a stupid error like atheism." Without mentioning Freud he scores (as psychologism) Freud's view of religion as illusion:

> The materialistic error was probably unavoidable at first. Since the throne of God could not be discovered among the galactic systems, the inference was that God had never existed. The second unavoidable error is psychologism: if God is anything he must be an illusion derived from certain motives - from will to power, for instance, or from repressed sexuality. (Ibid., 82, 85)

For Jung, then, religious experiences may well correspond to reality. It is the province of philosophy or theology to assess the validity of what they suggest. Certainly an intelligent person can acknowledge the existence of God. In fact during the last of a series of interviews on BBC, Jung was asked, "Well, then, do you believe there is a God?" The renowned psychoanalyst looked startled at the question, paused, and replied slowly: "No, I don't *believe* there is a God. I *know* there is."

Jung would, obviously, recognize the need and right of philosophy and theology to probe the question of God's existence. An affirmative conclusion would confirm his sense of the value of religious experiences and identify a religious dimension in human life.

His reply in the BBC interview suggests he personally has caught the common sense insight that all he knows by experience just doesn't make sense if there is no God.

Lepp

If these two giants of psychoanalysis differ so radically in their interpretation of religious experience, it seems clear that psychoanalysis is incapable of going beyond subjective experiences. This conclusion is confirmed by Ignace Lepp's study of atheism from a psychoanalytic perspective. Lepp, a Catholic priest and psychiatrist, carries marks of rare credibility. Until he was twenty-seven years old he was one of those people who had "always been atheists." His parents were free-thinkers and his environment was almost completely devoid of religious concern, not to mention religious practice. He joined the Communist party at fifteen, an experience resembling religious conversion. Indeed for ten years Communism played a role very similar to the role religion plays in the lives of believers. The Stalinist regime alienated Lepp and, like a number of other intellectuals, he left the party. A year passed in which he anguished much like a disillusioned believer. Gradually genuine questions about the meaning of life disposed him to encounter the Christian message. (Ignace Lepp, *Atheism in Our Time*, Chapter I.)

Reflecting on his own experiences, he reports he cannot discern a neurotic element either in his unbelief or in the faith that succeeded it. In his view the majority of atheists he has known are no more neurotic than are most believers. In fact he has found that a person may be neurotic without his or her unbelief or faith having originated from neurosis. On the other hand he has dealt with many atheists whose unbelief was closely connected with the psychic conflicts of the individual. He also is convinced that the faith of some believers bears undeniable signs of neurosis. (Ibid., p. 35.)

His practice as a psychiatrist coupled with his study of diverse world-views equips him to report on atheists of multiple guises. Intellectual conviction and commitment to social reform may ground unbelief. But he finds unconscious motivations in some who embraced communism, socialism, and the philosophy of rationalism or existentialism - all of which involved atheism. In other words, psychoanalysis cannot answer our questions.

Theater attempts to present living people confronting typical human problems; it holds a mirror up to a segment of life and reflects it. Two plays raised our two questions. Psychoanalysis is simply unequipped to answer them. Jung acknowledges this; he leaves it to philosophy and theology to verify whether there is a God whom our God-images mediate. Freud pontificates that religion is mere illusion; however, he grounds his denial of God's existence not on psychoanalysis but on his philosophy of scientism. Lepp sides with Jung, finding that most atheists, like most believers, base their positions about God's existence on motivations other than psychic conflicts.

What seems to be at issue is how to know what is real. The present book aims to demonstrate that knowing what is real is not limited to the sciences, that philosophy is a valid source of knowledge which can indeed lead one to acknowledge that it is reasonable to interpret certain experiences as encountering God. If it succeeds, then Jung is right in identifying a religious dimension of the human person.

DEVELOPMENTAL PSYCHOLOGY

It seems obvious that the only way to investigate our two contrasting questions is to push on to the more fundamental question, "Is there a God?" If the validity of the question about God's existence can be established, investigation will reveal one of two things: (1) that there is no God and consequently the answer to the first question is, "No intelligent person can acknowledge there is a God, for reason cannot justify such an affirmation." Further, it follows that there is no religious dimension to being human. Only a life coming to grips with reality, that this world is all there is, can be truly human. Or, (2) investigation of the question about God's existence may reveal that there are convincing grounds for affirming God's existence and that the answer to our second question is, "It is reasonable to claim there is a religious dimension to being human, so it is natural to know God. Life without God is humanly deficient."

Is there a neutral starting point for believers and nonbelievers to discuss this fundamental question? Developmental psychology does provide such an acceptable approach for posing a question about God's existence.

We begin with how the question about God's existence arises for believers.

How the Issue Emerges for Believers

Our question, "Can an intelligent man or woman acknowledge there is a God?" is also addressed to people who already believe. First of all, there are believers who would love to have cogent, presentable reasons for belief. Firmly satisfied in their relationship with God, they feel helpless trying to communicate their faith to others, - especially when their own children are the "others."

Loss of a loved parent or friend, or serious illness, their own or a loved one's, may lead them to question this God who is professed to be so loving. Falling in love with a nonbeliever and perhaps meeting obstacles to marriage from their institutional religion may evoke re-examination of beliefs. A challenging study in various fields may contradict religious beliefs, including the very existence of God.

Researchers have identified the point at which the question of God's existence tends to emerge in the ordinary believer's religious development. There seems to be a very natural place in faith development where our question has a vital role. Fowler's third stage of faith development, "Synthetic-Conventional Faith," is found as early as the age of eleven, but for many adults it is a permanent place of equilibrium. At this stage interpersonal relationships are all important. Values and beliefs are deeply felt but tacitly held. An implicit, unarticulated ideology undergirds the value and belief system. It is a conformist stage in which people are very dependent on the community's shared commitments and beliefs.

Various factors may contribute to movement away from this third state: resentment at the "tyranny of the they," conflict or contradiction among authority sources. Transition from the stage of Synthetic-Conventional Faith to stage four, "Individuative-Reflective Faith" typically occurs in the 20's. Frequently the experience of "leaving home" pushes one to examine carefully the implicit ideology of the third stage. The person may find herself in a totally different environment in which her faith, formerly shared by and supported by her religious community, is not accepted or even respected. Under such challenge she is forced to break out of "they" living and take personal responsibility for what she believes. She reflects on the beliefs and myths and symbols she had been living by and insists on translating all into conceptual meanings. A young adult, she moves into the fourth stage, "Individuative-Reflective Faith." For the first time she clarifies precisely what is meant by "God" (and other pertinent religious terms like incarnation, salvation, grace) and insists on personal insight and grounds for commitment of faith. People at this stage welcome a reasoned justification for belief in God.

Fowler compares transition to this stage in individual lives with what intellectual elites in Europe and North America struggled with during the Enlightenment. Religion was under siege in this era. Deism proposed to replace Christian theism, followed by the explicit atheism of Diderot and d'Holbach. Fowler implies that the individual passing into this fourth stage grapples with these fundamental issues. Symbols and myths must be examined, fundamental beliefs tested and personally rejected or accepted with reflective refinements. A reasoned treatment of the issue of God's existence would provide a valuable service to a person at this stage.

This is not to suggest that reason *replace* faith. Rather it is presumed that a person at this stage desires to understand what she means by "God." Just what grounds does she actually have for affirming this God exists, - reasoned arguments, or faith, or both? Such a determination to take personal responsibility for what she believes would stimulate examination of all her beliefs - which depend on which.

Fowler's identification of a particular stage of faith development seems too formalistic. Many people move into personal assessment and assimilation with much less traumatic experience than he has intimated. Perhaps solid, wise religious education provides the stimulus and the process of personal assimilation of one's beliefs. On the other hand, a challenge about God's existence or about one's religious community may emerge at any and every period of one's spiritual history.

Granted even believers may experience the emergence of a serious question about God's existence, consider how developmental psychology provides a neutral starting point for believers and nonbelievers.

Emergence of the God-Question

The distinction between "belief in" and "belief that" is part of everyone's experience. Organizers of the march in Selma appealed to our "belief in" equal rights to rally support for the demonstration. Indian demonstrators "believed in" Mahatma Ghandi, followed him devotedly. The will and emotions get involved in such a response.

"Belief that" is intellectual, possibly evoking further emotional and volitional response. Today most people "believe that" the earth revolves around the sun. Before Copernicus, Galileo, and Newton, people "believed that" the sun circled the earth. Developmental psychology of religion shows how to start with subjective experiences of "believing in," of "setting one's heart on." It proceeds to distinguish ways of harmonizing subjective desires, eventually opening up the question of "belief that" God exists or does not exist.

We are interested here in determining what is the ultimate concern, what actually is the center of value and power. We do not respond to this object of desire just because we "ought" to but because desire is evoked.

In this context we can say that everyone "believes in" something. People "believe in" what they "set their hearts on." Using terminology from comparative religion, developmental psychologists divide people into polytheists, henotheists, and monotheists.

This is, of course, an adapted summary of what is meant in comparative religion. There, *polytheists* (*poly*-many+*theos*-god) are those who believe in many gods; *henotheists* (*hen*-one+*theos*-god) are those who worship one god without denying the existence of other gods (for example, the deity of an individual family or tribe); *monotheists* (*mono*-single, alone+*theos*-god) are those who believe in one God, the transcendent creator, ruler, and sustainer according to Jewish, Christian, and Islamic traditions.

Developmental psychologists of religion are primarily concerned about the psychological "form" of faith, not so much about the content of faith. They begin with what all human beings share, whether they think there is a God or not. There is a subjective "believing in" experienced by believers and atheists.

However, if we focus on *what* people do "believe in" or what they "set their hearts on" we can use the above threefold division in a completely neutral sense in order to describe the different ways of integrating subjective desires. Polytheists, then, have many "gods"; they scatter themselves, choosing pleasure and satisfaction in all directions. The "form" of their faith is found with a content of many objects of "ultimate" concern. The young pour themselves out pursuing excitement and fun in whatever is currently said to be exciting and pleasurable. Older polytheists, having suffered disillusionment in such pursuits, are "laid back" and "cool." They avoid commitment, but still try to satisfy every desire, relate with whomever they wish. As Kierkegaard observes, for them boredom is life's essential problem.

Henotheists, on the other hand, nurture their trust in and loyalty to *one* "god". That god may be success, power, or prestige in various fields of endeavor. In some cases, dread of death spurs them to dedicate their energy to projects of self-vindication, attempting to guarantee for themselves some sort of immortality. Instead of making personal success in business, sports, or art their "god," some henotheists go out of themselves and commit themselves totally to country, church, university, political party, liberation of minorities, or other noble objectives. They "set their hearts on," lose themselves in, such transcendingly important though finite causes.

In using the term "monotheism," psychologists call attention to the fact that the one being, the transcendent center of value and power, source of all things, has been symbolized in both theistic and nontheistic ways in major religious traditions. So in developmental psychology of religion, monotheism differs from the more noble objectives of henotheists in offering for supreme trust and loyalty a transcendent center of value and power that is neither an extension of ego nor a finite cause or institution. Monotheism in this sense implies loyalty to the principle of being and to the source and center of all value and power.

With "monotheistic" integration the question of God arises. In a life with monotheistic integration one is implicitly dealing with a world-view. A world-view involves "believing that" something is true - that one's world-view is true and makes sense of the whole of life. "To set one's heart" in a monotheistic integration eventually gives rise to the question whether "the transcendent center of value and power, source of all things" actually exists. Just what or who this center is, is the question about God.

Thus, focus on "belief in," (which involves an act of will, trust, commitment) becomes at some point a focus on "belief that" (which involves an act of intellect, understanding, assent to truth).

From "Belief in" to "Belief That"

How do people come to ask, "Is there a God?" Consider the three classes of "believers in." Polytheists, in the sense used here, inevitably find life empty and absurd. Pursuing different objects of desire makes sense until the appeal of these objects fades, one after another, because of sickness, financial disaster, or because of a general sense of futility. Then polytheists are at a crossroads. As long as they are healthy and prosperous, ignoring questions about life's meaning allows people to chase after desires; illusion covers the emptiness. But at the crossroads they must face up to reality.

It is clear how the question of God's existence can emerge when a polytheist arrives at the crossroads mentioned above. She cannot, I submit, long remain a polytheist without moving into despair or empty, hectic living - thereby only postponing the despair. Either she confronts the fundamental question of God's existence or avoids the question by making some serious commitments, moving into henotheism.

Perhaps she commits herself to some worthy cause - to country, university, political party, or she embraces the world-view and lifestyle of some "ism" like Communism. This latter may suffice. Implicitly though, she is affirming or denying God's existence. Whether it is actually addressed or not, God's being is logically presupposed here. And we shall see what is required for that presupposition to be consciously challenged.

Of course, she may accept as fact that life has no overarching meaning and revert to polytheism, living a life more hectic than before.

Most people, however, are not polytheists and most just assume there is some overarching meaning. A large proportion of them simply accept the world-view of the community they immediately identify with. They are like the expert who knew everything about butterflies. When asked what he thought was needed for a meaningful human life, he replied he had no time for such questions!

Many people pursuing an absorbing desire have no sensed need to ask about the meaning of life or God's existence. An artist like Sam Shepard, distinguished playwright, director, stage and movie actor, could find life so engrossing that the question of ultimate meaning might not arise. A businessman like Donald Trump could devote all his energy and time planning financial ventures so that he too feels no need to ask, "Is there a God?" An athlete like Monica Seles could practice such long hours, compete in so many tennis tournaments, study her own game and that of likely opponents so intently, - that she is simply too busy to ask about the meaning of life.

Normally we acquire our beliefs and values through community lifestyles, not through theoretical thinking. Henotheists like the above can organize their lives around their finite "god" assuming there is some overarching meaning to the whole of life and reality. This they may assume even while implicitly denying God's existence. What would prompt such henotheists to entertain a question about the meaning of life or God's existence? Only a challenge to their lifestyle - some unhappiness, conflict of lifestyles, or explicit contradiction of the intellectual presuppositions of their lifestyle.

Unhappiness might come by way of sickness or betrayal or lack of appreciation for all they contribute to a chosen institution or cause. Falling in love with someone who does not share their henotheistic commitment, especially with a devout Christian, might force examination of one's lifestyle. Hearing a lecture or a serious conversation in which atheism or secular humanism is intelligently rejected might provoke reflection on the God-issue.

The henotheist will need some such challenge if he is to entertain our questions. Unless challenged, he will not be interested in our investigation. Still, this book will be around when his lifestyle does come into question.

Monotheists in the present context will have to be very religious people, God being the one they "set their hearts on," or they must be people utterly dedicated to an ideal like Communism or ecology, human or general. Something similar to the challenge experienced by henotheists must occur for the satisfied monotheist to address the question of the existence of their "transcendent center of value and power, the source of all things."

"What do you believe in?" thus opens into the God-issue: "Do you believe that there is a God?" As noted above, inevitably just what or who this center is, involves the question about God. Later we shall recognize this involvement when, having established the logical necessity of affirming the existence of a necessary being, we ask, "Can the material universe as a whole be this necessary being?"

Developmental psychology of religion explains how the question of God's existence can naturally emerge for all human beings, whether they face it or avoid it. By starting with the subjective experiences of "believing in" some "god" (object of ultimate concern), under certain circumstances the issue of "belief that" God exists or does not exist naturally arises. In this way believers and nonbelievers can relate to the same experiences and to the God-question.

Beyond what developmental psychology has contributed, nonbelievers can be led to investigate whether it is reasonable to take the question about God's existence seriously. For them certain dispositive arguments can be proposed which challenge the intellectual presupposition of their lifestyle.

In this way we, believers and nonbelievers alike, can pursue the radical question, "Does God exist?" A person's answer to this will root her replies to: "Can an intelligent person acknowledge there is a God?" and "Is there a religious dimension to being human so that it is natural to know God?"

SUMMARY AND CONCLUSION

This opening chapter aims at awakening an interest in two contrasting questions: 1) Can an intelligent man or woman reasonably acknowledge there is a God?   2) Is there a religious dimension to being human - so that it is part of being human to know and relate to God? The only way to answer those questions is to face the radical and implied question, "Does God exist?" For, if God exists, it *is* reasonably intelligent to acknowledge there is a God and it is highly likely that there is a religious dimension to being human.

Evidently psychoanalysis is unable to answer our questions. Critical to the investigation is the question, "Is science the *only* way to know what is real?" We confront this challenge head-on repeatedly.

Since genuine questioning is what leads to deeper thinking, the modern adult is urged to look within:

"What do you believe in?"

"What do you set your heart on?"

"Do you recognize how reflection on these questions inevitably leads to questions about the meaning of life?"

Crucial to all overarching meanings, all world-views, is the affirmation or denial of God's existence.

The issue, however, has been significantly and subtly affected by contemporary mainstream consciousness. All of us are affected by this mainstream consciousness in which people increasingly live as though there were no God. Situations and events are interpreted, decisions are made without any serious consideration of God. As we look at this contemporary consciousness in the next chapter it will become clear why the prime question is, "Can an intelligent person reasonably acknowledge there is a God?"

CHAPTER 2

ATHEISM AND SECULAR HUMANISM

Being a believer today is socially and intellectually respectable. So what need is there to ask, "Can an intelligent man or woman acknowledge there is a God?" Any number of distinguished intellectuals, scientists, scholars, philosophers, and theologians profess belief in God.
Traveler in the Dark raised our second question: "Is there a religious dimension to being human, so that knowing God is part of being human?" How can the answer be "Yes" when there are so many intelligent professed atheists - who, in fact, are very concerned about their fellow human beings?
Convinced nonbelievers tend to change the first question to "*How can* any intelligent man or woman acknowledge there is a God?"
Some nonbelievers benignly respect belief in God but they explain belief away as the product of imagination or emotional need. Others, however, judge it hurtful to society when intelligent people fail to recognize how harmful belief in God is. Religion has indeed spawned harmful aberrations. Surely we do not want a religion which hunts down and kills witches as*Vinegar Tom* depicts. Superstition is out, but are all religions sheer superstition?
Believers, on the other hand, link much of human suffering to cultures based on atheism. And they find themselves challenged to

explain how atheism has gained such intellectual respectability. Much of this book aims precisely at meeting that challenge.

As we saw in Chapter 1, the only way to probe our two questions is to clear up the implied prior question, "Is there a God?" Only then does it make sense to face the challenge *how* intelligent people can hold the opposite position.

What makes the question, "Is there a God?" distinctive today is that atheism in its contemporary form - secular humanism - undergirds today's mainstream consciousness.

ATHEISM: ORIGIN AND TODAY

Profound changes are in process everywhere. Communism in Eastern Europe has been cast off and struggles are ensuing in all areas - political, economic, and religious. The Soviet Union itself is undergoing similar transformations. China shocked the world by the violence used in suppressing demands for liberty. In our own country the abortion conflict has heated up. Gay and lesbian organizations strive to change laws and the privileged status of the traditional family. Long-accepted public manifestations of Christian faith, like the Christmas creche, financed by state or city, wreaths in public schools, and reference to God at graduation invocations have all been attacked as violations of Constitutional rights of nonbelievers.

These changes are surface symptoms, repercussions of deep-seated conflicts about human nature itself, conflicts that have been building for years. In a sense we in the West are still grappling, perhaps more subtly, with the same centuries-old issue of faith and reason. The radical challenge, how to accommodate the liberating force of reason within Christian faith, must still be faced. In many parts of the world other than the West, people are thrilling to the liberating force of Christianity or experiencing revitalization of other religions even while Western science and industry are being introduced into their worlds. Not too far down the road, however, these people will inevitably face the conflict that now challenges us.

"Man come of age," Bonhoeffer's phrase and another by Swinburne, perhaps blasphemously intended at the time, "Glory to man in the highest, for man is the master of things" - both expressions capture valuable truth that stuns people of faith, obedient servants of God. Indeed, historically, some people embracing the truth in these expressions broke away from Christianity.

Both sides of the faith-reason issue have been affected by successive conflicts. Christians have come to perceive what was true and good in the demands for unshackled thinking and in the claim of human responsibility for this world. On the other hand, the optimism generated by successful rebellion against Church and authority has been extinguished by two world wars, Auschwitz, and Hiroshima, by the horrors of Soviet Communism, drug cartels, street killings, international economic imbalances, crises, and world-wide unemployment. People are aware that they need something else, something more.

Let me start back with the Enlightenment. Until that time the term "atheist" was a term of opprobrium. When the philosopher David Hume was dining with Baron d'Holbach in Paris around 1770, he remarked to his host that he did not believe in atheists, that he had never seen one. The Baron said to him, "Count how many we are here. We are eighteen...It isn't too bad a showing to be able to point out to you fifteen [atheists] at once; the three others haven't made up their minds." (*At the Origins of Modern Atheism*, M. Buckley, p. 256) D'Holbach may have exaggerated, but about this time "atheist" became a badge of honor - asserted, argued, and claimed for oneself.

For the first time learned men called themselves atheists; this commitment of a few became increasingly the mark of an elite. By the beginning of our 20th century, perhaps a few hundred thousand could be numbered. Now millions consider themselves atheists.

From its start in Paris about 200 years ago, the growth is startling. Under atheists, defined as those professing atheism, skepticism, impiety, disbelief, irreligion, Marxist-Leninist Communism, militant nonbelievers, anti-religious humanists, we find listed: (in 1970) 165,288,500; (in 1980) 195,119,400; (in 1985) 210,643,500.

If we combine those who profess no religion with those who profess unbelief or agnostic, freethinking, non-religious humanism, and the like, it is claimed they numbered (in 1970) 543,065,300; (in 1980) 715,901,400; (in 1985) 805,748,900.

It is projected that by the year 2000 atheists will be 4.2% (262,447,500) of the world population and the non-religious 17.1% (1,071,888,370). (Ibid., 375)

We are talking about a religious phenomenon never witnessed before. Protestant and Catholic thinkers see this as "the age of atheism." And the cultural form this atheism takes is secular humanism.

Seeing how this secular humanism emerged will help us understand contemporary consciousness and its influence on our question, "Is there a God?" Strangely, the direction Christian apologetics took in the modern era led to deism and atheism - the intellectual presupposition of secular humanism.

At the beginning of the 17th Century there was a sense that atheists were everywhere, secretly undermining religion and European culture. One apologist made the outlandish charge that in Paris alone there were 50,000 atheists. Why then was it difficult to identify them? Because law throughout Europe made profession of atheism a crime, actually the term "atheist" was a form of opprobrium hurled at enemies, real or imagined.

What is striking about the apologetic response to atheism is that it was not the scientific revolution in process which prompted concern. As a matter of fact, the outstanding scientists considered their work guaranteed the foundations of religion. And the theologians who engaged in apologetics had recourse to current scientific discoveries. Instead, concern about atheism was grounded on the religious divisions and their conflicts. Once the true religion was abandoned, once authority was rejected, the expected conclusion was atheism.

DESCARTES AND NEWTON

The two intellectual giants of the age were Descartes (1596-1650) and Newton (1642-1727). Descartes, the father of modern philosophy, emerged in an era of skepticism that was articulated by Montaigne who found human reason unable to attain any certain knowledge. Hence, one must rely on faith. Descartes faced the challenge head on, starting with universal doubt, and proceeding to establish the foundational, inescapable certitude of self-existence. [For even amid universal doubt I must think in order to doubt, and if I am thinking, I must be.] He then proceeds to reason metaphysically to the existence of God, who in turn warrants the validity of knowledge of an external world. The world is material, subject to mathematics and the science of mechanics. It is a godless world, the existence of which God guarantees. There is no need to advert to God to understand this material universe. Thus the idea of autonomy of mechanics entered our world of thought.

Surely Isaac Newton belongs near the top of any list of greatest geniuses in history. And he might be identified as the incarnation of scientist-perceived-as-philosopher. Descartes set out to build a metaphysics which would verify the existence of self, God, and the world; a metaphysics grounding a physics. Newton approached his problems by collapsing the distinction between metaphysics and physics into a universal mechanics. In the development of this universal mechanics Newton inquired into the existence of God from the evidence found in the appearance of things.

Scientist that he was, Newton began not with others' doubts but with the scientific achievements of others, especially Copernicus, Galileo, Kepler and Brahe. He brilliantly systematized their work and produced a synthesis of terrestrial and celestial motion, explaining the world as a mechanical system. This raised the question about "the Author of the System."

Five years after the first publication of his *Principia* he wrote, "When I wrote my treatise about our Systeme, I had an eye upon such Principles as might work with considering men for the beliefs of a Deity; and nothing can rejoice me more than to find it used for that purpose." (Cited in M. Buckley, "Newtonian Settlement and the Origins of Atheism," *Philosophy, Physics, and Theology*, 86)

Thus philosophy got a new start in this 17th century and science achieved a coherent, defensible conception of nature as a whole which supplanted Aristotelian thought. Many factors have contributed to the demise of Christianity's central role in Western civilization but among the intellectual factors none can compare in importance with the impact of the natural sciences. In spite of their intentions Descartes and Newton significantly contributed to that impact, even though they thought they had grounded the very foundation of Christian belief. Neither of these giants was primarily an apologist. Their metier was far different. But others did directly address the feared atheism and utilized their work. The earliest apologist, Lessius (1554-1623), appears on the scene before Descartes and, it may be said, set the framework for apologetics for centuries. He was a theologian and although what really was at stake was a rejection of Christ, Christianity, and the Church, he treated putative atheism as a philosophical problem. Not long after, Mersenne (1588-1648) followed the same route.

THE APOLOGISTS

In the Middle Ages, thinkers were primarily theologians. They were intellectuals seeking understanding of their faith. "Fides quaerens intellectum" (Faith seeking understanding) was the motto. But the Renaissance had discovered the riches of Greek thought, including that of Plato and Aristotle, the greatest ancient philosophers. Theoretical thinking, introduced by the Greeks, had entered Western civilization as "philosophy" (love of wisdom). In undifferentiated form it included mathematics, astronomy, biology, physics, as well as what we now call philosophy of nature and metaphysics. Christian theologians incorporated Greek thought within their search for understanding. During the Renaissance thinkers were recognizing the specific fields of philosophy as distinct from theology. Philosophy restricts itself to what reason can achieve on its own. Theology starts with faith and revelation. Mathematics and certain areas of Aristotelian sciences were being recognized as proper fields of intellectual efforts.

Therefore, it is not surprising that Lessius and Mersenne attacked the problem of atheism as a problem for philosophy. Like the theologians of the Middle Ages they lived and thought as Christians did. Within his *Summa* of theology St. Thomas, in the thirteenth century, for example, dealt with God's existence as an issue for reason to judge. But philosophy had now become differentiated as a distinct field of thought. These apologists were doing what Thomas did, except that the reasoning process was acknowledged to be the distinct science of philosophy. In principle, moreover, the approach is correct and appropriate. At a point in history when use of reason was being esteemed in the pursuit of science, to assume reason was incapable of establishing God's existence would be to acknowledge that the reasonable person ought to be an atheist. Besides, offering divine Revelation to people who deny God's existence would hardly dispose them to accept messages - from a non-existent God.

But these apologists made two mistakes. They assumed that theoretical thinking could satisfy a person who has a problem about God's existence. Someone says there is no God. The believer gets him to accept an abstract definition of God, - for example, a necessary being, cause of all things in the universe. He lays out a cogent, reasoned argument to establish that such a being exists.

And the person with whom he is discussing looks amazed. "I asked, 'Is there a God?' This cerebral exercise concluding to some abstract necessary being leaves me utterly cold." Anyone seriously concerned with the question of God is asking whether he/she can *know* God. One comes to *know* God as one knows any person - by meeting, by experiencing, that person. Reasoning can lead one only to *know about* a person. I *know* my friend. I *know about* Newton or living persons I've never met.

These 17th century theologians failed to incorporate lived experience - either religious experience or other experiences which can be unfolded to suggest an encounter with something (someone) transcendent. The reasoning process is meaningful only insofar as it relates to the lived experience, justifying the reasonableness of interpreting the initial experience as an experience of God. Thus, proof of God's existence must allow a person to realize he or she has already been knowing, experiencing God.

The second mistake in the apologetic program was crucial. It was in ignoring the difference between philosophy and the natural sciences.

Lessius and Mersenne, for example, worked within a philosophy of nature, incorporating many of the recent findings of the sciences - especially in terms of the argument from finality. In Lessius, natural theology is no longer part of metaphysics. Instead it appeals to common sense or philosophic maxims related to astronomy, comparative religion, mechanics, and biology.

The outstanding scientists themselves considered that their work powerfully justified religion. Robert Boyle (1627-91), chemist, physicist, and philosopher, insisted that science and religion focused on a single object, the existence and actions of God. Newton himself scatters insights of natural theology throughout his writings and argues to the need for God to give rise to the system of the world.

Newton in his universal mechanics, as developed in *Principia* and in *Opticks*, reaches the logical need of an intelligent, outside force to account for the origin of the system and its particular correlative parts. This is a providential God, not a deistic God. But his reflections on natural theology had been inserted as random insights.

Samuel Clarke, perhaps the greatest apologist of the era, tried to use Newton to build a cogent natural theology. A brilliant young man, he published a translation of a Cartesian physics textbook with annotations based on Newton. His annotations evolved through various editions into a systematic refutation of the textbook!

Ordained an Anglican priest, Clarke became an earnest student of theology. In 1712, after a series of theological publications, came a bombshell: an attack on the Athanasian Creed, which creed professes the coequality of Father, Son, and Holy Spirit. For Clarke, only the Father is self-existent and absolute; the Son and Spirit therefore are subordinate, not equal. Actually he was aligning himself with what Newton held privately about the Christian Trinitarian belief, and what an older theologian, William Whiston, who had befriended Clarke, publicly held. A serious polemic broke out as a result. Meanwhile Clarke turned his attention to the fundamental foe, atheism, having been invited to give the Boyle lectures for 1704, lectures that Boyle's will established "to prove the truth of the Christian religion against infidels, without descending to any controversies among Christians." (Buckley, *Origins of Modern Atheism,* p. 170)

Based on the universal mechanics of Newton, Clarke's systematic natural theology focused on the distinction between the apparent and the real. He followed the method of analysis and synthesis Newton employed as closely as the nature of this material allowed. The late scholastic method of "theses" he adapted in order to lay out his position in a series of twelve propositions.

His first seven propositions establish the necessary being of one God. He seems to think he is following Newton, translating inertial forces into intrinsic causes and impressed forces into extrinsic causes. The argument he constructs is effective if interpreted as presenting insight into being and the causing of being. After establishing the existence of the self-existent being (which process of reasoning, assuming it is on the level of being, is valid) he turns to conjoin divine existence with personal attributes in order to get to the God of providence, the foundation of all religion.

In the development of this further point he is deeply dependent on Newton's universal mechanics, appealing to "the system of the world" and the physical discoveries of Newton's system. His reasoning casts doubt on whether he really was on the metaphysical level of being in the first seven propositions. At this point, like Newton, he seems to be proposing a "God of the gaps" and philosophy has become physics.

This dependence on philosophy-turned-physics becomes even clearer in Nicolas Sylvain Bergier's efforts to answer the serious, explicitly atheistic attacks on religion. The General Assembly of the Clergy of France in 1770 attempted to organize all the forces of the establishment - the king as well as the bishops and the doctors at the Sorbonne University - to alert the people to the danger. The government, startled by the state of affairs reported, depicting religious collapse in France, ordered seven books to be publicly torn to pieces and burned. The Assembly, well aware that censorship and zealous bonfires would not suffice, appointed Bergier to address the principal adversary, D'Holbach and his *Systeme de la Nature ou des Lois du Monde Physique et du Monde Moral*. It was, of course, not known at this time of the burning that d'Holbach was the author. Esteemed for earlier publications attacking deism, Bergier set about confronting the atheism of d'Holbach. His two-volume work, published in 1771, has been praised as "one of the best pieces of critical writing of the century." During the Catholic revival in the nineteenth century some looked on him as the greatest apologist ever.

What is of great significance for our purposes was the insistence that the battle against atheism be fought on the evidence of physics. To catch Bergier's perspective one needs only to read, "As soon as it is evidently proven that movement is not essential to matter, that the latter is purely passive by nature and without any activity, we are forced to believe that there is in the universe a substance of a different nature, an active being to which the movement must be attributed as it is to the first cause, a Motor that is not itself matter." (Buckley, *op. cit.* p. 254) Not religion, not theology, but philosophy and philosophy-turned-physics confronts atheism. Is there a God? The answer depends on a theory of motion and matter. The study of physics was extolled as the way to cure superstition and atheism. Defenders of religion wagered that they could do physics better than atheists could.

EMERGENCE OF PROUD ATHEISM

Notwithstanding the sincerity and competence of the apologists, the two mistakes made in defense of religion brought about both deism and atheism.

Philosophy had remained a very respectable science - in name! It took well over a century for people to realize that starting with Galileo a radically new way of thinking had emerged. Philosophy was soon limited to natural philosophy - which became physics. Metaphysics was the first branch of philosophy to be discarded. Not only was metaphysical thinking abandoned, but Hume (1711-76) came along, building on Locke and Berkley, to justify and propose empiricism which holds that our only knowledge is that attained by the senses. "Awakened from his dogmatic slumber" by Hume, Kant (1724-1804) argued systematically that the very structure of human intelligence made attainment of the real impossible. All our speculative knowledge can attain is appearance. We are unable to know speculatively that we are free and immortal or that there is a God. For many intellectuals the death knell for metaphysics had been sounded.

Just in passing it should be noted that Kant, in his second Critique, argued for the existence of God, freedom of the will, and personal immortality as necessary postulates.

Metaphysics done away with, the philosophy which alone seemed capable of disarming atheists came to be the "experimental physics" of Newton and other scientists. The God arrived at by these later followers of Newton during the Enlightenment was a deistic God, creator of the world but thereafter uninvolved. Only deism could oppose atheism.

But something strange happened along the way. The "gaps" in scientific knowledge which seemed to need a God were closed by scientific explanations. The designs in nature which seemed to demand an intelligent designer were explained as trial and errors of matter in motion out of which the surviving kinds of beings arose. And

The proposal of a naturalistic world-view and life-style could never have been accepted without the bitter contemporary climate of opinion. Clandestine writings angrily attacked Christianity as exploitation and hoax. Scandals both hushed and blatant abounded: one man's body was broken before he was publicly strangled, another was tortured and beheaded for blasphemy. No wonder there was rising horror about religion and the cruelty and blindness it spread. People saw the tyranny on all sides - tyranny of the Church, of the nation-state, by clergy, nobles, and king. Tyranny and religious wars affected everyone, especially the "enlightened" segment of society. The hatred obviously provided no intellectual argument for atheism, but it did generate a welcoming atmosphere for atheistic demonstration and acceptance.

D'Holbach proposed no novel theses, just theses more defiantly stated and rigorously argued than ever before. More importantly, his book confronted the conflicting issues of religion and disbelief with the very evidence theologians had been using for so long to prove the existence and attributes of God. It took the arguments of Descartes, Newton, Malebranche, and Clarke, and turned them upside down. What d'Holbach stood for was an alternative world system constructed on the same foundations as before but concluding to an absolute materialism.

He offered an explanation of the world and all in it based on science, explaining religious belief away. With confidence and optimism he proposed a substitute for religion, urging people to live in a world without God, replacing all of religion's functions - intellectual, moral, social, and political. No wonder the Church took fright.

The System incorporated the most critical insights of the preceding decades. Central, of course, was exploitation of the two giants of the seventeenth century, Descartes and Newton. Neither of them would have been happy with the objectives of d'Holbach, nor would they have thought the undertaking possible. He was determined to destroy the dualism between matter and spirit, between extension (Descartes) or mass (Newton) and thought or spiritual reality.

D'Holbach has several trivial philosophical antecedents. For example, the collapse of the distinction between matter and spirit might be said to begin with Etienne Condillac. Inspired by Locke's reaffirmation of Aristotle's insight that all knowledge originates in our senses, Condillac denied the distinction between sensation and thinking. All processes we call thinking are, he argued, sensations or combinations of sensations. How do we know sensations truly put us in touch with the outer world? Not by confidence in God, as

Descartes taught, but by our sense experience of touch. Daring as Condillac is, he does not move all the way to materialism. Rather he finds a place for God as the supreme cause and for a spiritual soul, the center of human unity.

Claude-Adrien Helvétius did not hesitate to carry through the logic of Condillac. If all thinking can be reduced to sensation, which requires bodily organs, then why must there be a spiritual soul? By embracing the doctrine that all human actions are determined, Helvétius can propose that ethics be treated like all other sciences, like an experimental physics. No wonder Paris was shocked by Helvétius' book in 1758.

Meanwhile La Mettrie was developing this current of thought along another channel to complete materialism. Focusing on the way matter is organized, he judges he can explain operations of individual parts and powers, even the process of thinking. La Mettrie first traced the active principle in matter from elemental forms to developed sensibility in animals and thinking brains in human beings. In *Man and Machine* he takes Descartes's position that animals are automata and extends it to human beings. The "soul" makes the human machine an enlightened machine.

A skeptic, La Mettrie admitted that probabilities were in favor of there being a God. However, he considered this sheer theory, of little practical value. Not surprisingly he put in the mouth of an unnamed friend, "The universe will never be happy unless it is atheistic." The reasons his friend gave closely fit what d'Holbach was to hold. Under atheism all forms of religion obviously will be destroyed at their very roots; religious and theological wars will be things of the past. Nature will be recognized as pure. People at peace would follow their spontaneous desires. Only these desires, according to La Mettrie, generate true virtue and lead to happiness.

With these ideas and arguments D'Holbach has all he needs to work out his materialistic system: human happiness must be built upon atheism.

The System of Nature

D'Holbach's is a complete philosophical system of naturalism. A philosopher's theory of knowledge always parallels his theory of reality. what it is to be a person grows out of both theories. For d'Holbach human knowing begins and ends with sensation. Perception, experience, and reason give us universal nature. That is the way truth is attained in contrast to imagination, enthusiasm, habit, prejudice and authority - all possible sources of error. Nature consists of elements in "assemblages" - in other words, organized bodies. Anything other than nature is excluded from intellectual respectability. Reason, scientific reason that is, has won the day.

Nature, then, is made up of elemental bodies united or separated by movement. The world is ruled by universal mechanics. Knowledge is attained by discovering the causes of these movements. And cause is defined as a being which puts another being in motion or produces change in it. Effect is the motion or change produced.

This is a universal mechanics posing as a philosophy of nature and actually taking the place of a metaphysics - scientism, pure and simple. It is essential to realize that d'Holbach does not consider existence as such at all. [We shall be reasoning to God on the level of existence.] The ultimates of his world are material bodies in motion. There is no place for anything beyond nature. To be is to be matter in motion; hence no need of, no possibility of searching for an original *cause* of motion.

Accepting current belief in spontaneous generation of living beings from non-living, he sees no difficulty in human beings having a similar origin. Distinction between matter and spirit is gone.

D'Holbach considers he has explained nature and the whole of reality. But his ambition goes beyond explanation. To provide the way to human happiness he must explain away religion with its errors and horrors. Doing this requires close attention to human nature and human actions.

The human person, like other living beings, is an organization of matter, a machine. There is no spiritual soul. People experience two kinds of sensations - agreeable and disagreeable; the former leaves one feeling happy, the latter miserable. Love and fear are evoked by these two experiences, corresponding to the physical laws of attraction and repulsion. All that people do can thus be explained, for people's reactions are as mechanical as the movement of the planets. The fundamental drive is to self-conservation. Pain and happiness are signs of what will help or hinder self-conservation. One searches to pursue the source of happiness and remove the source of pain. The internal experience of need, either to get what makes for happiness or to avoid what hurts, provides the sense experience of pain and urges us to act.

Contrary then to Aristotle's view, philosophy results not from the desire to know but from the desire to escape the painful. As a matter of surprising fact, the evil of pain is necessary for people to become more than insensible machines.

People are exposed to all sorts of evils - poverty, epidemics, famine, war. Dread of these stimulate the search for their causes and the means to control our lives. Centuries of struggling to cope with these obstacles to happiness produced philosophy and the sciences. In the course of history many disasters occurred which raged beyond man's control. Ignorance and fear imagined powerful agencies at work beyond nature, behind nature. Thus religion, the magical way to control or at least to cope with the causes of human misery, came into human existence. First the elements of nature were deified. Then as agents they were differentiated from the material natures and personalized The multiple gods came to be assumed into one: a single agent, one sovereign intelligence, a supreme spiritual being.

Clearly d'Holbach anticipated Feuerbach and Freud in this explanation of the origin of religion.

Since such recourse to imagination was practical, religion as a lifestyle developed. Mysteries were insisted on to camouflage the ignorance of religion and to ensure obedience to its power. This personalized supreme God was given consciousness like our own, and the qualities expanded to reach infinity, with the help of metaphysicians and theologians. Rather than proving to be the triumph of religion, monotheism (now intellectually purified over nature) marks the last stage of religion before its dissolution. For the metaphysical attributes of infinity and omnipotence clash in contradiction with the moral attributes. Theology, with its infinite God, denies the very qualities in God that religious experience postulated. Religion needs a good, kind God who can be appeased and cajoled by prayer. These attributes are denied by an immutable, omnipotent God who does nothing to prevent evil.

Religion is based on ignorance and deceit, born of imagination in order to cope with unmanageable disasters. It develops through theologians into self-contradiction. All this confirms the reasoned explanation of the universe: matter in motion, organized nature is all there is. Given time, illusions and strife will be banished and people can get on with building a civilization of freedom and dignity, with science providing human control of nature for human happiness.

Finally, d'Holbach effects a brilliant tour de force, taking the acknowledged theologians as well as the two intellectual giants, Descartes and Newton, and showing how their basic principles, properly understood and corrected, justify atheism. Meeting Clarke head-on he shows, for example, that the theologians' first three theorems actually can and should be absorbed into d'Holbach's atheistic *System*. That there is a being, eternal, immutable and independent as well as self-existent or necessary is indeed true. This being is material nature. Clarke's pivotal theses are shown to justify what d'Holbach has laid out as atheistic naturalism.

In other words, d'Holbach attempts not to refute the theologians but to demonstrate that their secret was atheism. He judged he could remove Descartes's disguise and show he really espoused atheism. Let Newton be consistent in his own science of mechanics and he, too, would end up godless.

SUMMARY AND CONCLUSION

Is there a God? Diderot and d'Holbach not only assert a resounding "No," but propose a life-style to replace religion. Now this life-style is called secular humanism. The "No" and its attendant secular humanism, at the time not widely heard or attended to, has found support in philosophical, scientific, technological, social, and political changes since then. By the year 2,000 it is projected that over one billion - 17.1% of the population - will explicitly espouse the non-religious world-view.

Undergirding this Atheism of Enlightenment is the philosophy of "scientism" - which we shall repeatedly address. The Sciences, natural and social, have brought the human race to awesome control of nature bestowing astounding life-giving, life-enhancing benefits. The intellectual giants who launched the scientific revolution thought their work guaranteed the foundations of religion. As we shall see in Chapter Three successive options prepared the way to scientism. Metaphysics and philosophy of nature gradually disappeared as reason became identified with scientific reasoning. Diderot and d'Holbach, combining the findings of science with common sense and common logic, led to atheism as the necessary condition for human liberation and development.

Paradoxically, Christian apologists empowered these shapers of the Enlightenment. Rightly relying on reason to argue God's existence, they mistakenly worked with philosophy of nature-turned-physics. Diderot and d'Holbach accepted their perspective, turned their arguments upside down, and demonstrated that they really led to atheism.

Unfortunately, we are not reporting merely interesting historical facts. This atheism was the root of secular humanism that in turn generated our contemporary mainstream consciousness which blocks out thought of God, making today's God-issue distinctive.

Understanding this root and development of contemporary consciousness is essential.

CHAPTER 3

THE ROAD TO SECULAR HUMANISM

Diderot and d'Holbach and the Enlightenment have been with us since the eighteenth century, strengthening the community of secular humanists. It all began in the 13th century, ironically, with St. Thomas Aquinas, the great Catholic theologian and philosopher.

Thomas succeeded in bringing ten centuries of thought about God into systematic form. He articulated the problem of God in four basic questions.

The first question to be asked about God, as about anything, is *whether* God is.

The second question normally asked, once the first has been answered, is *what* the thing is. But since we cannot know what God is, we take the opposite approach and ask what God is *not*.

Third: *How* is God *known* by us?

Fourth: *How* do we talk about God or *name* God?

What is most significant, however, is that Thomas transposed the problem of God into a problem for philosophical intelligence. Daringly and for the first time in history, the quadriform problem was put squarely to human reason.

In approaching the problem of God this way, Thomas made axiomatic, for all time to come, the *distinction* between faith and reason. In view of what happened, it is essential for us to remember that "distinction" is not the same as "separation." The shape of my finger is "distinct" from my finger, but obviously it is not separated from it. Sight is a faculty separate from hearing, each of these faculties having its own bodily organ: eyes and ears. Thomas conceives the human intellect as an immaterial faculty for attaining truth. Both faith and reason function through the human intellect to bring us to truth, but they travel by different and distinct routes. Faith is our supernaturally-aided, human response to God's testimony: God's statements about God and about ourselves. Mysterious as they are, we assent to them as true because of their source. Reason, on the other hand, is our human response to evidence comprehended by our unaided human intelligence.

Thus what grounds the intellect's affirmation may be either faith, empowering the intellect to accept as true what God reveals, or reason, personal intellectual insight into the evidence. These are not two *separate* faculties, like sight and hearing, but one intellect capable of attaining reality through natural insight or through supernatural empowering faith.

Aquinas insisted that people should carefully attend to what is involved when they affirm anything. Do they affirm it through intellectual insight or through faith without direct insight? Confident that truth cannot contradict truth, Thomas feared no discrepancy between what reason showed and what faith could tell us.

Despite his reverence for reason, Thomas did not exaggerate its worth. For Thomas, faith held first place, based as it is on God's revelations mediated through Christ's church. Therefore, whenever contradiction between claims of faith and reason occurred, faith functioned as a negative norm. Obviously the first step was re-examination of the entire issue. Not infrequently the contradictions were recognized as only apparent.

In summary, Thomas made clear the distinction (not the separation) between faith and reason and he acknowledged faith's priority in determining truth.

BEGINNING OF NATURAL SCIENCES

Some three hundred years after Aquinas the scientific age dawned with the rise of modern astronomy, physics, and chemistry. It must have been an exciting time for those intuitively aware of what was happening. Certainly, looking back, we recognize a true revolution took place, one of the greatest transformations in all of history. Because of what Galileo introduced, and what Francis Bacon set forth as its program, we enjoy the incredible benefits of science, technology, and industry.

Galileo turned from the study of motion as being to measurement of motion. Bacon insisted that knowledge was pursued for power, for dominion over nature. Thus knowledge would contribute to human welfare and progress.

All this had gradually been prepared for, especially with the development of mathematics and with a focus on quantity or extension (which lent itself to mathematical analysis) rather than on substance. The key to understanding nature was mathematics.

Galileo (1564-1642) is considered the pivotal figure with whom modern science began. To the theory of Copernicus he brought the practical test of the newly-invented telescope. In his work on dynamics he combined observation and induction with mathematical deduction tested by experiment. The true method of physical research was thus inaugurated.

But it was Isaac Newton (1642-1727) who defined and demonstrated the ideal that scientific investigation continues to pursue today: the mathematical description of nature's processes. Building on the insights of Galileo and the data provided by Tycho Brahe (1571-1630) and John Kepler (1571-1630), Newton was able to "systematize the universe in a synthesis of terrestrial motion and celestial motion...Newton wrote a mechanics of the world that also explained the world as a mechanical system." (Buckley, 101-2)

During this period, as Galileo led the revolt against Aristotle, Servetus and William Harvey (1578-1657) broke free from the authority of Galen and established the function of the heart in the circulation of the blood through the lungs and body.

Robert Boyle (1627-1691), Joseph Priestley (1733-1804), and especially Antoine Lavoisier established the science of chemistry. Modern physiology began with Albrecht von Haller (1708-1777). Abbe Spallanzani (1729-1799) proved spontaneous generation of animals did not occur. John Ray (1627-1705) and Linnaeus (1707-1778) founded systematic botany.

Systematic exploration of the world began to be approached scientifically in the 17th and 18th centuries. This not only improved geography and navigation, but the increased knowledge of the earth led to study of its structure and history, and so to geology.

As observed above, these were exciting times when intellectual authority was thrown aside and discovery after discovery was made. Although the new ways of thinking met opposition from Aristotelians and only slowly worked their way into the universities, scientific academies sprang up to lend support. These academies helped science to grow rapidly by discussion of research findings, and especially by means of periodic publications.

Since education was not widespread, this excitement was not directly or immediately felt by the populace. Nonetheless the broad ideas must have circulated. What must people have thought and felt when they learned that our earth was not the center of the universe? No doubt the discovery of the New World and reports about new peoples had somewhat prepared them for such radical changes of perspective. Development of commerce must have been liberating minds too.

However, the impact of the scientific revolution increased as thinkers agitated against government and Church, pushing for greater freedom in the areas of research and people's rights. The impact intensified during the 19th century as science produced technological benefits. Previous to this time, inventions which contributed to better living sprang up independently of science. But in the 19th century scientific discoveries began to lead directly to industrial benefits. Experiments in electro-magnetism led to the dynamo and electrical engineering. After years of experiments Maxwell's electro-magnetic equations would lead to the wireless, broadcasting, and radar.

Science by its very nature is intrinsically related to technology, which in turn leads to industry. Today advances in communication, in travel, and especially in medicine are breath-taking, all reinforcing respect for science.

Furthermore, Darwin's evolutionary findings must have strongly influenced people, affecting their sense of human importance, even their faith. They realized not only that the earth is not the center of the universe, but that we are descendants of animals.

ADVANCEMENT THROUGH OPTIONS

The exciting new discoveries in science attracted many of the best minds in Europe. Merely listing the names of famous scientists of the era and their discoveries suggests why. And it all began with the sense of liberation from the authority of established Aristotelian ways of thinking. Advance became possible when Galileo and Newton discarded the entire Aristotelian scheme and *chose* length, time, and mass as new *fundamental* ideas. Scientists now thought in terms of matter and motion; nature was mathematized.

The fruitfulness of research seemed to warrant the *option* of working with those ideas. This new way of thinking was so successful that reason became *identified* with scientific reasoning. At first it functioned as a philosophy - the philosophy of nature. After all, people did not recognize how radically new this scientific way of thinking was. Philosophy of nature soon became the science of mechanics.

In the enthusiasm for the rigor and possibilities opened up by the new sciences, no effort was made to *prove* that science was the paradigm of reasoning or that people had purified previous methods and finally discovered the way to philosophize. This cultural option had the farthest- reaching effects.

Thus the foundation of scientism was laid. For Thomas and the medievals, there was one universe of truth, containing different kinds of truth. The correspondingly different methodologies stood distinct from one another yet in unity. Whether truth was attained by reason or faith, and within reason by philosophical or Aristotelian scientific reasoning, there was acknowledgement of the truth and harmony among truths. Now an option was taken to restrict reason to scientific reasoning more or less exclusively.

Innocent and well meaning as this option was, the consequences were momentous. Natural sciences, structured to discover and explain the sensible, the material, and the quantitative, are simply incapable of attaining God. After all, God by definition is *im*material and *non*sensible. As it has been picturesquely phrased, to claim there is no God because science neither discovers nor needs God is like pulling a fishnet out of the ocean and proclaiming, "There is no water in the ocean!" A fishnet is fashioned to capture practically anything else except water. It was designed to let water *escape*. Natural sciences are able to capture only sensible and quantitative things. Their "net" lets everything else escape.

This implication of atheism did not unfold for a long time, but something else did develop very soon. As thinkers established the validity of the natural sciences, they gradually tended to extol reason above faith. Bruno, burned at the stake in 1600, believed in God. He could not accept Christ and the Trinity, knowable only by faith. Newton and Samuel Clarke, employing Newton's work as a Christian apologist, quietly rejected traditional Christian doctrines. Casually, with no awareness of the seriousness of what they were doing, with no intention of radical change, people tended to *separate* reason from faith. Distinction between reason and faith became separation -- by a kind of cultural *option*, not by intellectual conviction. Esteem for the new thinking also inclined thinkers to treat reason as judge of the teachings of faith.

Another contribution of Thomas influenced the development of thought and contributed more directly to the development of contemporary consciousness. He insisted that all knowledge is good and worthwhile, and that the material universe, with its own laws, merits study for its own sake. The new intellectuals *opted* to concentrate on the natural sciences and to set their sights on explaining the universe without recourse to religion or faith. In its early stages, science, when confronted with phenomena which the science of the time could not explain, eluded the difficulty by having recourse to God. This so-called "God of the gaps" offered a convenient by-pass whenever scientific investigation ran up against a blank wall. This gambit was justifiably abandoned in the early 19th century, an event immortalized by the famous exchange between Napoleon Bonaparte and the astronomer, Pierre Laplace: "God? I have no need of that hypothesis." The scientific community discovered that it could manage its own affairs without appealing to God. This quite legitimate development, however, conjured up an illicit and unwarranted conclusion: *Since science* does not attain or need God, *therefore there is no God.* No water in the net? Aha, water does not exist! Such dependence on science contributed to the rise of atheism.

The vast run of humankind, however, ignored that reasoning and conclusion. They stubbornly continued to believe in God. So here was a new problem: how explain *that* fact, their continued belief? The solution was quite ingenious. It was prepared for by the casual, unwitting transformation of Thomas's *distinction* between faith and reason into their *separation*. Since reason, now restricted to scientific reason, does not and cannot validate belief in God, faith must be a function not of reason but of *imagination* !

Christianity, within which the sciences emerged, was a religion of events; Christian faith was based on historical happenings. It is also a religion of dogmas, affirmations assented to by faith as true. Being true, they put us in touch with reality, with God, and God's will for men and women.

For modern intellectuals all this seemed nonsense. Christianity, like all religions, they judged to be the product of imagination, a religion of myths. The events on which Christians take their stand never *really* happened. People must have projected into history their experience of themselves-in-the-world. As Sisyphus never lived or kept rolling a stone up a hill, so there never was a Christ, so never his resurrection from the dead. The function of myths like these is to account for human experiences - frustration in this world or hope for a higher life. Myths do embody a sort of truth, but not truth of historical order. Neither the myth of Sisyphus nor that of Christ states a fact. Therefore both are fantasies. So the thinking went.

Similarly, Christian dogmas do not express ontological truth, are not statements about the objective order of reality, about God, or

God's will for us. Dogmas have only pragmatic, emotional value as statements about the subjective order of religious experience.

Within the intellectual community, then, scientific reasoning inexorably swept the field. Because in their estimation science was the supreme human achievement, and since science is equipped to deal solely with sensible, quantitative, perishable reality, it followed that any entity which science could not apprehend just was not worth apprehending. No wonder our consciousness tunes out anything other than the contingent, the relative, and the temporal, thus blocking even the possibility of God.

Note, the significant steps were all options without any attempt to justify those steps by proof. For a long time there was no explicit rejection of God. Many intellectuals retained their Christian faith, failing to recognize the developing contradiction between their faith and reason as currently misunderstood.

FURTHER OPTIONS DEVELOPED

It must, of course, be conceded that the remarkable achievements of scientific reasoning affected practically everyone, even the most religiously devout. The mind-set of the laboratory spilled over into the market place and legislative chamber. From both spheres God was gradually eliminated. And clearly people's consciousness is more directly affected by what goes on in these latter spheres than in academic circles.

Commerce burgeoned with "The business of business is business" as the shibboleth of economics. Concern about God or God's laws was gradually dropped from commercial enterprise. Missionary activities in South America and India, for example, often were thwarted by those in pursuit of wealth even at the cost of human lives. Slavery flourished.

In politics also, the rise of the secular state separated religion from public life. The state was to be godless, so that religion, if practiced at all, became appropriate only for the sanctuary and the individual heart, not for the civic community. Governmental decisions were made without the slightest regard for faith, for God - even without regard for morality it seems.

The disposition to prescind from God in intellectual enterprises, and to palm God off as an unwarranted distraction from the efficient conduct of business and government actually became a campaign under the Enlightenment. The Enlightenment espoused Deism, belief in a God who began the universe but had no further involvement with it. The Christian God and especially the Christian Church had no place in this world. No place, both because Christian faith demanded reason be subject to it and, more immediately and emotionally, because Church authorities were so closely identified with the establishment. Deists were determined to remove power from Church authorities so they could not impede scientific research or the structuring of the purely secular state.

The option to identify reason with scientific reasoning laid the foundation of scientism - found in Diderot and d'Holbach. The option to change Thomas's *distinction* between faith and reason into a *separation* of the two empowered the Enlightenment to assume the priority of reason over faith, now a function of imagination, not reason, allowing reason, scientific reason that is, to judge the truth-value of faith. Option to explain the universe without recourse to religion or faith prepared the way to Deism and Atheism.

It took centuries for the secular humanism of the Enlightenment grounded on scientism and Atheism to shape contemporary consciousness. Contributing was the work of Nietzsche who, perceiving the corrosion of belief in the foundations of Christian life, announced "the death of God." This same corrosive development we have been describing inevitably culminated in something far more sinister, "atheistic Communism" and "atheistic Existentialism." In both movements God is not merely irrelevant and ignored; in these movements God is an obstacle to be destroyed. Practical atheism and secular humanism created an environment from which emerged these *anti*theistic movements.

Existentialism in its antitheistic form, as exemplified in Sartre, flourished in Europe after the Second World War. Echoes of the "Existential absurd" are found in American literature but American intellectual life never embraced Existentialism. Marxist Communism burst forth in the Soviet Union first; later it took root in China and Eastern Europe, but never sank firm roots in the United States.

Happily, Communism has been abandoned in the Soviet Union, a nation striving to re-insert itself among Western democracies. It would be premature, however, to conclude that all is well. All is not well. The vast population of China still groans under the heel of Communism. Closer to home, there is a determined effort throughout the West to slough off the remaining vestiges of a Christian public morality, especially as regards marriage and the family. Will Communism in the Soviet Union and Eastern Europe be replaced by secular humanism in the free marketplace package?

Although they failed to achieve widespread, permanent embodiment, these two movements contributed to the shaping of contemporary consciousness. Not only their antitheism but also the insistence on freedom in Existentialism definitely help explain why our consciousness is what it is.

The "counter culture" movement of the '60's and '70's rearranged the consciousness so far developed. Accepting the dismantling of Christian religion and culture as we have described, the "counter culture" rearranged the elements, to make feeling and self-indulgence more prominent. Those spearheading the movement had no doubt that everything is contingent, relative, and temporal. They exploited the freedom and autonomy within the dominant consciousness.

It is within that atmosphere, which we are calling mainstream "contemporary consciousness," that our inquiry is to be conducted. Since the intellectual presuppositions of that consciousness never have been proved, the challenge now stands exposed: intellectual integrity demands we face the God-question.

SECULAR HUMANISM AND CHRISTIAN RELIGION

The struggle for people's souls between believers and nonbelievers goes on constantly. Believers, of course, far outnumber nonbelievers. What is more pertinent and interesting is that a conflict of two "religions" is at issue.

Religion is a holistic response of all aspects of the person - intellect, will, emotions, way of living. Ordinarily it involves community and community life-style: a system of beliefs, approved practices, common worship, community activities for members of the community as well as by the community for others.

Secular Humanism structures a lifestyle on scientism, a philosophy which contends that science *alone* attains reality. The resulting community functions as a religion. It has a system of beliefs, approved behavior and practices, sometimes certain services resembling church services and so forth. As with traditional religion, this lifestyle evokes a holistic response. Certain secular humanist organizations, as a matter of fact, are registered as religions receiving tax-free standing.

Conflict indeed there is between secular humanism and traditional religion. These two religions, like lifestyles in general, cannot resolve conflicts with one another because the warrant of lifestyle response is that it "feels" right. Any position or activity that is in accord with one's lifestyle "feels" right. It follows that when one's lifestyle is challenged by a conflicting lifestyle, recourse to the lifestyle itself is futile.

Repeatedly, secular humanists and Christians come into conflict over established practices and assumptions based on the Christian religion. Secular humanists try to structure life and community on what science and common sense propose for human welfare and find their efforts in conflict with countless traditional practices based upon the Christian religion. Why, for example, should prayers be said in school? Why should religious institutions be tax-free? Why should marriages be monogamous, or only between male and female? Having grown sufficiently numerous, secular humanists challenge these and other traditional assumptions and practices. Since it is the very nature of human persons to incarnate their beliefs in customs, secular humanists seek in their turn to establish customs based on atheistic humanism.

Christians have taken for granted all these assumptions and practices, incarnations of Christian beliefs. They have not had to consider or justify them. As a result, many professing Christians, affected by the dominant, contemporary, mainstream consciousness, feel insecure about being able to justify these practices. Worse, some Christians take contemporary perspectives and values as standard and reinterpret Christian doctrine in the light of these secular standards. Then they defend and embrace the secularist lifestyle.

It is essential to recognize that secular humanists *feel* these traditional assumptions and practices are wrong and harmful. Christians in general *feel* the assumptions and practices are right. Hence the conflict cannot be resolved by appealing to the lifestyles themselves. For the most part efforts to resolve these conflicts have involved litigation or boycott, or socio-political-economic pressure. However, the only civilized way to resolve the conflict is to disengage the strands of pertinent theoretical presuppositions and discuss them intelligently.

The primary theoretical presupposition involved is, "There is a God." Understandably I focus on Christian religion but the conflict exists between secular humanism and all theistic religions. Although many other theoretical presuppositions need to be disengaged, clarified, and assessed, I limit my efforts to this primary one.

If there is no God, our Christian religion (indeed all theistic religions) and all the logically connected customs are ungrounded and some may be fundamentally harmful to people. If there is a God, secular humanism is radically ungrounded. Life based on secular humanism is not life within truth; inevitably it becomes harmful.

THE ROLE OF PHILOSOPHY

Buckley's magisterial study on the origins of modern atheism claims that modern atheism took both its meaning and existence from the self-alienation of religion. Such a claim raises the question, "How do we investigate whether there is a God or not?" At the time the natural sciences were developing, so the author reports, on all sides there was a perception that atheism was emerging. Christianity recognized the need to account for its assertion that God exists but refused to claim that faith alone justifies acknowledgment of God's existence, as though reason were incapable of doing so. Instead of insisting on religion's ability to justify itself, Christian apologists turned to philosophy for its vindication. They abandoned what is intrinsic to Christianity - religious experience, the reality of Jesus Christ, personal witness. The author of the study concludes that in its efforts to justify itself religion "fathered its own estrangement" and generated modern atheism.

What the study fails to make clear is that people in that era did not recognize the difference between philosophy and science. The philosophy engaged in became natural philosophy and this in turn became the science of mechanics. The error was in using science rather than philosophy to vindicate religion's basic assertion, that God exists.

Religion is able to justify its positions by disengaging the theoretical presuppositions on which religion builds, then establishing the truth of each presupposition. Thomas, at a time when theology and philosophy were not separate sciences, employed philosophy to establish at least the initial fundamental truth: "God is." Religion, as a lifestyle, definitely has room for philosophy. And philosophy, since it has recourse only to reason, must be the means of justifying the basic theoretical presupposition, "There is a God."

For secular humanists deny the validity of faith as a way to know what is real. Identification of the kind of reasoning to be used is essential to the project. It will not be the kind used for the natural sciences but one appropriate for the subject, the reasoning used in philosophy.

Why insist on this role of philosophy? Doubtless an encounter with Jesus Christ in the New Testament or through the witness of somebody respected and loved would be a faster way than philosophy to lead a person toward belief. A mystical experience or a strong religious experience might accomplish it. God's "graceful" action would be involved in such instances and we have no control over God's actions. But I am not primarily focused on the psychology of leading a person to belief. Besides, such new believers would, in principle, be faced with the issue of determining they are not suffering illusions but are truly encountering God. I say "in principle" for the individual might be convinced the religious experience was self-authenticating and not challenge that interpretation. Furthermore, like Jung, such a person very probably would have caught the insight that life and reality don't make sense if there is no God.

It simply must be faced that our culture so esteems reason that unless belief in God is intellectually respectable a person will have difficulty even considering the issue. Further, the community of believers has the responsibility of establishing for their members as well as for nonbelievers that it is reasonable to acknowledge there is a God.

Finally there is a significant distinction between "convince" and "persuade." The objective of preacher and pastor is to persuade. Emotional considerations are involved. The objective of the philosopher is to convince - to lay out explanations and steps of argumentation in as clear a manner as possible, enabling self and others to catch the significant insights. Persuasion itself insofar as it respects the person's integrity must be based on genuine conviction.

Philosophy then must be employed to resolve the conflict between the two lifestyles by addressing the pivotal intellectual presupposition: There is (is not) a God. Note that never before in the West has atheism been so strong that it has generated a lifestyle able to compete with traditional religious lifestyles. But showing that philosophy, not the sciences, offers the appropriate kind of reasoning will require extensive treatment.

SUMMARY AND CONCLUSION

The road to Diderot and d'Holbach has been described - starting with St. Thomas in the 13th century. Inescapably clear is the fact that naturalistic Atheism would not have entered intellectual history but for these cultural options:
- to identify reason with scientific reason,
- to change *distinction* between faith and reason into *separation* of faith and reason,
- to treat reason as superior to faith, and
- to undertake explaining the material universe without faith.

Mediating these options were misguided apologetic attempts to prove God's existence.

As a result we now have a conflict between two "religions," Christianity and secular Humanism. Such a conflict can only be resolved by disengaging the radical theoretical presupposition, "There is a God." and arguing its truth or falsity. Philosophy alone provides conditions acceptable to all. Intellectual integrity, granted that options not intellectual proof undergirds the scientism of secular humanism, would seem to demand that the question be faced, "Is there a God?"

But first we must examine the contemporary consciousness shaped by secular humanism which causes today's God-question to stand forth as uniquely distinctive.

CHAPTER 4

CONTEMPORARY CONSCIOUSNESS

Atheism having become the foundation of a lifestyle competitive with traditional religious lifestyles, has also been enormously influential in structuring mainstream contemporary consciousness. At times it even retains religious language, all the while distorting or obliterating traditional belief in God. Because today's mainstream consciousness tends to block out any consideration of God, it transforms the God-issue.

To illustrate how consciousness functions consider, "Should the United States search for a man of royal blood to be appointed our king?" Many people think that question no more absurd than this one, "Can an intelligent man or woman acknowledge there is a God?" Democracy is so imbedded in our mindset that we refuse to entertain even the *idea* of a king. In the same way our dominant contemporary consciousness is so structured that it blocks out the very idea of a necessary, absolute, eternal being.

Consciousness, of course, refers to the deep, preconceptual attitude people take toward reality and events; this attitude characterizes a community's response to what is and to what happens. It is the unquestioning way people interpret what they experience.

CHARACTERISTICS OF OUR CONSCIOUSNESS

Three major historical changes shaped our mainstream contemporary consciousness.

1. The twin developments of technology and urbanization, growing out of the scientific revolution and industrial age --
This is the first epochal change.
2. Realization that institutions and cultures are historically conditioned --
This particularly accounts for the dimension of relativism in our mindset.
3. Loss of the sense of the sacred, ushered in by the scientific revolution, emptying the world of spiritual beings --
This constitutes the third epochal change.

Obviously, secular humanism developed within these changes, which changes gradually produced a consciousness with four characteristics. Absolutely everything is considered *contingent* (That is, nothing *is necessary*). *Relativism* is the second characteristic, and how pervasive it is! Whatever is studied must be viewed from the perspective of its relationships and all thought, all beliefs, all morals are merely relative. (That is, nothing is *absolute*.) Needless to say everything real is *temporal*. (That is, nothing is *eternal*.)

Clearly these three - contingency, relativism, and temporality - go together. Since the consciousness of an age prisms everything people experience, our consciousness just described, simply excludes God, traditionally understood as necessary, absolute, and eternal - completely the opposite of the characteristics just mentioned. The *idea* of such a being is not even entertained.

I call attention to the fact that never has it been *proved* that everything is contingent, relative, and temporal-- that there exists nothing necessary, absolute, and eternal. Intellectual integrity would seem to demand we face the challenge: What *evidence* is there for the *pre*suppositions in contemporary consciousness that reduce belief in God to superstition?

The fourth characteristic, a sense of *freedom and autonomy*, is obviously present today. I love this aspect of our culture. It liberates and empowers. People feel far less shackled by historical structures and procedures. We are free to dress as we like, shape our lives as we like, change laws, institutions, procedures as we like. What can be done is not restricted to what has been done.

However, things are not so ideal as they seem! This freedom is freedom to do-as-one-pleases, not freedom of self-determination. Because of the naturalism and materialism undergirding the sense of contingency, relativism, and temporality, our lives are assumed to be fully conditioned, pre-determined. Ironically, men and women of the Middle Ages knew they possessed freedom of self-determination so that their lives were ultimately in their own hands (wills/choices) even though at the same time they possessed very limited freedom to do as they pleased. Today although enjoying freedom to do as they please in many areas, people have a sense that ultimately their lives are utterly conditioned. Also, it seems to me that the autonomy they sense is generally autonomy within a group. Few are strong enough to exercise genuine freedom and autonomy; confidence in being autonomous rests on confirmation by a person's community of significant others.

FURTHER CHARACTERISTICS

Intermingled with those four characteristics of dominant mainstream consciousness is an anthropocentric culture: focus is upon the human person rather than on the universe as a whole or on being. More significant is the understanding of knowledge. An earlier culture focused on abstract, universal concepts and stressed deduction and logic. Today's culture prefers the approach of the natural and social sciences, focusing on the concrete and the empirical; not deduction but scientific method is stressed. Rather than the deductive, look to the empirical; rather than being static, knowledge is dynamic; rather than focusing on the abstract, today we are concerned about the concrete; not the universal and unchanging but the developmental.

The natural sciences - physics, chemistry, biology, and the others - have come to be looked on as the crown of all human knowledge - and, most pertinently, as the ultimate judge of truth. To know what is the fact, to know what is real, we are expected to turn to science. In any challenge to religion by a scientific finding, it is taken for granted that religion will be proved wrong or will need re-interpretation. For example, the claim that human beings evolved seemed to conflict with the statement about creation in the book of Genesis in the Bible. This conflict forced believers to open their eyes to the fact that they had been misreading Genesis. Believers had read the account of creation as a scientific report rather than as a religious message--namely, that everything depends ultimately on God.

Science has become so influential that few people regard philosophy, especially metaphysics, as valid knowledge. Some intellectuals and even teachers of philosophy restrict philosophy to reflection about other fields: to philosophy *of* science, philosophy *of* art, philosophy *of* history and so forth. Some people hold that philosophy is of no direct help in knowing the real.

What has happened is subtle: science and the scientific method have been expanded into a separate philosophy, scientism, the implicit philosophy of most people today. So fruitful have the sciences been and their findings so generally accepted that some people regard them as the *only* way to have solid knowledge of reality and as the ultimate determinant of all truth. Scientism is this exaggerated trust in the scientific method to attain truth in *any* field.

Nonbelievers, explicitly or implicitly secular humanists, will resonate with this description of what constitutes knowledge. As a matter of fact, secular humanism builds upon scientism as its philosophy.

There should be no need to call attention to the fact that sciences deal with the sensible and with mathematical analyses. People steeped in the sciences may have problems with their faith. Trained to test the truth of any proposition by sensible verification or mathematical deduction, they consciously or unconsciously respond to the fact that neither the existence of God nor any of their religious beliefs can be verified this way. Conscious realization of this can cause some people to lose faith. (Unless, of course, they realize there are other ways to know reality and that to deny there is a God because science does not discover God is like pulling up a *net* out of the sea and proclaiming there is no water there because the net doesn't show any.) Others who have applied scientific criteria to their faith tend to compartmentalize their lives. Rigorous, intelligent testing in all areas of their lives *except* religion! The mistake of "Fideism" is the result, the position that faith alone justifies any part of religion.

Implicit or explicit espousal of scientism creates the greatest obstacle to any reasoned approach to God. Obviously, **if** scientism is true, there can be no reasonable justification of God's existence.

This is not to reject or even criticize science itself. Without the sciences we never would be able to live with the security, comforts, medical procedures we enjoy today. Not the sciences, but scien**tism** is the danger! This philosophy I reject as utterly and (as I will show later) demonstrably false. If secular humanism and Christianity are to dialogue, the validity of scientism must be vigorously debated.

ANTITHEISM

Something is missing in one's understanding of our historically distinctive mainstream consciousness if a person is ignorant of the antitheistic element involved. The whole modern culture evolved within a context first of indifference, then of outright hostility toward God and religion. Many intellectual architects of the culture such as Freud and Marx, were atheists, indeed antitheists. Their influence explains how so much agnosticism and atheism have been woven into the basic fabric of contemporary culture. We know that the insights and perspectives of intellectuals and artists cascade down to the general public through media and entertainment; they become the "common sense" of an age. People's political experience disposed them to accept this "common sense" because at times they did have to struggle against religion to acquire certain rights and liberties involved in the development of modern society.

Contemporary dominant mainstream consciousness, then, is accurately designated by 1) contingency, 2) relativism, 3) time, 4) freedom and autonomy. That makes the problem about God's existence historically distinctive. Even believers must make an effort to overcome the consciousness they breathe; they must refuse to slip into fideism, the position that reason is *unable* to establish God's existence.

George Santayana once said, "We cannot know who first discovered water. But we can be sure it was not the fish." Shock is needed to break out of what we take for granted, never questioning.

Recalling how options rather than intellectual proof paved the way to scientism should provide that shock. For it will make clear that options built the characteristics into our consciousness. Hence the challenge, "Where has it ever been proved that there is nothing necessary, absolute, and eternal?"

MAINSTREAM CONSCIOUSNESS

The shock needed may also come from identifying precisely what is meant by mainstream dominant consciousness. After all, to claim that contemporary consciousness blocks out the very idea of God, may strike some as absurd. Not only do millions regularly attend Church and greater millions profess belief in God, but even atheists cannot escape media coverage of religious events and issues. Refinement obviously is required. Reference is to mainstream consciousness.

In any large nation numerous communities each have their distinctive identifiable consciousness. But what may be termed the historically distinctive dominant mainstream consciousness - communicated today especially through the media, entertainment, and the academic community - normally affects every other consciousness. Thus members of religious communities with, for example, their own Catholic, Protestant, Jewish, Moslem, or Hindu consciousness, are influenced by this dominant mainstream consciousness.

There is a religious dimension in this historically distinctive contemporary consciousness, for, as will be argued, to be a person is to have this religious dimension. But the vibrancy of this aspect may be so diminished that it has little effect on a person's life. On the other hand, the religious dimension may be given a non-transcendent object. Secular Humanism proposes to do just that. Offering a world-view restricted to this world and this time without God, it proposes to focus human energies and efforts on developing this material universe, on building socio-economic-political structures which improve our human lives in all aspects. In both cases people live as though there were no God. In fact diminished vibrancy of the religious dimension tends to converge with explicit secular humanism.

There are at least three different ways to describe what has happened. One way is to acknowledge that American culture has blended three traditions: Christian biblical religion, civic-minded republicanism, and individualism. Culture and language are intimately intertwined and these three strands of our inherited culture each give birth to a language. More fundamentally, the strands of culture never completely disappear because human nature remains the same, human needs persist even if suppressed or repressed. If suppressed or repressed, the proper language will be muted. At present, individualism is so dominant that the biblical and republican traditions have become dormant. People speak comfortably in the language of individualism; the other two languages have been muted.

Thus in the distinctively historical mainstream consciousness the religious dimension is dormant and it lacks the language to express this religious dimension. The flourishing language communicates secular humanism - a lifestyle without God.

As each of us belongs to multiple communities, so we all share multiple consciousnesses. Devout Christians, Jews, Moslems, and Hindus are conscious of God, but they tend to isolate concern about God within their private lives. Not only does the God-less mainstream consciousness structure their attitudes in the public arena but it subtly affects their religious lives as well (if only to prompt them to refrain from involving God or Christ in public issues).

Another way to describe what has happened is to note that from the beginning of our nation we have had a distinctive "civil religion." This civil religion affirmed the existence of God, the life to come, the reward of virtue and punishment of vice, and exclusion of religious intolerance. We are talking about a God-based religion, neither sectarian nor Christian in any specific sense, yet by no means antithetical to Christianity.

Thus there was genuine affirmation of a transcendent being (Deistic for a limited number; theistic, even Christian, for most). Not only did Americans believe people's rights derived from God, but they considered that our obligation, collective and individual, is to "carry out God's will on earth."

This civil religion was not intended as a substitute for Christianity. As individuals, people might believe and celebrate whatever they judged true and good. But national officials were to operate under the guidance of civil religion.

However, the word "God" has come to mean so many things that it is almost an empty sign. The meaning of "God" - at one time universally accepted in reference to a transcendent being - has become so vague as to lack reference. For many it has become a dangerous word and one to be dropped from the vocabulary. Deism became atheism which became antitheism. The conflict has, for the most part, remained somewhat muted, but the godlessness of secular humanism has become dominant in our mainstream culture. That world-view, that religion, is communicated through our public school system where reference to God is prohibited. This development explains what is meant by the absence of God in the historically distinctive mainstream consciousness.

Sociologists have warned what this change could effect. Presidents, for example, are inaugurated by taking an oath before the people and before God. Thus their obligation extends not only to the people but to God. Accordingly the will of the people is not the criterion of what is morally right or wrong. The people's will is to be judged by a higher criterion, God's judgment. And the rights of men and women derive from the hand of God.

If or when "God" is an empty symbol, if and when presidents and the nation do not believe there is a God before whom they form their judgments, whose will they are obliged to carry out on earth, what happens to the rights of individuals or minorities?

In the 1950's a prescient Will Herberg identified "The American Way of Life" as the religion actually operative in our nation. He captured the foundation and orientation of Americans drifting into the secularization of religion. Although polls at the time reported almost universal (97%) belief in God, still at the same time Americans acknowledged that their religious beliefs had no real effect on their ideas or their conduct in the decisive areas of everyday life, business, and politics. However, while Americans did not let their Protestant, Catholic, or Jewish doctrines influence their approach to business or politics, Herberg uncovers an unacknowledged religion which does provide Americans with a fundamental normativity and meaning in all they do. This is the third explanation of what has happened.

This "common religion" is "The American Way of Life," the operative faith of Americans as a people. This "Way of Life" is "at bottom a spiritual structure, a structure of ideas and ideals, of aspirations and values, of beliefs and standards." What Americans effectively consider the right, the good, and the true in actual life is found in "The American Way of Life." "Sociologically, anthropologically, ...[the American Way of Life] is the characteristic American religion, undergirding American life and overarching American society despite all indubitable differences of region, section, culture, and class."

This common religion affirms the supreme value and dignity of the individual. It emphasizes activism with the goal of "getting ahead." It is pragmatic; "deeds, not creed" count. Needless to say, "The American Way of Life" is generous and humanitarian. It provides a mood of optimism, believes in progress (General Electric's "our greatest product") and is fanatic in its belief in education. Materialistic we are surely, but striving for worldly success needs to be justified in higher terms, - of service or general benefit to the country. Americans are idealistic and most of them see issues and struggles as a crusade for the right and the good. At the very core of "The American Way of Life" is a sense that a "new order" of things was begun and perdures in this New World of ours.

Herberg discerns the interrelationship of this "common faith," "common religion," and mainline churches. He suggests "The American Way of Life" can best be understood "as a kind of secularized Puritanism, a Puritanism without transcendence, without sense of sin or judgment." He finds Americans have a sense of responsibility "before God." However, he finds that Jewish and Christian churches have tended to become secularized - as parts integrated within the large whole, "The American Way of Life." In fact, in his mind Christian and Jewish faiths in America have ceased to be the ultimate value; rather they are perceived as good *because* they are *useful* in furthering the major values in "The American Way of Life." Going further he states that when reference is made to the "God" in whom all Americans believe and of whom the churches speak, actually the term denotes sanction and underpinning for the supreme values in the American Way. "Secularization of religion," he says, "could hardly go further."

All this is crystalized in President Eisenhower's crusading call: "Our government makes no sense unless it is founded in a deeply felt religious faith - and I don't care what it is." Americans heard this, not as a call to indifferentism but as the expression of their own conviction that the three faiths were ultimately saying the same thing - affirming the "spiritual ideals" and "moral values" of "The American Way of Life." The Americans' devotion to religion is *not to "God" but to "religion."* "The faith is not in God, but in faith."

Thus Protestantism, Judaism, Catholicism are three diverse but equally legitimate and American expressions of an over-all American religion; they stand for the same "spiritual values" and "moral ideals."

To state the same insight another way: Democracy, (a synonym for "The American Way of Life,") has three religions, like three species of the one genus, Democracy. The step is easy but fateful from "the religions of democracy" to "democracy as religion," erecting "democracy" as a superfaith under which the three prominent religions fall as species. (As Muslims dedicated to Islam increase in numbers, will their faith become merely a fourth species?) Not only have many intellectuals taken that step but the public school system is given the primary responsibility to teach the democratic ideal as religion. We see in this how the logical conclusion of "The American Way of Life" - this "common religion" of American society - is realized. This conclusion reveals the true inner meaning of "The American Way of Life" as our common religion.

Finally, the "common faith" of Americans has its personal as well as its civic aspects. This inner, personal religion is grounded in "faith in faith." Because the historic faiths have been progressively devitalized under the common faith of the American Way of Life, faith in faith serves as a kind of "miracle drug." It is important to utter only two or three words - "I believe" or "I have faith" - *with nothing added.* By "faith" (object omitted) I reach peace of mind; anxiety and guilt are dissipated. I live in the land of "normalcy" and "self-acceptance." Here we have the triumph of the therapeutic. Faith in faith provides "positive thinking" - confidence in oneself and all one's activities. Not faith in God who empowers but a "man-centered faith, a worldly, lift-yourselves-by-your-own-bootstraps doctrine" and therapy.

Whatever the explanation of what has happened, Americans now share this historically distinctive mainstream consciousness from which God is absent, - simultaneously holding their individual religious beliefs. And this contemporary mainstream consciousness affects the way we interpret our specific religious beliefs.

As acknowledged above, there is no single consciousness in a culture. Our great nation is a community of communities. And each community fashions its distinctive consciousness. The religious communities certainly are open to God in their consciousness. Polls report how large a percentage of Americans profess belief in God. Religious activities and moral positions are often covered on television news as well as by radio, newspapers, and magazines. There are regular religious programs on radio and television, not to mention religious television networks. Nonetheless over and above this religious consciousness there is a historically distinctive mainstream consciousness which affects even this religious consciousness.

Apart from the fact that many "believers" are so affected by mainstream consciousness that their profession as Catholics, Protestants, or Jews is belied by their beliefs and behavior, believers today do not experience the support and security in their belief that believers in an earlier age had when the mainstream consciousness included awareness of God. One reason for this is that academic intellectuals and the media tend not to pay attention to religion, treating its teachings and practices as atavistic epiphenomena of contemporary culture.

CONTEMPORARY CONSCIOUSNESS, THEATER, MEDIA

Sociological studies like those explanations of what has happened alert us to the reality of the mainstream consciousness and help us understand how it affects us. And a moment's reflection on today's theater, movies, and television confirms the absence of God from this mainstream consciousness.

Years ago Eugene O'Neill, certainly one of America's greatest playwrights, revealed a sensitivity to the developing consciousness. "Most modern plays are concerned with the relation between man and man, but that doesn't interest me at all. I am interested only in the relation between man and God." Reference to God can be misleading, for elsewhere he said,

The playwright today must dig at the roots of the sickness of today as he feels it - the death of the old God and the failure of science and materialism to give any satisfying new one for the surviving primitive religious instinct to find a meaning for life in, and to comfort the fears of death with. It seems to me that anyone trying to do big work nowadays must have this big subject behind all the little subjects of his plays or novels, or he is simply scribbling around the surface of things and has no more real status than a parlor entertainer. (*Nine Plays by Eugene O'Neill*, Introduction by J.U. Krutch, p. xvii)

Today's consciousness had not yet developed, but O'Neill (1888-1953) reveals awareness of a significant stage of its development. Raised a Catholic, he had lost his faith in an era when sophisticates professed atheism, even though the dominant mainstream consciousness still incorporated belief in God. O'Neill knew that God's existence was being denied and intuitively he sensed "the sickness of the day."

From the time language emerged, allowing people to be conscious of being selves, questions about the meaning of death and life demanded answers. Without answers here, people become sick. O'Neill knew that religion had provided answers to those questions; he knew that although science and materialism were undermining religion, they were unable to substitute alternative ways to heal "the (resulting) sickness of the day."

Denial of God and profession of materialistic atheism came to be so taken for granted that the mainstream consciousness is no longer *aware* of any such "sickness."

A study of today's theater provides a glimpse into this contemporary consciousness. With few exceptions our playwrights present characters living as though there were no God. An echo of O'Neill can be discerned in Tony Kushner's *Angels in America,* (1991), winner of the Pulitzer Prize and of the Tony Award two years running. Very much aware of the "sickness" in body and heart *Angels* makes clear that the myth of God and heaven no longer serves: gay lifestyle is here to stay and people without faith will struggle on. So explicit a denial hearkens back to the late nineteenth century. Perhaps Kushner sensed a need to defy religion as interest has awakened among the unchurched, among business leaders, and so forth. Such renewed interest, however, cannot be said to have yet changed today's dominant mainstream consciousness.

Movies certainly present people living as though there were no God. And television not only reveals the same consciousness but significantly shapes it. Because TV must win audiences for business and government, it must appeal to people's desires. By careful study of viewers' opinions and wishes it discovers how to present entertainment, commercials, and even news in forms that feed those opinions and desires. It selects out what characterizes Americans in general. Sales and ratings confirm its judgments. By letting these characteristics shape what it presents, television both reflects and reinforces those same outlooks and values.

The dominant contemporary consciousness so revealed would have us interpret life's events and problems without reference to God. According to a 1990 study at the University of Dayton "Religion is an 'invisible institution' on primetime network television." Socioeconomic and political events are reported in the media without reference to the human dimension of relationship to God. Most recently ABC seems to have discovered something happening, possibly a resurgence of religious practice. Will the other media make the same discovery? Will interest in it last? Tax-supported schools are prohibited from referring to God and thus they reinforce the secular, godless, humanistic world-view.

This secular humanism is not proposed and argued. It is taken for granted, providing the framework of what is considered real and of value. Everyone admits the dimension of reality and value so portrayed. Christians perceive a deeper dimension, a wider scope of reality and a richer, more expansive spread of values. Secular humanists could complain if these added dimensions were included. When, repeatedly, in all sorts of contexts, reality and values are limited to what secular humanists acknowledge, people tend to interpret events and problems as though reality and values really were limited to what secular humanism professes.

The God-question takes on a distinctive form because of this mainstream consciousness. Hence it is essential to describe this consciousness, to underscore how its characteristics result not from intellectual proof but from cultural options, and finally to clarify how it is distinctive by excluding even the consideration of God.

SUMMARY AND CONCLUSION

Certainly it is odd to claim mainstream consciousness blocks out the very idea of God in a country where 90% plus profess belief in God, where the media report religious happenings and the proclamations of religious leaders.

Granted each distinctive community generates its proper consciousness and so members of religious communities share awareness of God, the dominant mainstream consciousness affects even religious people. What has happened in American culture verifies this: "The American Way of Life" dilutes all affirmations of God.

Characterized by a sense that all is contingent, relative, and temporal (as well as by a sense of freedom and autonomy) our dominant mainstream consciousness tends to prism out any attention to even the idea of God. Today's God-question, therefore, is historically distinctive. People have to be challenged to question the effect of such a consciousness. Remembering that it results from options - not proof should open people to the demand of intellectual integrity to investigate whether there may not be something necessary, absolute, and eternal.

"Is there a God?" The insight is simple so that everyone can, indeed in some way does, know God. One has only to look with "the eye behind the eye," with intelligence. The appeal to intellectual integrity will be encouraged by demonstrating that the existence of God is an intellectually respectable issue.

CHAPTER 5

FACING THE QUESTION TOGETHER

How can we get people to look with "the eye behind the eye" at the issue of God's existence? That is what we've been trying to do - to make clear how unwarranted it is for contemporary mainstream consciousness to block out consideration of God; to demonstrate that secular humanism developed by options, not proofs, and from mistaken appeal to science, not philosophy, to prove God's existence. What more would dispose people to investigate whether or not God exists? We shall try to clear a path from where nonbelievers are standing (comfortably living in the mainstream consciousness which blocks out any thought about God) to a spot where the world lies before them as a panorama they've never observed before. There the question of God cannot be avoided. So that nonbelievers will not hesitate to follow this path, each step of the way will be on solid ground and intimately connected, one step leading to the next, leaving the path open for re-inspection or retreat at any time.

A schematic outline of the steps along this path makes clear how the topics to be treated successively are intimately related, developing one from the other. We begin by pointing out that today the question of God's existence must be faced in a collaborative effort with philosophers, scientists, theologians seeking a common perspective. But immediately there emerges a challenge to the entire project. Is it possible to prove God is? Or is "fideism" right, only faith allows one to say there is a God? Related to fideism are two other issues: (1) the assumption that feeling warrants judgments and (2) the place of agnosticism at the heart of knowledge of God.

After clearing away these obstacles we examine a series of "dispositive arguments" aimed at stimulating a keen sense of how intellectually responsible our question is: Does God exist?

A COLLABORATIVE EFFORT

At this point in history all educated people esteem and appreciate science and technology. That is a given. Pope John Paul II agrees the time is right for increased collaboration between religion and science.

> Turning to the relationship between religion and science, there has been a definite, though still fragile and provisional, movement toward a new and more nuanced interchange. We have begun to talk to one another on deeper levels than before, and with greater openness toward one another's perspectives. We have begun to search together for a more thorough understanding of one another's disciplines, with their competencies and their limitations, and especially for areas of common ground...It is crucial that this common search...grow and deepen in its quality and scope.
>
> John Paul II, "Message of His Holiness Pope John Paul II," *On Science and Religion*, ed. R. J. Russell, Wm. R. Stoeger, S.J., and George V. Coyne, S.J. (Notre Dame: University of Notre Dame Press, 1990), M4.

Pope John Paul invites scientists, philosophers, and theologians to address issues the Church and human society in general are faced with. The Church and the Academy, he states, bear "before God enormous responsibilities for the human condition" because of the profound influence both have "on the development of ideas and values and on the the course of human action." The booklet cited contains the responses of nineteen distinguished intellectuals, Catholic and non-Catholic, believers and nonbelievers. All applaud the Pope's initiative and daring, although some remain quite critical of any prospects for immediate success.

In 1987, at the Pope's directive, an international research conference was convened at the Vatican Observatory in honor of the three hundredth anniversary of the publication of Newton's epoch-making book, *Philosophiae Naturalis Principia Mathematica*. Scholars in the respective fields indicated in the title of the published papers, *Physics, Philosophy and Theology* (1988, distributed by University of Notre Dame Press), came from the United States, Canada, United Kingdom, Poland, Denmark, and Switzerland. Pope John Paul's invitation for extended collaboration was first published as a foreword to this publication.

The present Pope, a scholar in his own right, has consistently been concerned at encouraging such open dialogue. After the conference mentioned above, he told the Vatican Observatory staff that besides continuing their excellent work in communicating the Church's perspective on science he wanted them to take steps to communicate the perspective of the scientific community to the bishops. Accordingly, in the summer of 1991 a workshop on Galileo and galaxies was held for bishops from around the world.

Nonbelievers, especially those shaped by the sciences and aware of the historical conflicts between science and religion, may be surprised to learn that this conference and the subsequent invitation are not extraordinary or without precedent. In 1936 the Church established the Pontifical Academy of Science, which traces its origin to the Academy of the Lynxes (Linceorum Academia) founded in Rome in 1603, reorganized in 1847. The Pontifical Academy is the only supranational body of its kind in the world, with a Pope-selected, lifelong membership of outstanding mathematicians and scientists from all over the world. Exceptional competence is required, but not belief, Christian or otherwise. Its purpose is to honor pure science and its practitioners, to promote the freedom of pure science, and to foster research. Popes are able to rely on the Academy for the most authoritative current scientific findings. Confident that truth cannot contradict truth, the Church has always supported and encouraged science, learning and art - in spite of impressions many have had to the contrary. In that spirit Pope John Paul II instituted a parallel academy in 1995 for the social sciences.

Pope John Paul proposes "a more thorough-going dialogue" between the community of world religions and the scientific community, "a dialogue in which the integrity of both religion and science is supported and the advance of each is fostered." What objective prompts such daring collaboration? "To build a culture that is more humane and in that way more divine." *(Op.cit.,* M7-8)

The present work aims at contributing modestly in two ways to this objective. First, it specifies the kind of reasoning appropriate to the God-question, showing how this kind differs from scientific reasoning.

The international research conference convened at the Pope's directive devoted part of its time to that precise issue. Later I shall attempt to spell out the kind of reasoning required for pursuing our radical question, "Does God exist?" At that point I shall refer to some of the pertinent insights of the research conference.

Second, this work aims at establishing the existence of God, thereby improving the climate for dialogue between the scientific and religious communities.

IS IT POSSIBLE TO PROVE GOD IS?

A collaborative effort, yes, but since that fateful slippage from "distinction" to "separation" of faith and reason, people have not expected to reason to God's existence.

Both the nonbeliever and some believers may be surprised at the proposal to "prove" that God exists if they assume that science is the only way to establish *what is the case*. As we have seen, science has no need of God in its projects. Since it was developed and structured to deal with the sensible and quantitative, it simply can never attain the immaterial and spiritual. For secular humanists, of course, the case is closed - unless appeal to intellectual integrity succeeds.

Furthermore, if the model of proof is mathematics or chemistry, obviously proof of God's existence will seem impossible. But take history as your paradigm and proof of God's existence becomes more plausible. Possibility of proof becomes still easier to accept if the method of determining guilt or innocence in judicial trials is taken as the model.

In other words, no reasoning to God's existence will offer the compelling rigor one generally meets in mathematics or chemistry. Even in sciences reasoning is not so compelling when peers discuss the outer reaches of these fields.

As for history, certainly numerous facts and interpretations of events have been accepted as proved. But the marshalling of evidence differs significantly from procedures in mathematics or chemistry - and the conclusions are not so compelling.

During a court trial facts, motivations, circumstances, and witnesses all contribute to the process of proving guilt or innocence. Frequently the evidence is far less forceful than what grounds conclusions in history or the sciences. That terrible miscarriages of justice have occurred when the innocent have been found guilty does not warrant saying that no truth can be obtained by a court trial. Prudent caution is necessary and careful reflection on the force of evidence is essential.

The kinds of data and warrants proper to each of these fields differ. Consequently people have to open their minds to the fact that the kind of data and warrants invoked in reasoning to God's existence

necessarily will be proper to the God issue. If there is a God, God is unique and in unique relationship with things. It should not be surprising that the process to discover God will likewise be unique.
This is not to suggest settling for something less than rigorous reasoning. Rather, the reasoning will be different, still rigorous, but appropriate to the unique relationship of "beings" to ultimate "Being." Formal proofs move on the metaphysical level where the force of reasoning is difficult to experience. If one catches the proper perspective on the data of the God issue, then he'll recognize the rigor of the arguments.

FIDEISM AND PSEUDO-FIDEISM

Among believers, the problem may be fideism - that is, reliance on faith **rather** than reason. For Protestants who hold that original sin left human reason corrupted, it makes sense to say that reason cannot be trusted. Consistently they contend that there can be no philosophy of God. Philosophy of religion, perhaps, but not what Catholics have long taught as Natural Theology, a philosophy concerned with what we can know about God by reason. Such a stance leaves those Protestants vulnerable to the charge of being *un*reasonable. If reason is unable to establish that God exists, then isn't the *reasonable* position that of atheism?

Many Catholics talk as though they are fideists. But look what follows, implicitly. If there is such a gulf between faith and reason, then the philosopher, who by profession deals with reason, ought similarly to stand for atheism. If it is impossible for the universe of reason and the universe of faith to intersect at any point, then it is *unreasonable* to accept any of the affirmations of faith, even the first, that God is. The reasonable position for the philosopher is atheistic denial. For Thomas, the cardinal point of delicate intersection is the instant that reason affirms what faith also affirms, namely that God is.

Granted reason is able to affirm that God is, it may be reasonable to believe God has spoken to us, has revealed truths about God and about what we are, what our destiny is, how we ought to live. But if reason is unable to affirm that God is, then there can be no *reasonable* grounds to believe God has revealed anything.

One may still continue to believe but one is then a fideist (believing blindly), vulnerable to the legitimate charge of being *un*reasonable.

Actually, most people do have an intellectual element in their religious response. They know the world and life do not make sense unless there is a God. They're convinced, probably without being able to marshal evidence sufficient to convince others, that God has protected them in certain situations or provided for them in special ways. Because they've been gifted with faith and especially if they're living a life of prayer, the reality of God is woven into all they do. And they may never disengage the intellectual strands of evidence for God's existence.

Normally they have no need to raise any question about God's existence. Untrained in philosophy or theology, they may stammer in any attempt to articulate why they believe. They have no need to apologize. Most people who enjoy Beethoven and Mozart are unable to explain why. Believers probably feel equally incapable of justifying their preference for Capitalism over Communism, equally incapable of justifying the way they raise their children.

Two important points must be made. Like most holistic responses (such as contemporary sensitivity about germs) and lifestyles, religious response involves intellectual elements that are fused with imaginative and emotional elements. It often requires specialized training to extricate the intellectual elements and assess their truth. Second, faith has a role in the final committed acceptance of the reasoned conclusion that God exists. Some time will be devoted to explaining this subtle role of faith in the proofs.

Two failures underlie the pose of some believers as fideists:
1) failure to recognize that there is an intellectual element in one's religious response and
2) especially failure to distinguish between the reasoning process and the committed acceptance of the conclusion with the help of grace.

Believers are wrong and do serious disservice to religion when they claim they "just do" believe in God and give the impression that there are no intellectual grounds for affirming that God exists. The fact probably is that they feel inadequate to identify those grounds. But to hold that reason has no valid status in religion is to hold that religion has no reasonable status in human lives. It follows that being religious must be unreasonable, that the reasonable person is the atheist! They may think they escape the need to justify their beliefs and lifestyles. Instead, they denigrate their faith, putting it on the level of their taste in food and music.

Catholics have the assurance of the first Vatican Council that reason can indeed establish the existence of God. Whether an individual believer is able to articulate reasonable grounds for his belief has nothing to do with whether it is possible to have reasonable grounds for one's belief. I have full confidence that the earth moves around the sun and full confidence that this can be established by reason, even though I myself am completely incompetent to prove it.

Similarly the believer can modestly acknowledge certainty about his belief along with his inadequacy to prove it. This is very different from suggesting that God's existence is something human reason cannot establish.

"FEELING" VS. "KNOWING"

Cognate with the fideistic and pseudo-fideistic (confused believers) attitude is the appeal to "feeling" that it is not possible to prove God's existence. Feeling has always been the source of many judgments and decisions, but it became emphatically the warrant in the counterculture of the late '60's and '70's.

"Feeling" as warrant was "feeling" in the sense of affective response or "feeling" in the sense of response in accord with one's lifestyle. Rock music, drugs, and sexual indulgence released repressed spontaneity among people living on "feeling" in the former sense. These were "with it," they were "swingers." Love, for such people, meant "You make me feel good." The worth of any idea or activity was judged by whether it "turned them on."

Warranting judgments and choices by "feeling" in this sense is destructive for the individual. It constitutes living on Kierkegaard's aesthetic level. Despair is inevitable. And society would simply collapse if this way of life became common. Although the counterculture disappeared, reliance on feeling still affects many lives.

The latter sense of feeling is an ordinary way to warrant judgments and choices; it simply is not the last recourse. The authenticity of a lifestyle response as warrant depends on the validity of the presuppositions incorporated into that lifestyle. After all, one judges as one is. The wise, the just, the continent person almost instantly and intuitively perceives what justice and temperance require in a given situation. They "feel" what is the right thing to do. Of course the habitually unjust and incontinent person responds with equal spontaneity and intuition to the same situation in the opposite direction. And there exactly is the problem. In each case things "feel" right!

Much harm actually resulted from using feeling as basis for judgments and choices even on life-style response. Families were broken up when it felt good to change one's life, even though this involved disloyalty to spouse and children. Many Catholics, theologians included, embracing attitudes and lifestyles based on secular humanism, found it "felt" right to *accept* certain doctrines and to take certain moral stances. Since these doctrines and moral evaluations were in accord with the current thought, it felt right and comfortable to adopt them.

Theoretical thinking must be reincorporated into our holistic response. What is the role of this theoretical thinking? It comes into play either through the desire to know or when habits, institutions, or lifestyles are challenged. Challenge comes in the form of unhappiness or conflict or because the presuppositions built into a lifestyle are denied or questioned.

Exposition of the conflict between secular humanism and Christianity in Chapter Three exemplified the issue and process of theoretical thinking.

If then one "feels" it is not possible to prove God's existence, the preceding section on fideism will at least have forced a re-examination of why a person "feels" that way.

The Place for Agnosticism

Too often believers, comfortable in their belief, ignore the profound "agnosticism" involved in all knowledge of God. Those skeptical about the possibility of proving there is a God may find that explicit acknowledgement of the unknowableness of God is really the truth they want to preserve.

St. Thomas Aquinas, strong in affirming reason's power to discover God's existence, is equally firm in insisting that we cannot know *what* God is.

Recall that Thomas reduced all possible questions about God to four and posed them to reason itself. Whether fideism is true or false depends on whether reason is able to answer those questions.

The four questions are:
"Does God exist?"
"What God is not?" [This question replaces the usual second question:What the thing (in our case, God) is?]
"How do we know God?"
"How do we speak about God?"

Most pertinent to the issue of fideism is his claim that after we prove *that* God is, we cannot know *what* God is, but only what God *is not*. Is that an arbitrary claim? By no means. It rests firmly on the fact that reason has only one road to attain God. Since our knowledge originates in sensation, our knowledge is limited to whatever sensible things can lead us to. Sensible things can only lead us to God as cause and they necessarily are inadequate representations of their cause. Hence everything we know about God is reached through a threefold predication: affirmation, negation, supereminence. Thus, for example, God is intelligent (for God created intelligent beings). But God also is not intelligent (in the limited, contingent way people are intelligent). God is supereminently intelligent, in a superior and utterly mysterious way. Every effort to know anything about what God is involves this threefold predication. Always utter mystery!

A profound agnosticism, an ignorance, is at the heart of our knowledge about God. This is the truth some people are certain of, the truth they insist on (fearing it is being denied) and intend to affirm by claiming it's not possible to prove God's existence.

Let them hold onto this truth, while still reflecting carefully on the precise questions being asked. The question about what God is not arises only after we answer the first question: Does God exist? It is absolutely crucial that the agnosticism start after the affirmation of existence. Knowledge that God exists, yes, but ignorance of God's essence. And even to know God's existence we must apply the threefold predication. God is, but at the same time God is not (like anything else I know). Still God is in a supereminent way which escapes my comprehension.

This ordering of questions, this distinction between knowledge of existence and ignorance of essence is not restricted to the God issue. Because I don't know what light is (Is it a wave or a particle?) doesn't mean I don't know that there is light. Because I don't feel comfortable with any definition of love doesn't mean that I don't know whether there is love in the world. Even more striking, ask yourself if you know who the person is that you love most in your life! Not only do you know the loved one exists but you easily identify him/her as this body, this way of smiling, walking, even this way of reacting to situations. But the person, him/herself--who is he/she? Mystery! And yet you relate on the deepest level with this loved one.

The order of questions is important. Because I can come to know that God is (even though I know God only as Other) I can know God is present to me, to us. I'm able to cultivate a relationship with this Transcendent Other. And the utter mysteriousness of what God is leaves me humble and awed. At the same time all I learn about God from revelation I associate with the mysterious Being so known.

The religious lifestyle built on faith, prayer, community worship and living provides the holistic response which generates a sense of intimacy with this utterly mysterious God. Probably this sense of intimacy also lies behind the claim that it is not possible to prove God's existence by reason. Once again the role of theoretical thinking is apparent. If conflict warrants it we can disengage the intellectual component of a religious lifestyle and try to establish the truth of the underlying intellectual presupposition. But it is equally important that discovery of intellectual truth be somehow incorporated in a religious lifestyle. Certainly, living religiously is far more important than arguing intellectually.

For those who have been "turned off" by religious institutions, this is not an argument for church membership in order to relate to God. Rather the point is simply that a holistic response involves far more than intellectual assent to the truth: God exists. There is an emotional dimension, an appetitive element of love, of desiring union. The final chapter will address this issue of institution and the value of finding a community of people who share one's convictions about God's existence and one's desire to be united with God. Not that God needs our worship, but *we* need to respond to what we know is true: that God exists. *We* need the support of people who think and feel as we do.

DISPOSITIVE ARGUMENTS

We spoke of a path for nonbelievers, stretching from where they stand now to a spot with a panoramic view. With fideism and its cognate positions disproved, the path is clearer. Now it seems that proof of God's existence may be possible - in a form proper to the issue - though not in the form of the natural sciences.

To encourage nonbelievers in this search, consider some dispositive arguments, proposed not as probative, but as evidence that the question deserves to be considered. Believers will find these same "arguments" not unrelated to their own state of mind. For believers, these ideas are psychological aids. Before any proof they do not constitute rigorous proofs; after a satisfying proof they roborate and flesh out the metaphysical reasoning and conclusion, allowing one to feel comfortable with the reasonableness of affirming God's existence. In the midst of believers it's easy to retain faith in the existence of God. But in our secular humanistic culture it takes genuine effort to keep belief vibrant. For example, the perspective of history shows that the vast majority of *all* people who *ever* lived believed in God!

NATURAL SCIENCES

Discoveries of science can allure one to raise the question of
God as creator. Seventeenth and eighteenth century attempts to base belief in God on the findings of science have been seen as both error and disaster, but certain scientific findings have opened up the

question about God - a question to be investigated by philosophic rather than scientific reasoning.

Having learned this, Christian scientists warn against making much of the "anthropic principle," a term coined in 1974 referring to the result of applying the elementary particle and quantum theories to the first moments of the "Big Bang."

> ...[A] 'life-bearing' universe...was extremely unlikely... Estimates varied of just how unlikely, but the Cambridge theorists who first developed these ideas...thought it could be much less than one in a million."
> (E. McMullin, "Natural Science and Belief in a Creator,"*Physics, Philosophy and Theology*, pp.70-71)

act it has been estimated that "If the rate of expansion one second after the Big Bang had been smaller by even one part in a hundred thousand million million it would have re-collapsed before it reached its present size."

(Ian G. Barbour, *Religion in an Age of Science*, San Francisco, Harper & Row, 1990, p. 135)

The author of the article quoted just above holds that a design argument based on the "anthropic principle" relies on a "gap" [as in God of the gaps]: "the inability of contemporary physical theory to explain the original tight specification of the initial cosmic state." Already nontheistic theories are being offered to explain the data. (E. McMullin, ibid.) Nonetheless, certain scientific findings can be used, not as proofs but as ways to open up the question, "Is there a God?" Two of the three most respectable theories of the origin of the universe, for example, open neatly into the question of God as creator. The first is that of the expanding universe. Pope Pius XII developed this theory in order to lead to the insight of God as creator. The expanding universe theory, together with the diverse but converging methods of dating the universe, as well as the Law of Entropy, pictures the universe as starting at some definite time (perhaps 15 billion years ago), expanding to the present state and due at some future date to lose all its energy. The famous scientist, Edmund Whittaker, also works with this data in treating the question of God's existence. Is it possible that there be absolutely nothing (15 billion years ago) and the universe just came into existence? Can something arise from absolute nothing? Or mustn't there be something (one) causing the universe to come into existence? But the need for creation is a philosophical insight, even though common sense can grasp it. The distance between the expanding universe and its creative cause is a philosophic step.

Another general theory is the "constant state universe" which demands constant creation of hydrogen atoms. Although he no longer holds this position, Hoyle proposed the theory claiming it does not prove the existence of God. As a scientist he is perfectly logical. In the capacity of scientist he has only to postulate the succession of new hydrogen atoms coming into existence. To deny the existence of God, however, in this context is illogical. From a philosophical perspective the coming into existence of new atoms of hydrogen raises the obvious question: Must there not be a creator of these, since something cannot come from nothing?

Neither of the preceding theories postulated or proved there is [or is not] a God. As scientific, **neither theory even raises the question**. The philosophical questions evoked by the two scientific theories are what lead the mind to the insight that there must be a creator, a being existing independently of anything else and able to produce being from absolute nothingness.

The theory of the "pulsating universe" does not lead to God so easily. An entirely different treatment is required. This theory postulates that once the universe expands to a certain point it returns in the opposite direction. Unlike the expanding universe theory, this theory does not presuppose a time before which the universe did not exist. It therefore does not evoke the philosophical question: How did the universe come into existence from not being? No new atoms are postulated. So the philosophical question of creation does not come immediately to mind. A subsequent chapter of this book will deal with the impossibility of the pulsating universe being self-sufficient.

Science, then, can awaken wonder and curiosity about the source of the marvels uncovered by science. And the nonbeliever can be encouraged to pursue the questioning by reflecting on three striking facts: billions of believers, witness of great thinkers, and witness of the mystics.

UNIVERSAL BELIEF

There is little controversy about our primitive ancestors believing in gods, indeed little controversy about peoples in general believing in transcendent beings, till this post-modern era of history. Thus billions upon billions of people have held religious belief in God or gods.

As for today's population, consider the various world-wide studies and polls about belief in God's existence. Without pursuing the full meaning of that belief just remember that the vast majority of people on our planet profess belief in God. Projections for the year 2000 estimate that the vast majority of the population will profess there is a God.

Someone may ask, "How can this be true and yet the dominant mainstream consciousness excludes the very idea of God?" In Chapter Four we identified the dominant mainstream consciousness as that historically distinctive consciousness mediated today by the media and academics. It affects practically everyone, but by no means cancels or replaces the consciousness of the different communities. Without question it structures our government, business, education, our social, economic and political perspectives and is palpable in our media, art, and entertainment.

And the countless people who take their religion seriously do not escape the impact of our mainstream consciousness. Believers today do not experience the support for their belief that believers had a century ago and earlier. They do not meet God in the economic, social, and political spheres, nor in entertainment nor in the media. Believers themselves must add a religious dimension when they engage in those spheres and they must reinterpret what they see and hear in movies, media, and theater.

The dominant mainstream consciousness reveals a practical atheism - a way of life with little or no attention to God or God's existence that encourages people to act as though there were no God. This, I submit, is compatible with a theoretical affirmation of a God, especially an affirmation without deep, serious conviction.

Furthermore, consciousness prisms everything through itself - but does not question itself. Consider what our American Constitution proclaims: All men are created equal. Yet for almost a century Americans used slaves! For almost two centuries Americans, equal all, refused women the right to vote. Contradictions *can be ignored*. Most of us live with contradictions in our lives.

Back to the striking fact: the vast majority of people on our planet, including people in the West, profess belief that there is a God. Even optimistic atheists only project 4.2% of the world population to be atheists by the year 2000. Moreover it is worth calling attention to the fact that no entire people has totally denied God or has been totally ignorant of God's existence. Even Marxist-Leninist attempts to wipe out belief in God in the Soviet Union obviously failed.

WITNESS OF GREAT THINKERS AND MYSTICS

Numbers obviously do not make anything true. Suppose only *un*enlightened people could believe in God. The numbers, which certainly do consist for the most part of simple people, become much more convincing when added to the remarkable agreement of outstanding thinkers of *all* ages on the question of God's existence. So alongside the naive, quasi-spontaneous assertion of God's existence in polls and the universal belief in simpler times, we have the reflective positing of the same belief by thinkers of the stature of Plato, Aristotle, Plotinus, Augustine, Thomas, Descartes, Leibnitz, Kant, Whitehead, James, thinkers who have profoundly influenced civilization.

Just as the understanding of what God is differed in the course of history, so the ways varied by which thinkers arrived at an understanding of God's existence. Still it is very significant that almost all great thinkers up until now, the post-Christian era, arrived by independent, profound reflection at the same conclusion: There is a God. And even during this post-Christian era most intellectuals hold belief in some sort of God. Certainly for every outstanding thinker who denies the existence of God, as did Sartre (although near the end of his life he acknowledged that there might be a transcendent being), there is another thinker of equal stature who professes belief in God as did G. Marcel. This is true among scientists as well.

The evidence is reassuring. Not only have billions of people today and throughout history believed in God but also the question has been examined by the most profound thinkers in the world and agreement has generally been reached that there is a God. Reassuring for believers and challenging for nonbelievers! The weight of evidence can be increased by looking at the mystics, men and women who report extraordinary religious experiences. Today concrete experience is highly esteemed.

What is the scientific value of the testimony of these mystics? Science accepts the testimonies of unique experiences when the persons involved provide sufficient guarantees of honesty and competence. Many mystics are clearly superior persons and witnesses worthy of respect. Not only are they recognized as persons of integrity and holiness but also as people who have made outstanding contributions in various fields. I think of St. Ignatius of Loyola, St. John of the Cross, and St. Teresa of Avila. The list is long. And there are non-Christian mystics as well. There is a fundamental accord among mystics when they describe the experiences themselves, the successive phases of the mystical life as well as the object of their intuitions. The basic point of God's existence is one of remarkable convergence among the mystics.

Keep in mind the purpose of this listing of "dispositive arguments." By no means proofs that God exists but undeniable facts that deserve to be faced.

SUMMARY AND CONCLUSION

The aim of this chapter has been to encourage nonbelievers to pursue seriously the question: Does God exist? After identifying how the present work shares in the collaborative effort of scientists, philosophers, and theologians, we removed a common confusion about what "proof" means in the God-issue. The path to the panoramic view has been cleared of certain misapprehensions like fideism and its cognate positions, while the proper place for agnosticism of God's essence has been preserved. Dispositive arguments provided serious reasons to interest nonbelievers in looking at the issue.

At this point we have met the overall objective of Part One: to stimulate genuine readiness to address the radical question: Is there a God? The two contrasting questions, symptomatic of our era, have been resolved into that radical question. "Can an intelligent person reasonably acknowledge there is a God?" captures the likely focus of nonbelievers. "Is knowing and relating to God a basic part of human nature?" reflects the concern of believers. It seems clear that to answer these contrasting questions we must engage the radical question. By starting with "belief in" we were able to establish how nonbelievers and believers alike have to propose "belief that" which provides needed overarching meaning for life. Crucial, of course, to all overarching meanings is the affirmation or denial of God's existence. In another era that might have sufficed, but it was necessary to deal with contemporary mainstream consciousness, undergirded as it is by secular humanism. The entire God question today has a distinctive perspective since such a consciousness blocks out consideration of even the possibility of a God. Detailed treatment of consciousness and secular humanism has uncovered the challenge to intellectual integrity to acknowledge the effect of today's consciousness and to recognize how unwarranted its blinding characteristics are.

Chapter Four built on all this. And assuming nonbelievers are disposed to argue the radical question of God's existence we are ready for Part Two.

PART II

Open to addressing the radical question, "Is there a God?" we must be clear about and agreed upon two things:
1) What the term "God" means and
2) The kind of reasoning that will be used here.

We first deal with the meaning of "God" and at the same time identify how reason functions in our issue, relating it to actual experiences which may be understood as encounters with God.

For the kind of reasoning involved we consider knowing as a form of awareness within which reasoning takes place.

To make the process of proof successful, this kind of reasoning calls for three "conversions": intellectual, moral, and religious. As shown earlier, the kind of reasoning used in the sciences will not be used here since it is inappropriate for this subject.

Disqualifying scientific reasoning for our purposes is an occasion for describing the philosophy called scientism. Scientism will be treated at length in Part Four with five chapters on Naturalism.

CHAPTER 6

MEANING OF "GOD" AND PERSONAL GOD-QUESTION

Assuming that the objectives of Part One have been achieved, let the dialogue begin..

First we must be sure we are talking about the same thing when we use the term "God."

Second, if the investigation is to be significant, each person must have a clearly articulated question. Obviously, the questions must be cognate.

Third, it is critical to understand just how reasoning functions in our issue.

(Since reasoning grounds the conviction that certain experiences can be interpreted as encounters with God, we must,)

Fourth, identify just which experiences are pertinent.

MEANING OF "GOD"

In any sophisticated process of reasoning, the nonbeliever and I must agree that the being attained by the reasoning, if valid, does indeed qualify as "God."

Everybody, nonbelievers as well as believers, must be familiar with the word "God." But the meaning of the word depends on personal history, on how it fits within their "form of life." Human response to a term is more than intellectual grasp of a concept. Imagination and emotion clothe our concepts.

What I have in mind can be illustrated by the word "father." Imagine how differently the word rings in the ears of people who idolized their fathers and in the ears of those who grew up not even knowing them. Again, what does "love" mean to those who have never experienced it? Or to those who have become cynical because the supposed love of their parents dissolved and they watched one parent suffer because of love betrayed by the other?

To relate our definition of God to people's lives, first look at a few scenarios in which God plays significantly diverse roles - thus affecting the understanding of "God." Next, since the term's natural habitat is religion, consider what "God" means in Christian living. Finally, we shall distil a definition of "God" from that lifestyle which will, I am sure, be acceptable to believers and nonbelievers.

For the devout believer "God" refers to a Being ever present, loved above all, the center of life. All day long this believer walks with God, talks with God, turns to God especially in needs, relishing God's presence. The richest moments of life are spent in God's presence - in prayerful joyful union, in making important decisions, in shaping all of life.

"God" for a non-devout believer is still real. Probably he does not walk with God or frequently talk with God. Secular, worldly realities

primarily occupy his attention. Still, in serious moral decisions he does face God. In regular worship he acknowledges God's reality. Evidence of his sincerity is his concern that his children learn about God and the church, synagogue, or mosque he attends. His financial support of the religious institution is also evidence.
What about nonbelievers? Consider the man who, although raised in a believing family, has lost all faith in God. He will react very differently to the term "God." He lives as a negative or as a positive atheist; he simply *lacks belief* in God (negative) or he *believes* there is no God (positive).

The former, or *a fortiori* the child of negative atheists, may have a lifestyle very similar to that of a believer but lacking any sense of the divine dimension. He "sees" things and events "as" natural, simply human things and events. The believer, in contrast, "sees" similar things and events in her life "as" related to God. Supposing contented lives in both cases, he feels fortunate; she, blessed by God. Contemporary consciousness conditions people to experience life like the negative atheist. Believers have to make an effort to incorporate the divine dimension into their lives .

For the negative atheist, references to "God" are like references to "father" for the fatherless person or like references to "love" for the one who has never known love. When negative atheists watch television coverage of religious services they're respectful, but prayers to "God" and exhortations to belief are like archeological reports of primitive tribal worship or like discussions about "transmissions" and "heat shields" to the nonmechanical, except that in the latter case the reference is to something admittedly real, even though they haven't a glimmer what the things are..

The positive atheist responds very much like the negative atheist in her daily living. If she belongs to an atheistic humanist society she may see belief in God as something harmful to society, herself and her family included. And she may actively attempt to ensure her family is not affected by religious activity. Whenever possible she may seek to give her totally secular interpretation of events.

"God" to such a person may evoke the image of an anthropomorphic deity or an oriental potentate-like god or a terrorizing image. "God" means a non-entity projected by believers as real - and belief in which harms or diminishes the human person.

To the *anti*theist, Communist or Existentialist, who looks upon belief in God as the source of human blindness and suffering, God is the enemy to be cast out of people's minds and hearts. Banish God so that private property may disappear and a new species of human beings may arise is the Communist attitude. "How can a person be truly free if there is a God?" expresses the Existentialist concern.

For a sophisticated antitheist the God-myth is assumed to have been successfully falsified and rejected. The idea of God seems concocted through alienation and a projection of human attributes (a la Feuerbach) or by an unfounded option (a la Sartre). This person wants to banish the idea entirely because he sees resultant harm to human nature or human freedom.

Let me add one last category of persons, the alienated theist. Such a person may seem to resemble the antitheist but is at heart a believer, probably a very angry one. I have in mind the person who has experienced evil in his life - perhaps had a parent, a spouse, a child ripped from his life. This, maybe after earnest prayers for help. Or there is the believer dismayed at human suffering - starving children, rank injustice, perhaps ecclesiastical complicity. Think of the rabbi who declared, "After Auschwitz how could I believe in God?" In both cases denial, angry denial, is on the lips but hurt belief in the heart. At the word "God," a guard goes up. He or she turns away to human concerns, like the father who has cast out his offending child and declares he no longer has a daughter, refusing even to talk about her.

Agreement?

How is it possible to reach agreement on the meaning of "God" if God has been absent in some lives, the very idea of God hated by others, yet real in the lives of still others, indeed intensely loved by some? I have confidence it is possible, though difficult. Why? In my judgment agreement can be reached on the meaning of "God" because we are all human and to be human involves knowing God, even though we may not realize it is God we are knowing.

I am convinced both that God exists and that there is a religious dimension to being human. These convictions explain why I find the following schematic argument valid. The nonbeliever would require considerable development of the argument, but still he may find it suggestive.

Built into our very natures and wantings is a fundamental thrust, the desire for perfect happiness. (Certainly nonbelievers acknowledge they want to be happy!) Only union with God can satisfy that desire. (Thomas Aquinas argues this point by calling attention to the nature of our intellect and will: desire for unlimited truth and desire for unlimited good. Only God can satisfy these desires.) What is naturally desired must be - in some way - naturally known. Therefore all human persons naturally know God.

Obviously not everyone knows or recognizes that it is God they know in wanting happiness. All sorts of obstacles, inner and outer, hinder that recognition. People set their hearts on riches, or pleasure, or honor, identifying these rather than God as the object of perfect happiness. Yet, in wanting perfect happiness it *is* God a person knows. But that is not simply knowing God. It is similar to an experience of seeing *someone* coming toward me. That someone actually is Mayor Jones. But I don't know that until get a clear view of him. Only then do I know that *all along* I have been seeing Mayor Jones coming toward me. So, too, everyone knows God, since everyone wants to be happy, even though he or she may not know it is God they want in wanting happiness.

DEFINITION OF GOD

Some readers may consider that argument just a slick ploy. No matter. If valid it at least suggests why everyone is able to agree on what is meant by God - to affirm or deny God exists.

Behind the question as to whether agreement can be reached on the meaning of "God," lies the difference between the holistic response of religious lifestyle (involving imagination, emotions, practices, as well as intellect and community) and the partial, abstractive response of theoretical thinking. The term "God" belongs properly within religion, within religious lifestyles. Search for a definition is an exercise of theoretical thinking.

Far from any conflict between lifestyle and theoretical thinking, they are ordered one to another. Belief in God is at the bottom of living religiously. Bizarre or humanly harmful practices in religions such as human sacrifice, are obviously related to erroneous understanding of God and human relations with God.

Hence it is appropriate that we derive our definition of 'God" from the term's natural habitat, religion. From this holistic understanding of "God" can come a theoretical definition which both believers and nonbelievers can accept.

Many people are correct in denying God's existence! Why? Because what they think of as God is ridiculous or even harmful to human living! Perhaps my treatment may help if they have been repulsed by false images of God.

Let me speak as representative of believing Christians. The God we meet is not the god of primitive myths but the God who was gradually revealed to the Jews as creator of the world, master of history. Beyond human comprehension, our God is spiritual, transcendent, vastly different from anything else we know. This is not a superstitious belief in gods or spirits intruding everywhere in life. Nor is God like some oriental potentate before whom I am to grovel in abject fear. Our God is a God of love calling each person to a relationship of love, so that fear is cast out; we exult in our dignity and freedom and increasing power. We do not live with taboos. Moral prohibitions are consciously rooted in reason or in explicit reference to Scripture. Ultimately, morality for us is a call to love from a personal God.

We do petition God for help and success, but it is not a question of bargaining with God or ritually rejoining the Great Time. The certainty of God's listening rests on faith in Jesus's directive, "Ask and you shall receive." Always, of course, we try to ask within the framework of "Yet, not my will, but thine be done."

Appreciating the power of technology and social organization, we ask without expecting miracles. For while we believe God can effect changes by miracles, we know God ordinarily leaves it to people to do what is necessary. Incidentally we think of God not as a gap-filler, but as the source of being.

God has invited us to an intimate covenant in Jesus, the God-man. This covenant is intended for all peoples, *none* excluded. Empowered beyond human virtue we are to love all, including enemies.

God has overcome death through Jesus Christ and promises beatific joy forever. Living for eternity, however, does not take the eyes or heart or mind away from the present world and people's needs. We are members of the human family and bring God's dealings with us to the human family. Joining forces with all others we discover how God has been dealing with them and this enlightens us and deepens the understanding and appreciation of the relationship with God. And we bring the light of the Gospel and the forces of Christian life to help all people build a truly human civilization.

This is the God who exists within the richness of Christian faith. Extended reasoning, faith, and indeed religious living are needed to reach that understanding of God. As mentioned at the outset, "God" is a word within a religious context and the false images of God which many people have need to be eliminated.

However, from this rich, lived understanding of God we can disengage a definition of God that any reasonable person can accept in the claim that God exists. If the reader recognizes how the abstract definition is embedded in a full religious lifestyle, it will generate a sense that the God-question is real and related to human living. At the same time it must be clear that we're discussing only one theoretical presupposition of a religious lifestyle; we are not investigating any other factor involved in a religion, and certainly not religion itself.

In religious experience I encounter something existing. I know what "something existing" means because I know I am something and existing. This *something* existing which I experience, however, exists as entirely *different from anything else knowable.* I know this is so because I reason to this something as the cause of limited, contingent things. So this something must exist, must have whatever is necessary to cause all contingent things to exist and cannot be contingent like the things it causes, for then it too would require a cause. To apply Thomas's threefold way of predication: God is something existing, but is not something like anything else, but something existing in a supereminent way, escaping all human comprehension.

Here then is the definition of "God" which everyone, believer or not, can accept: *Proof that such a being exists warrants agreement that God exists.* **God is something existing, entirely different from anything else, cause of contingent things, possessing whatever is necessary in order to cause contingent things to exist -- and so, not contingent but necessary.**

An entire course or more would be required to draw out the implications of all this and to show this existing something is immaterial, infinite, intelligent, able to will, intimately present through knowing, loving, and preserving everything in existence precisely by knowing and willing.

I shall link the existence of this "something" to certain lived experiences people certainly have, arguing it is reasonable to interpret those experiences as encounters with the living God.

In whatever classification readers consider themselves, negative, positive atheist, antitheist or alienated theist, not to mention believer, they should be able to agree that we have established there is a God *if* we can establish such a being exists as described.

WHAT IS THE READER'S QUESTION?

Does the reader have a genuine question about God defined this way? No one fully understands a proposition or a truth, without knowing it as an answer to a question. Whatever we learn and accept as true, we do not make our own until we discover it answers a genuinely experienced question.

At present God is very real to me. I sense God's presence; I pray; I want to live as God's instrument in all that I do, undertaking whatever

I do because it is God's will. Is there any point for me to try to prove that God exists? I do not have a genuine question about that, for I know the answer already. Perhaps sharing the following events will help the reader to choose a question.

Twice in my life I have had to face the challenge: Is there really a God? Twice this has been a genuine question and I needed an answer.

The first surge of doubt occurred, strangely enough, in the third year I was a Jesuit. After two years of intense religious experience during my noviceship, doubt arose in my mind. Looking back from my present position I think the doubt was not very serious. It troubled my intelligence, but not my heart. I consulted, I read, and the doubt dissipated in a year or two. But the second time was more disturbing. I had been ordained a priest a number of years when a dear friend left the Church. Suddenly I was shocked into facing the entire structure of my life. If my friend, who was very intelligent, gave up the Catholic faith, was I living an illusion? This challenge to my faith in Jesus Christ grew into a doubt about God.

When that occurred, I was seriously asking, "Is there a God?" That experience gave me great pause about proofs for the existence of God. I had been teaching the traditional proofs for God's existence for some years. Now as I turned to them in serious need they seemed to lack vital significance. My mind was dark those days and my heart was sick. Here I was a priest and a religious and I didn't know whether God exists or not.

I studied. I tried to pray. Time went on and gradually the living witness of a friend - the witness of one to whom God was real - somehow opened my eyes again to the living reality of God. This did not involve argument or reasoning at all. It was sharing the lived experience of God encountered. Incidentally my friend was unaware of being such a grace- filled witness and gift. Faith restored, the proofs rang true when I went back to them. I also realized the importance of keeping vibrant the sense of God's reality and presence.

Years later a student with a similar experience approached me. He had been raised a devout Catholic but belief in God had become disturbingly dull, if alive at all, and he felt challenged in his integrity as a person. He confessed serious doubt about God's existence and asked me to direct a specialized course in a tutorial relationship. I assigned authors who I thought might provide insights to rekindle his knowledge and belief in God. We met weekly and discussed his reactions to the readings as well as his own insights and concerns. By the end of the semester he had confidence enough to trust his inclination to believe. The readings and discussions did contribute something; they probably provided assurance that it was intellectually respectable to assent to the proposition - God is. But what really inspired him to assent was another person, the girl he started dating. Later she married him. But at the time her warm faith, the experience of sharing in the liturgy with her, transformed her into a living witness of God experienced. The role of reasoning was subsidiary though still of value.

Today I do not have any serious question about God's being. However, a genuine question I do have is: Since God is so real to me, how can I communicate this realized knowledge to someone who doubts or denies God's existence?

THE NONBELIEVER'S QUESTION

Rather than sharing my distress at the onslaught of doubt about God's existence, nonbelievers have been living comfortably without God. It is essential that the nonbelievers have experienced a challenge to their non-belief, - that they recognize, perhaps, that they have been too comfortable in their assumption that intelligent people rightly live without God.

Presumably they are awakened to the validity of the question, and the "dispositive arguments" have stimulated a sense that intellectual responsibility demands they face the question, "Is there a God?"

If the previous chapters have shaken nonbelievers enough to have them face the question, they may approach it merely as an academic question. To face it truly and seriously they will have to want or need an answer. Personally experienced emotional need or perhaps desire for harmony with a loved one may be the catalyst.

Thus they have the same question I faced years ago - minus my emotional distress. That question is definitely cognate to the question which genuinely concerns me now - "If God is so real to me, how can I share this knowledge?"

THE BELIEVER'S QUESTION

Does it seems strange to ask believers what their question about God's existence is? For a serious investigation it is essential to identify the precise question one is hoping to find an answer for. In my own case I take my question most seriously. This book is my attempt to pull together the work of years shaping an answer to it.

Supercilious people sometimes look down on believers as though the more admirable stance were one of questioning. I respect the need of constant openness to questions. But the only value of raising questions is to stimulate the search for answers, for truth. If one already has the answer, is in the truth, there's no need of questioning. If a man knows someone loves him, it's only harmful for him to keep asking if that person really does love him. At times I wonder if some people prefer the pursuit of truth to the possession of truth. Do they *want* the truth? Possession of truth about God demands conformity of the possessor's life with this truth. A person can use questioning as an excuse to avoid reforming his life or to put off growing in prayer. Maybe subconsciously the thinking goes like this, "If I continue to question, I can avoid choosing!" Maybe what they fear is commitment.

Certainly I do not wish to raise doubts. Someone in quiet possession of God may use her time more profitably by nurturing her union with God by prayer, worship and loving service. Such a person may prefer to pray and to read the masters of the spiritual life.

Believers should, of course, live this union with God aware that questions about God's existence never need to be repressed in fear. They should be confident that it is reasonable to affirm God's existence, indeed they should know that some members of the community have asked (and do ask) these questions and have found adequate grounds for the affirmation and are ready to explain each step, answering objections as well.

Believers whom I see engaging in our investigation probably phrase their question in one of two ways. First, there are those who have engaged in serious discussions about God's existence and would dearly love to be able to explain to others in a cogent way just why it is reasonable to believe. They ask, "Can a cogent argument for firm belief in God be clearly articulated?" The second group includes those committed Christians eager to live as "countersigns" in their culture. To be a sign they must speak the language of the day, giving evidence they appreciate the attitudes and values people esteem today. Today's consciousness demands respect for reason. So some such question as "Just how can the existence of God be demonstrated to people today?" must be real to Christians serving as countersigns.

Conviction that God does exist obviously could change the lives of one-time nonbelievers. But here are three ways in which believers also can profit from understanding a proof that God exists.

> **First**, as I sketched out above, the reasons for positing the existence of a Transcendent Other
> 1) imply that God must have whatever is necessary to be the ground of all existence and
> 2) enable us to know what God is not.

These two steps anchor all knowledge of God and identify what/whom Scripture is talking about in its revelation of who and what God is. The threefold way of predication assures us that God is and is present, but shrouded in utter mystery and darkness.

Second, sometimes the light of faith shines so brightly there seems no need of reason's light about God. At other times the light of faith fades; we have to struggle to preserve our faith. At such times it can be very supportive knowing that it is reasonable to interpret certain experiences as encounter with God; which in turn encourages us to remember that the experience in faith once was very tangible.

Third, is to give the believer assurance that it is intellectually responsible to believe. In a culture where God seems absent from the dominant consciousness, a culture where science (incapable of discovering God) commands such respect, the third reason may become the most important.

Whether believer or a nonbeliever, it helps to articulate precisely one's own question about God's existence. Since all the above questions are cognate, my efforts to cope with my own question could prove helpful in answering others.

SUMMARY AND CONCLUSION

Since the word "God" belongs properly within religion, we first described its meaning for believing Christians. False images and ideas about God eliminated, we derived a definition of "God" which everyone, believer or not, should be able to accept.

Autobiographical vignettes of two actual challenges to belief in God may have helped readers to crystallize their own God-question. Nonbelievers perhaps recognized how unwarranted has been their feeling comfortable in unbelief. For some, personally experienced emotional need may ensure that their question about God's existence goes beyond the academic. Believers will have crystallized their specific perspective on the God-question.

The next two chapters clarify the kind of reasoning involved in the God-question.

CHAPTER 7

WHAT KNOWING IS

Insight into God's existence is not difficult - unless preconceptions block out the light. Remove the mistaken preconceptions and very often insight follows. In the process of reaching agreement on the meaning of "God" and the function of reasoning about God's existence, certain mistaken preconceptions were removed. As we strive for agreement on the kind of reasoning the God-question requires we have to unveil the mistaken preconception that science is the *only* method of reasoning which allows us to know what really is.

The intent is to open minds to a broader understanding of what it is to think, to reason, to know. We begin by situating knowing as a form of awareness and reasoning as a form of knowing.

KNOWING AS FORM OF AWARENESS

To be a human person is much more than to be a knower. It is to be a physical body, a chooser, a culture-maker as well. The self unifies all we are and do. As unique selves each of us cares for the body and adapts the material world for our lives and community. Knowing does transfuse all we do, but all knowing is in turn ordered to holistic living. Besides knowing, we experience, desire, love, work, we live. Knowing as a specific activity comes into play only when something happens to evoke a question.

In my thinking, "knowing" is one of eleven ways of being aware.

1) Awareness of feeling,-- for example, pain or pleasure or general well being;
2) Awareness of emotions,-- of fear, hope, joy, love, resentment;
3) Awareness of wanting, desiring, needing;
4) Awareness of conflicts of desires or needs;
5) Awareness of choices, of willing among conflicting wantings;
6) Awareness of conscience,-- directing, accusing, approving, regretting;
7) Awareness of sensing,-- seeing, hearing, touching, etc. -something(s);
8) Awareness of peace of soul;
9) Awareness of doing -- walking, exercising;
10) Awareness of making--building, repairing, establishing;
11) And ultimately, awareness of knowing, which can come into action amid any of these awarenesses.

How, then, does knowing awareness differ? It is the only awareness capable of questioning and it is one's ultimate arbiter of the relation of other forms of awareness to reality.

Normally I walk through the day aware of all I experience as "being." Only if a question arises does "knowing" take place. Questions arise only if curiosity, unhappiness, conflict of lifestyles or challenge to the assumed truths undergirding one's lifestyle - evokes them.

An example: Suppose I'm accustomed to walk across a frozen pond on my daily winter stroll. Normally I move along with awareness of ice being. One day I hear crackling sounds when I'm in the middle of the pond. Immediately a question arises: Is it safe to walk on this ice? I reflect on those sounds. Are they the sounds of ice firming up under intense cold? Or sounds of ice cracking up as it begins to melt? Since it's 15 degrees Fahrenheit I judge the former is the case and I continue my walk.

Again, routinely I pray during the day, aware of God being. As I prepare to engage in a reasoned process to God's existence I recognize the challenge: How do I *know* there is a God? At this point I find myself examining what I do whenever I know anything.

Close attention to what I experience in such situations reveals that *knowing*, as a distinctive form of awareness, is a complex of question, understanding, assessing, affirming or denying. From beginning to end, a proposition is involved.

When the crackling raises that question I obviously have formed a proposition "It is safe to walk on this ice - Yes? - No?" I have *understood* "ice" - "walk on ice" - "safe." Immediately I assess the proposition: I look to evidence for and against the proposition being true. Attending to the temperature and so forth, I move on to affirm the proposition. "It is safe to walk on this ice - Yes."

Consider the "understanding" aspect of knowing. It transfuses all other awarenesses. In the ice scenario I normally move along merely aware of ice being. But the experience of seeing, feeling, maybe tasting, as well as sliding or feeling the slipperiness does not give me "ice"! My community, of course, taught me to call this thing ice. But what did I understand by that word? The process of understanding is subtle. With regard to anything I understand a "something" which is subject of multiple predicates: "hard," "slippery," - and then "water frozen". I never reach an intellectual intuition of 'ice." (or anything else!)

The natural curiosity of the child generates multiple questions to which community gives answers - at least names of things. But gradually the person acquires understanding behind the names. *Awareness* of "stomach tight", for example, includes *understanding* of that area of my body as stomach, for awareness does not give me "stomach."

All awareness is awareness of something and something being. As I walk down the street I walk with awareness of trees (being), road (being), cars (being), breeze (being). Sensing each of those things I am aware of them - transfused by understanding that such and such sense experiences are related to and are understood as trees, road, cars, breeze.

What about this awareness of "being"? As I walk through the day aware of all I experience as "being," I do not explicitly affirm anything (which is the crucial, ultimate aspect of knowing). Only if a question arises, do I move to affirmation or denial. Suppose in walking along I am surprised to hear my name being called. I look around to see who called me. I see no one. I become convinced I was mistaken. The awareness of my name being called must have been awareness of sounds which I *imagined* were sounds of my name.

Obviously I can be in error in other ways as I walk in awareness of being. For instance, because normally I have good reason to let awareness of houses being go unchallenged I may do the same erroneously if I experience the identical awareness of houses being when actually what I am experiencing are set pieces on a movie lot. Bank tellers or store owners can accept awareness of policemen being when actually thieves are wearing police uniforms. In such experiences nothing in the experiences evoked a question.

To sum up, knowing awareness does not explicitly come into action unless a question arises about or within another form of awareness. Knowing always operates on other awarenesses. Hence one always knows in reference to the concrete and to the imagination. Knowing provides the understanding which transfuses all other awarenesses and is ready to go into action about the "being" of other awarenesses, monitoring one's awareness of house truly being or pain truly being or ice being safe.

To set the stage for explaining reasoning as a form of knowing I must first treat language and proposition.

LANGUAGE AND KNOWING

From beginning to end in "knowing awareness" a proposition is involved. To understand the reference to "proposition," start with sentences, as distinct from words and phrases. A sentence is a group of words expressing a complete thought. Written sentences are signs of spoken sentences, called utterances. So when we talk about language, strictly speaking we are directly talking about utterances. Whether people are print- or sound-oriented, they start with what is sensible and undeniable.

Language so permeates our lives that we fail to appreciate it, to marvel at it. And it functions in many ways: it communicates moods, emotions, biases, etc. But a central function of language is to communicate what one thinks, what one knows, because through knowing we touch the real. The most important thing I did in the ice example was to know the ice was not melting. If someone on the other side of the pond were debating whether he should cross on the ice, what he needs to know from me is whether the ice is melting or not. My emotional reactions to the crackling sound would be of little help.

So sentences interest us precisely inasmuch as they are signs of propositions. They express propositions. Propositions are interior, mental acts of knowing. Different sentences can express the same proposition. Obvious proof lies in the fact that the same proposition can be expressed in different languages. But the point can be made more impressively by considering the following. Suppose three people are planning a picnic and some dark clouds float onto the horizon. A question awakens the knowing awareness: Is it prudent to continue their plans? Imagine one of them looking at the sky and saying, "It's going to be raining at four o'clock, an hour from now." Another immediately agrees, "He's right." The third listens to their prediction and says, "No way! There'll be no rain at four o'clock."

Three different expressions of one and the same proposition. This example should help to get behind sentences to the interior act of knowing. The function of a proposition is to "pick out" a state of affairs. One person picks out the state of affairs that at four o'clock rain will be falling and affirms it. Another takes a positive stand toward that proposition and affirms it. By her sentence she refers to the identical state of affairs of rain falling at four o'clock and likewise takes a positive stand of affirming it. This becomes clearer if we spell out what her sentence means. "He's right" is shorthand for "What he just said is true." And this is the same as simply repeating his sentence. As for the third speaker, he picks out the exact same state of affairs, namely that at four o'clock rain will be falling but takes a negative stand toward it by denying the proposition.

Notice that there are two different parts of the proposition involved. One, the name, identifies what the knowing refers to. The other determines the sense or what is at least being entertained about the referent. This gives the sense and can be called the predicable. Name and predicable need not correspond to noun and verb. In the example above, "rain" or the interior act corresponding to the word identifies what we are thinking about. And we are thinking that it will be falling at four o'clock. We could have the same name, rain, and be thinking of its chemical composition. Same name, different predicable. However these two knowing parts form a whole and as a whole they do one thing: as a whole the proposition presents a delimited content. *This delimited content is a state of affairs.* Thus a proposition presents a state of affairs or picks out a state of affairs. It "proposes" a view of reality to be examined by the mind.

To pick out a state of affairs is distinct from the knower's attitude toward the proposition. The knower may have the attitude of merely agreeing with the proposition. He may have the attitude of asserting it, of denying it, of doubting, hesitating about it, wishing, fearing, swearing at it. Clearly then the act of knowing inasmuch as it is the *proposition* is distinct, though not always separate, from the knower's *attitude*. In terms of the complex of knowing awareness, all acts are distinct from, but pivot around, the proposition. Questioning, assessing, affirming, denying relate to the same proposition.

In our case the primary concern is with the acts of asserting and denying propositions. To assert or to deny a proposition is to do something within one's mind. One takes a stand toward the proposition.

Asserting or denying propositions is the primary concern because this is the way to attain truth and when we attain truth we know what is real, what is the case. A proposition is true when the state of affairs it picks out exists or is the case. A proposition is false when the state of affairs it picks out does not exist or is not the case. The proposition remains the same whether the state of affairs picked out by the proposition exists or doesn't exist. And the proposition remains the same whether the knower asserts it or denies it. A proposition can *be true* (the state of affairs picked out by it exists) and *not be known* to be true. When the proposition *is true* and is asserted then the knower has knowledge. The knower knows what is the case. When the proposition is true but the knower denies it, the knower is mistaken. The knower does not know what is the case.

In reverse order, when the proposition is false (the state of affairs picked out by the proposition does not exist) and is denied, the knower has knowledge, this time knowledge of what is not the case. And of course, when the proposition is false but is affirmed, the knower is mistaken.

The distinctive way of being aware called "knowing" then begins with a question. As the question arises a proposition is formed. In the ice example, "It is safe to walk on the ice.--Yes or No?" The terms in this case are so clear I'm sure all are understood. Assessing the proposition, I listen intently to the crackling sounds, distinguishing by memory the sounds associated with freezing and sounds associated with melting. Attending to the 15 degree temperature I conclude the crackling is a sign of freezing and so I affirm, "It is safe to walk on the ice. Yes." If the evidence pointed to melting I would deny the proposition, "It is safe to walk on the ice. No."

In other words, human knowing which begins with a question consists of the mind making a "proposal" for consideration. The word, "proposition," comes from two Latin words, "pro"-before, and "positus," a form of the verb -to place. The mind places before itself a proposition. Evidence is sought for and against the proposal. Then the mind takes a stand on the proposal; it asserts the proposal or proposition, or it denies it.

KNOWING AND REASONING

We human beings, then, are "propositional knowers."

As for the assessing aspect of knowing, some propositions are immediately evident: "The whole is greater than any of its parts." "Things equal to the same thing are equal to each other." Some are evident in the light of immediate sense experience: "This chair is brown." Some come to be affirmed by reasoning: "At some time I shall die -- (Because every human person is mortal and I am a human person.)"

That God exists is not an immediately evident proposition, nor is it evident in the light of immediate sense experience. If it is true, it can only be so because reasoning provides evidence of its truth. Reasoning proceeds from proposition to proposition.

I shall spell out every proposition of the reasoning process we're engaged in, and suggest that advancing from one to the other is like climbing a mountain. When we reach the top of the mountain and I declare, "God exists, Yes," I shall know what is the case, provided the proposition picks out a state of affairs which exists. If someone does not agree, she will use the same proposition and deny it, "God exists, No." She will be judging that the reasoning does not provide evidence for the proposition and will judge that the state of affairs picked out by the proposition does not exist. One of us will know the truth, will know what is the case. One of us will be mistaken. To *deny* a proposition which is *true*, one which does pick out a state of affairs which exists, is to be mistaken. So supposing that the reasoning is valid, then the proposition, "God exists," picks out a state of affairs which does exist. To deny *that* proposition is to be mistaken. If, of course, the reasoning is not valid, the proposition "God exists" does not pick out a state of affairs that exists, and to affirm that proposition is to be mistaken.

In Chapter Six we identified precisely how the question about God emerges for believers and nonbelievers. So we have the question -"There exists a God - Yes or No?" And we realize that the evidence must be assessed by reasoning.

Hence the utter necessity of reaching agreement on the *method* of reasoning. Nonbelievers trained in the sciences feel well equipped*appropriate* to test claims about what exists. Whether or not they have actually attempted to test the claim that God exists, they have little doubt that any such claim will fail their scientific test. For almost two centuries scientists have been in agreement that their work needs no God-hypothesis. They recognize I must intend to use a method of reasoning other than that of the sciences. And they feel skeptical whether any other method can survive serious scrutiny.

It is important not only to admit but to insist that the method of reasoning to God's existence is different from the method used in the sciences. If God exists, God exists as absolutely unique, so it should come as no surprise that the method of reasoning to God's existence is distinctive. By making explicit everything involved in each step of the reasoning from personal experience up to the affirmation that there is a God, we shall be describing the method *while* using it. The reader will be able to weigh every single step. For the present readers are urged to recognize the limits of science and note the distinctive kind of question philosophy probes.

NOT SCIENCE BUT SCIENTISM IS THE PROBLEM

At this point we confront not science but "scientism," the extrapolation of the sciences into a philosophy.

Surely this is not a rejection or degradation of science. An intelligent person simply must recognize and appreciate the tremendous achievements and benefits of science. It is logically inconsistent to disdain the natural sciences while accepting the blessings of modern medicine, radio, television, air travel, telephones, computers and so many other benefits we enjoy. Likewise one recognizes the objectivity of science so that in principle everyone has to agree with firm scientific findings. Apart from research on new issues and from the outer fringes of scientific knowledge there's practically universal agreement on the findings of the sciences. There is, moreover, confidence that constant progress is built into science, present findings serving as the basis of future developments. Maxwell's equations (mid 19th century) were verified in laboratory tests, then led to Marconi's telegraphy at the turn of the century which led to radio and television. Without question, the discovery and development of the sciences are among the greatest achievements of the human race. And increasingly we are being equipped by science to conquer almost any practical problem.

The profound, widespread esteem for science is eminently deserved. But to extrapolate the sciences into a claim that this is the only way to attain knowledge is a philosophy, and is called scient*ism*. It is appropriate at this point to demonstrate how unwarranted and false is a philosophy which holds that natural science is exclusively the way to reason to what is real.

Although it is difficult to find people explicitly proposing or trying to justify scientism, nonetheless the mindset affects most people today, especially those who never think about philosophy.

This extrapolation of sciences into scientism is logically unfounded and profoundly destructive--of knowledge and human fulfillment. Serious charges!

LOGICALLY UNFOUNDED

The series of options described in Chapter Three through which reason came to be identified with scientific reasoning laid the foundation for scientism. The conviction that only science could be trusted to obtain truth led the way to scientific treatment of areas traditionally the province of philosophy, namely psychology, logic, and cosmology. And, of course, the conflict between science and religion generated attitudes receptive to scientism.

Notice that none of the above offered intellectual, logical justification of scientism. A thorough treatment of the issue would require confronting British Empiricism, the tendency to consider that Kant eliminated metaphysics as insight into reality, and especially Logical Positivism. Scholarly works do confront and, in my opinion, thoroughly refute all of these.

But Logical Positivism, the logical climax (and dead-end) of Empiricism and scientism, needs some explanation. Its proponents in the middle of this century excitedly proclaimed they had uncovered the reason that thinkers easily reach agreement in science but practically never in philosophy. Their reason is simple: philosophical propositions are meaning*less*. And obviously a proposition must be meaning*ful*, must actually state something, if it is to be tested as true or false. A principle of verification was formulated (indeed over and over re-formulated) as a "litmus" test for meaningful propositions. "A proposition is meaningful if and only if it is verifiable (i.e., empirically)." But propositions about the soul or God or moral principles cannot be so verified. "Therefore they are not meaningful. Rather they express emotional attitudes or preferences. Thus we can put aside philosophy and get on with learning more and more about our world."

Contemporary consciousness conditions people to find philosophical, ethical, and religious propositions meaningless--so the *im*plicit philosophy of many is scientism.

The beginning of the end of Logical Positivism occurred when someone asked: "Is the principle of verification verifiable" Obviously it is not. At best it's a rule, in fact an arbitrary rule. Once again we discover that what seemed to ground scientism has no logical justification. Only the successive options of past centuries, roborated by the marvelous achievements of the *sciences*, account for the influence of scientism. Some people equate scientism with science.

DESTRUCTIVE OF KNOWLEDGE AND FULFILLMENT

Later chapters examine Naturalism, the atheistic philosophical correlate of scientism. The arguments critical of Naturalism confirm the present claim that there is no logical justification for scientism. My second charge, that scientism is also profoundly destructive of all knowledge and human fulfillment, will not be developed at length. The charge is based on the atheism it generates. Without an absolute being, there can be no absolute truth and so all knowledge is undermined. And without absolute truth there can be no absolute moral principles or inalienable rights. As for fulfillment, only God can fully satisfy the human person in mind and heart. Only absolute moral principles and inalienable rights can adequately guide us in our personal decisions and in structuring a just and effective society.

Incidentally, among those who espouse scientism, explicitly or implicitly, philosophy is considered merely private opinion or is reduced to a philosophy of language and to the philosophy of science, of history and so forth. Philosophy in itself is denied any proper insight into reality, limited to ordering the findings of these other fields. This is a serious error and a great loss.

LIMITS OF SCIENCE

Besides being logically unfounded and profoundly destructive, scientism is simply inadequate. Scientism, as stated, is a philosophy which extrapolates from the proper fields of scientific inquiry to claim that science suffices for the whole of life. Training in the sciences can incline people to scientism, if they are not alerted to other ways of knowing. Actually in our culture most people seem to experience responsive echoes to the claims of scientism. Consider the fact that science as science does not require any reference to God. This can encourage sliding to the *unproved* claim as though it were a conclusion: "Therefore, there is no God."

Recall two things from our earlier treatment of contemporary consciousness. First, science throws out a net structured to catch what is sensible and quantitative. This makes it incapable of investigating whether there is a God, who/which by definition is *neither* sensible *nor* quantitative. Second, only by a series of options did our culture reach the point of trying (a) to explain the world without God, by scientific reasoning alone, and of trying (b) to conduct business and society without God.

Such observations should counteract the inclination to adopt scientism. Now to some illustrative facts that challenge a person to recognize the limits of science in people's lives and certain other facts that identify philosophy as a distinct and valid source of knowledge.

To start with, people build their lives on truths they accept without scientific evidence, some without the *possibility* of scientific proof. Take a couple who love one another. They're certain enough of their love to commit themselves to each other for life. How do they know they really love each other? Science cannot prove it for them. Again, who demands scientific evidence that he is the child of his father? Yet this knowledge is taken absolutely for *certain*. Lives are built around these truths.

All of us take on trust the scientific and technological claims, let's say in medicine. For example, people accept their doctor's statement on the latest state of the art for a certain operation. Or again, a person takes on human faith the claims of knowledge which geneticists propose. It's true, of course, that all of the claims of sciences can in principle be verified. Nonetheless, we don't even attempt to verify them but assent to the claims without verification. Knowledge of reality then is not limited to what any of us personally knows scientifically.

Those mundane facts alert a person that what is accepted as true is not limited to what there is scientific proof for. Now some facts which can lead to recognizing philosophy as a distinctive source of knowledge. Everyone knows there is not *a science* but there are many sciences. Each science deals with a specific field of inquiry. Thus there is no "natural science" of the whole of reality, a point developed in a later chapter. We need philosophy to study reality as a whole. But consider that philosophy raises questions which no science addresses, the answers to which science must presuppose.

Two of these questions must be answered affirmatively or science is an illusion. (1) Is knowledge possible? (2) Is there a real world? Science *presupposes* an affirmative answer to both questions; philosophy alone reflectively establishes the answers. Linked with these two fundamental questions are the first principles of knowledge and of being, such as the principle of noncontradiction (the same thing cannot be affirmed and denied of the same thing at the same time) and the principle of causality (whatever exists contingently has an efficient cause). Only philosophy can deal with these first principles. Science has to presuppose them.

Another question grounds our personal and community lives: What is the ultimate basis of moral judgments? Science cannot provide the answer. It can only report what many people do or what they say they think is right or wrong to do. Without a philosophical answer we're locked into a cultural relativism: behavior is right or wrong depending on what a given culture approves. Not many want to admit such utter relativity in morals. Today scientists are raising philosophical questions occurring within the area of their scientific concern. Since the questions are philosophical, scientists may push scientists to ask them, but scientists as scientists cannot answer philosophical questions anymore than dentists, for instance, can answer socio-political questions about health care.

Very important in relation to the moral issue are two other questions: What is it to be a human person? And are we free with freedom of self-determination? To answer the first we have to ask how to explain that our intellectual knowing includes the characteristics of *universality* and *immateriality* (which allow insight into the spirituality of the soul). And unless we are free, all question about morality is meaningless. Philosophy addresses these two questions.

Finally, grounding the philosophy of religion and the issue of God's existence are the ultimate questions: Why is there *being* rather than *nothing*? How explain *why* anything (the self, for example) exists? It is not enough to say, "Why not?" because there is in a person no necessity to be. It is not enough to give reasons why that person is human or child of these parents, for the question is *not*: Why is he *what* he is, but why *is he existing*? Nor does it suffice to point to material supports of his present existence, since those material things don't have to exist either.

The fact that many people don't realize how such questions touch their lives and so have no interest in them doesn't invalidate the questions. Thousands of questions fail to interest people; still they are valid questions. It's a mark of the philosopher to wonder about matters such as these just discussed. These questions, which only philosophy asks and is able to answer, definitely pertain to the meaning of *each* life.

Galileo rebelled against metaphysical analysis of motion. What good is it to contemplate motion as the amazing act of a being in potency precisely inasmuch as it is only in potency? To him the issue was futile and useless so long as motion had not been mathematically defined. Fortunately he did rebel for he ushered in the new scientific way of thinking, which has given us such material benefits. But the dialectic has brought us to the opposite extreme. Quantitative analysis of the world has interposed another world of mental constructs between us and our world so we hardly see nature any more; and it has blotted out *the wonder that anything exists*, including motion. Not too much reflection is needed to see that philosophical questions are valid and that study of them requires a method different from study of the sciences.

SUMMARY AND CONCLUSION

We touched on many issues but focused on one objective: to reach agreement on the method of reasoning to be used in the God issue. We widened the understanding of what it is to think, to reason, to know.

Knowing is a distinctive way of being aware. Explanation of the term "proposition" led to considering the difference between propositions immediately evident and those affirmed through reasoning.

Since "God exists" can only be affirmed by reasoning, we made an initial step toward explaining the kind of reasoning involved in reaching such an affirmation - or denial. Scientism, the philosophy that holds that knowledge of what is real is limited to scientific reasoning, was argued to be ungrounded and harmful. The limits of science were suggested and this opened into evidence that philosophy is a distinctive source of knowledge.

What kind of reasoning, then, will we use? The sciences and scientific reasoning having been ruled out, it will have to be philosophical reasoning. The next chapter attempts to generate a clearer understanding of the kind of thinking needed. Even this will not define the kind of reasoning. What constitutes this kind of reasoning will be evident only in the actual *process* of reasoning step by step from a very simple, sensibly perceptible fact to the affirmation itself: God exists.

CHAPTER 8

KIND OF REASONING IN THE GOD-QUESTION

It might seem that agreement on the appropriate method of reasoning in the God-question should have been reached by now. And yet the truly critical reflection remains to be done. **Philosophic reasoning requires changing one's perspectives.** Most people have to undergo an intellectual conversion to change their perspective and to engage in *reasoning* about the question, "Is there a God?" Without this conversion one cannot follow the reasoning proposed. Two other conversions, moral and religious, are also needed, but they are not intrinsic to the process of reasoning as is the intellectual conversion. Just what they involve will soon become clear.

"Conversion" seems strange in a philosophical context, until we recall how Plato in the morning of philosophy suggested the need of such an experience. In his famous example of the cave, prisoners are chained in their seats watching shadows of images of natural objects on the wall in front of them. To free the prisoners someone must get them to "turn around" (con-vert) in order to discover the shadows for what they are. What they thought reality are but shadows, not of actual trees and other objects but shadows of replicas of trees, horses, and people cast onto a wall by the light of a fire behind these imitations. The "converted" prisoners are led beyond the wall of replicas, outside the cave, to see the natural objects.

Ours has been described as a "sensate culture." The real is identified with "bodies" and knowing with "seeing, taking a look."

The axiom "Seeing is believing," is not a totally new phenomenon. St. Augustine in the 4th century struggled for years before he realized he had identified his notion of the "really real" with "body." Today's culture has been structured by the natural sciences which are concerned with the sensible. It is not easy for persons shaped by contemporary consciousness to break out of the assumption that the real is limited to bodies, to the sensibly perceived.

Augustine, in the struggle of religious conversion, slowly caught the insight that "the name, real, might have a different connotation from the name, body." Both Augustine and Plato transcended their imaginations to acknowledge that the real and the body are not identical.

INTELLECTUAL CONVERSION

"Conversion" always involves upheaval and profound reorganization. So it is not surprising that nonbelievers, their outlook shaped by contemporary consciousness and the sciences, face an extremely difficult obstacle to philosophical investigation of the God-question.

Today people still need to overcome the spontaneous tendency to think that everything real is body. It is essential to move out of the world of the immediately sensible into the world of the intelligible and being. In this new world, the actual world, the real is recognized as that which is known through intellectual understanding, assessment, and judgment.

To do this constitutes intellectual conversion and it is rare. Since it must be intimate, radical, conscious and deliberate, it is a matter of personal grappling with oneself. Yet in our question, "God exists - Yes or No?" intellectual conversion is an intrinsic condition if one is to be able to reason to a firm "Yes" or "No."

Intellectual Conversion and "Knowing" Awareness

Intellectual conversion demands eliminating the pervasive myth that knowing is "looking" and that the real is what is out there to be looked at. This myth fails to distinguish between the world of immediacy and the world we live in with meaning. The former is the sum of what the senses give us.

To break free from the myth and to effect the necessary conversion, one must attend carefully to what happens when he knows. As developed earlier, knowing is not just looking, seeing, sensing. Knowing as a distinct way of being aware undergirds all awareness, comes into explicit action when a question arises. Question leads to understanding, assessing, and judging.

Chapter 7 developed "knowing" as a distinct form of awareness, which, however, transfuses all other forms of awareness and constantly monitors those other forms in relation to reality. I described how we walk through the day with awareness of the seen, heard, touched, tasted, smelt and felt - being. The myth would have us believe that's all there is. In fact, the myth ignores the transfusion of all this awareness with meaning and understanding by knowing awareness. As I pass a red car - unless something evokes a question about it - I am aware of red car being - but sense awareness gives me only "red"-"extended"; knowing as understanding transfuses that sense awareness and I relate to it as "red car."

Furthermore, the myth likewise ignores the fact that we as knowers monitor all awareness, implicitly affirming awareness, for example, of red car "being." As knowers we are ready constantly to affirm or to correct the implicit affirming that the red car really is, if anything connected with the spontaneous awareness evokes a question. If, for example, I've heard of a cardboard model of a red car so cleverly devised it easily deceives people, I may look more carefully to determine whether what I see really is a car.

Corresponding to this revised appreciation of knowing is the realization that reality is *not just* what is looked at. Reality is what is related to awareness but organized by questioning, understanding, assessing, and posited by judgment or affirmation.

As for the God-question, intellectual conversion means one is ready to acknowledge as real whatever reason leads him to recognize as real, whether body or spirit.

AIDS TO INTELLECTUAL CONVERSION

A first step is to reflect on the knowing awareness of the previous chapter, the complex, interiorly developing process from questioning to affirming or denying the identically same proposition. Surely the reader had no difficulty recognizing how scientific reasoning fits into the description of human knowing. Science starts with the experience of the sensible. Questions arise, creative hypotheses in the form of propositions are presented for consideration. Sometimes the hypotheses are not even imaginable. Assent to them is not a matter of looking or sensing, but of grasping the evidence as compelling. Experiments are devised to provide grounds for affirming or denying (or modifying) them. When sense experience is the confirming factor, it is not seeing but intellectual insight that confirms that the sense experience is compelling evidence of the truth. The scientific method is most effective in providing such evidence. The mistake is to assume that reasoning to compelling evidence is limited to the scientific method - apart from the failure to perceive that intellectual insight, not seeing, is essential even in science.

As human persons we all share the general way of knowing as well as the specifically scientific way. Reasoning to God's existence involves a way of knowing radically different from *scientific* reasoning, a way most people find difficult, and yet as thoroughly human as common sense and scientific knowing are. An intellectual conversion is required and no one can convert to what is not human.

Next, reflect on what a person actually experiences when he knows something. Since neither in common sense nor in science do we know by "taking a look," then reflect on how one does know what he knows. The mind will then be open to accept as true whatever the intelligence compels a person to admit, even when the reasoning differs from scientific reasoning.

Here is a common sense example of knowing. Imagine a man, let's call him Harold, who has broken up with his girl friend, Helen. He misses Helen desperately. I tell him that Helen is attending a lecture in the next classroom. Does he know that Helen is in the next room? Assuming he trusts me he will accept my word and without a doubt affirm to himself: Helen is in the next room.

He is so sure he starts planning how he can meet her and what he'll say. Going into the corridor he looks through the window in the classroom door and sees her in the front row. Does he *know* anything more by seeing her than by believing me? No. He affirms the exact same proposition: Helen is in that room. There is now another dimension to his knowing, a more satisfying ground for his affirmation--sight. The lecture finishes, Helen remains alone in the room. He approaches her and sensing her readiness he hugs her. Does he know anything more by touching her than by believing me or seeing her through the door? No. There is, obviously, still another dimension to his knowing and another, absolutely convincing, ground for affirming the proposition that Helen is here--touch.

To emphasize that his knowledge is not seeing or hugging Helen, consider the possibility that it might be a look-alike actress hired to deceive him when he looks through the window; or it might be her identical twin whom he hugs. So when he thinks it is Helen it's his intellect which not only accepts the evidence of sight and touch but also implicitly rules out all possibilities of error.

Eliminate the seeing and touching. I tell him that Helen is in the next room and that she urgently needs a car to get to the airport after the lecture. So certainly does he know that Helen is in the next room that he'd rush out to arrange to drive her to the airport.

Knowing, then, is not taking a look or touching. Knowing is forming a judgment that such and such is the case. What is involved in judging? First, an understanding sufficient to form a proposition, for example, that Helen is in the next room. Second, an understanding of what has to be the case to know that the proposition is true, that the state of affairs picked out by the proposition exists. Third, a recognition that what has to be the case actually is the case.

There is little difficulty in understanding what forms the proposition. He and I both know who Helen is. To be in the next room is easily understood. But what has to be the case for him to know that the proposition is true? To look through the window and see her would be sufficient grounds for him to know Helen is in the next room. For him to hug Helen in the next room would warrant his knowing that she was there. But also just accepting my word would be enough to allow him to know that Helen is indeed in the next room. What's necessary for him to accept my word? Whether he attends to it explicitly or not, he makes two judgments about me: that I am in a position to know the fact; and that I have no reason to lie, indeed good reason to tell the truth. Granted he knows these two facts, then he actually *knows* that Helen is in the next room.

Not much reflection is needed to recognize that our lives are based on propositions like this. A person acknowledges them as true because he cannot escape the experienced necessity to affirm them as true. In technical language, they are "virtually unconditioned."

One further point about the common sense affirmation that Helen is in the next room. There is a difference between what her friend knows by seeing or hugging her and by believing me. There is immediate awareness of Helen and of Helen being present. And in that awareness his intellect affirms Helen is and is in that room. When he knows Helen is in the room *because he believes me*, there's no awareness of Helen or Helen's presence. There is awareness of the proposition, "Helen is in the next room," and awareness that he knows the proposition is true.

When we advance proposition by proposition to acknowledgement that God exists, we shall not have new awareness of God and God being present. We'll be aware of the proposition, "God exists," and aware it is true. The conviction that God exists, reached by reason, has to be brought back to and linked with some awareness in which a person is actually *experiencing* God. At that point we find it is reasonable to interpret that experience as an experience of God. The awareness of God and God's presence will have been present from the beginning in the same experience that can now *with conviction* be interpreted as awareness of God.

TECHNICAL DESCRIPTION OF INTELLECTUAL CONVERSION

As we attempt a more technical analysis of intellectual conversion, keep in mind how Harold knows Helen is in the next room.

Let's begin with what is inescapably true. Each of us is a self. I am I. I am one self. It is this "I" which unifies all I experience and do. This "I" I'm aware of in all the different kinds of awareness. We all share levels of awareness. There's the *empirical* level of awareness when we sense, perceive, imagine, feel things. On the *intellectual* level we inquire, ask questions, and understand. The *rational* level is where we reflect on what is proposed on the intellectual level, assess evidence, and reach judgment on the truth or falsity of a proposition. Finally, on the *responsible* level, we are concerned with ourselves, with our operations and goals and so we evaluate and decide about possible courses of action and carry out our decisions.

Clearly, our awareness of self differs and expands from level to level. Awareness of self takes on a new dimension when, after sense awareness, we question and try to understand what we've experienced. Still a third dimension emerges when we try to form a judgment about whether we've correctly understood our experience. We are more fully aware of being a self when deliberating what we're going to *do* about what we've judged to be true.

These many levels of awareness are successive stages of a single thrust, the drive-to-be of the human self. They are all dynamically ordered toward knowing and doing what is good. But to know what is good, one must know what is real - which requires that one know what is true - which means one must know the intelligible - which can occur only by attending to the data of experience. In reverse order, the person attends to what is experienced and the attentive observation awakens questions. Questions answered result from insight, but diverse insights can emerge from inquiry, so the further question arises: Is this insight correct? Granted that truth is achieved, what is the person to *do* about the state of affairs? What is the truly good thing to do?

Up to this point, there probably has been agreement with the description of oneness of self, levels and dynamism of awareness.

People usually recognize and acknowledge what it is to be human - and precisely in the matter of knowing.

What is not so easy, and few people realize its importance, is the next step. If a person is to undergo the intellectual conversion required to engage in the reasoning that leads to the existence of God, besides being attentive, intelligent, reasonable, and responsible, she must heighten her awareness by objectifying each aspect of it. This, each person must do for herself or himself.

Let me spell out the process of objectifying in orderly detail. Remember, 1) a person experiences, 2) a person understands, 3) a person judges, and 4) a person decides. To objectify awareness of these activities:

A. One is to *experience* his four human responses: the experiencing, the understanding, the judging, and the deciding.
B. One is to *understand* the dynamic unity of the four human responses: his experiencing, understanding, judging, and deciding.
C. One is to *judge* (affirm) the reality of the four human responses: his experienced and understood experiencing, understanding, judging, and deciding.
D. And he is to *decide* to operate in accord with the norms of his experienced, understood, and affirmed experiencing, understanding, judging, and deciding.

Attentive reflection will alert readers that this detailed schema for objectifying their awareness of what they do when they "know" anything simply formalizes the description of how Helen's friend "knows" she is in the next room.

To interiorize this focus, let's imagine a person standing by the window looking at a red barn. I ask him what he sees and he says, "A red barn." Another person present laughs for she knows it is just a prop for a TV commercial. "It only looks like a barn," she observes.

What happened? Clearly aware of the color and shape before him and recalling past experiences of seeing such color and shapes related to barns, he brought to bear his understanding of "barn" to his experiencing of it. Because he had no reason to question what he was experiencing, he falsely assumed that he need ask no further questions and so affirmed, "That's a red barn."

On the other hand his friend, like him, experienced color and shape, but because she had watched the crew erect the frame in preparation for the commercial, what he *experienced* she *understood* as a cleverly disguised red frame structured to suggest a barn.

Because of all this she raised a question beyond what it looked like and denied it was a barn.

Interiorizing one's reflections makes clear that to know is to experience, question, understand, assess, and affirm or deny. To know scientifically obviously involves this process. Now, even though the attending, understanding, judging, and deciding in philosophy are done somewhat differently from the way they are done in the natural sciences, still the differences never imply there is inattention rather than attention, stupidity rather than intelligence, irrationality rather than rationality, irresponsibility rather than responsibility. Consequently, in reasoning about God's existence one should be ready to follow the process of knowing, attending to the data appealed to, intelligently assessing the way the data are understood, and reasonably assessing whether to affirm or deny that understanding.

ATTAINING THE VIRTUALLY UNCONDITIONED

The process of knowing leads to reasonable affirmation or denial: to truth, to reality, to what is the case. This process can be viewed from the perspective of self-transcendence or from insight into the virtually unconditioned.

Self-transcendence is the way we achieve authenticity. We break out of ourselves first through sense experience. But unlike brute animals we ask questions. We wish to understand what things are, why they are. Gradually through understanding we construct a world-view, in part or in whole. Then there follow questions for reflection: moving beyond imagination, guesses, ideas, hypotheses, we ask if this world-view is really so. At this point self-transcendence has new meaning. Self-transcendence goes beyond the subject-self and seeks what is independent of the subject. Rather than reporting what appears to me or what I imagine or even what I think or wish, judgment of reflection reports *what is so*.

And the self-transcendence achieved in reasonable affirmation or denial results from grasping the virtually unconditioned.

The *unconditioned* is that which is and has *no* conditions; it *cannot not be*. Traditionally God is understood to be unconditioned. The *virtually* unconditioned is a something which is only *if* certain conditions are fulfilled, and the conditions *are* fulfilled. It is called virtually unconditioned, because, granted the conditions are fulfilled it, like the *unconditioned*, cannot not be. Take a simple example. John returns home one evening to find fire engines in front of his house, the front windows broken, black soot everywhere. He makes the cautious statement: "Something has happened." This proposition is the conditioned. What is involved? John witnesses the present appearance of the house. He remembers what it was like when he left in the morning. He understands the meaning of "happen." He knows the happening occurred because he knows the conditions which would make his statement true are fulfilled. John knows the proposition is true because he knows it is virtually unconditioned.

That's very simple. How does one know in more complicated propositions what the conditions are and whether they've been fulfilled? When one recognizes there are no more reasonable questions to ask! But how does a person know whether or not there are further reasonable questions to ask? Familiarity with the area of knowledge equips a person to know this. After all, I could stop asking questions about genetics much sooner than a biologist or chemist could. And I could thus accept as true what is really false.

In the scenario used earlier Harold knew Helen was in the next room; he knew what was meant and knew the proposition would be true when I told him she was there, *if* two conditions were fulfilled: (1) if I were in a position to know the fact and (2) if I had no reason to lie. He formed a judgment that those two conditions were fulfilled and recognized Helen had to be in that room. When he looked in through the window, he knew that was Helen sitting there - if he could trust his eyes and if there were no one who looked so like her that he could be mistaken. He implicitly judged he could trust his eyes and that no one could look so like her that he could be mistaken. Knowing this, he knew that had to be Helen sitting there. In both situations he implicitly realized it would be unreasonable to ask further questions.

In the example of the red barn, the conditioned once again was the proposition, "That is a red barn" or "I see a red barn." The first person erred because he assumed, as we usually do, that no questions needed to be asked granted the experience of seeing that color and shape. Walking down the ordinary street we are aware of houses, trees, and so forth, being. We do not normally question whether we are being deceived since our multiple experiences warrant the assumption of awareness of real houses and trees. His friend, having observed the framework being built, had reason to question and go on immediately to deny the proposition.

Questions and familiarity may seem terribly vague, but they provide a realistic framework for an understanding of the process of knowing. When there are no more reasonable questions to challenge a proposition then a person feels the need to affirm it. There is, of course, a spectrum of situations stretching from where it's rash to affirm a proposition all the way to where it's stubborn stupidity not to affirm it. For me to take a definite stand in affirming a proposition like, "We should spend billions on the Strategic Defense Initiative," would be rash. I simply don't understand all that's involved. For me to refuse to affirm that the building across the road is real is stupid. I can conjure up bizarre possible ways in which I may be deceived about it. But I have more than sufficient warrant to make the affirmation. There are many propositions in between. Some, a person ought to affirm even though less certain than the proposition about the building; with others it's extremely difficult to know whether they're true or false. This is the area of *probable* truth.

Familiarity refers, of course, both to common sense and to specific areas of competence. Ordinary living provides familiarity with most practical matters. Competence in specific areas of knowledge requires learning and experience. Often the ordinary person must form a judgment indirectly by determining which "expert" he will follow. Obviously this is not a course on the theory of knowledge. It is an attempt to show that knowing is affirming what is recognized as virtually unconditioned. It is not seeing or sensing even when sense experience provides compelling evidence which the intelligence grasps. When we come to reason about the existence of God, sense experience will not be appealed to as compelling. There will be reasoning to support affirming the proposition, "God exists," as virtually unconditioned. Each step will be explained, the data and perspective identified, the grounds for affirming each step clearly specified. The individual alone can judge whether he grasps the compelling evidence, the virtually unconditioned.

People are so unaccustomed to interiorizing their reflections this way, so conditioned to verifying by the scientific method, that a genuine intellectual conversion is normally required to reason to God's existence. A person must recognize that to know, one intellectually grasps the virtually unconditioned.

Required also in this intellectual conversion is an opening of the mind to view the data from the perspective of being, ready to follow wherever the virtually unconditioned leads us within or beyond categories of the sensible and quantitative. In other words, we cannot arbitrarily limit *being* to the sensible. In a certain perspective the God-question pivots precisely on this: Is there being beyond this world of sensible being? Such a conversion enters intrinsically into the process of reasoning to God's existence.

Far from manipulating people or asking them to abandon their intellectual integrity by this conversion, I ask them to be open-minded and form a judgment about God's existence on the same basis they form common sense and scientific judgments - by insight into the virtually unconditioned.

MORAL CONVERSION

All would be in place now if we were simply knowers. But we are physical bodies, choosers, and culture makers unified by the self, as well as propositional knowers. And each aspect of the self has its own desires and wants. The body seeks its pleasure and gratification. As culture-maker, the self is immersed in the objectives, values, and world-view of the culture. As chooser, the person wants many, many goods. Emotions and desires can control, or at least strongly influence, what we think about and what we accept as true.

A person who has suffered from alcoholism in the family finds it difficult to discuss calmly the need for moderation and the acceptability of moderate drinking. Having had a loved one viciously killed, a person finds it difficult to discuss calmly the morality of the death penalty. Any search for truth requires a readiness to accept what intelligence reports as true, no matter whose ox gets gored, one's own or that of loved ones, no matter how it affects positions dearly held.

Unless there is harmony among our desires, unless biases and prejudices are recognized for what they are and challenged, then the pursuit of truth will be seriously hampered.

The completely amoral person cannot seek to know God. Wrapped up in self he is unable to transcend self in pursuit of the true or the good. Self-satisfaction, not objective good, is the standard in his life. Concomitantly, the true is identified with what enables him to obtain self-satisfaction.

The morally mature but evil person has no concern for knowledge of God or ultimate truth. She too is preoccupied with self, uninterested in ultimates. The morally mature good person may be in error, but genuinely strives to have her actions correspond to what she judges is good and right.

Because each of us is one person, intellect and will must be in harmony. Our oneness and reasonableness demand consistency between what we know (intellect) and what we do (will). There is a volitional appropriation of truth which consists in willingness to live in accord with it. Newman's aphorism is true:

"A man convinced against his will
  Is of the same opinion still."

Attaining truth calls for harmonious cooperation of all one's powers - the subconscious, perception, imagination, memory, and the rest. When bad will is at work all our powers conspire to bring forth doubts about truth and evidence for error. Without good will a person cannot proceed to the attainment of truth.

DO WE NEED MORAL CONVERSION?

I presuppose that readers are committed to some objective moral standards. Most people seem to recognize the importance of commitment to *accepting* truth, once found, no matter what consequent changes in one's life it may demand. Emotional determination *not* to change one's lifestyle, regardless of the truth discovered, will block the ability to "see" the evidence.

Our question is so fundamental that re-examination of one's moral commitment to truth is needed for all involved, believers and nonbelievers, if there is to be serious dialogue. A believer like me must face the reality that it would be most difficult to change my lifestyle structured so completely around God. Undoubtedly, momentous changes are at stake in a nonbeliever's life also.

How can we all be stimulated to become fully authentic in our investigation? Questioning opens the self to go beyond immediate awareness and leads to further questions as one assesses evidence. Self-transcendence demands we go beyond bias, wish-fulfillment, to acknowledge what actually is so. As unified human beings we are not just knowers, but doers and lovers. So questions demanding decisions arise: Will we act in accord with what we know?

How ready are we to take responsibility for the serious judgments about what is real? Do we back away from a firm "yes" or "no" answer to the question, "There is a God - Yes or No?"? After arduous, detailed reasoning do we have the courage to affirm or deny? Will I appeal to my faith (and pretend it is insight), if I do not actually perceive intellectually the necessity of affirming, "Yes, God exists."? Will the nonbeliever follow each step to the conclusion and lose courage, letting the absence of mathematically or sensibly compelling evidence excuse him from saying "Yes!"? Will bias perhaps slip into agnosticism?

Furthermore, the challenge of conforming our actions to what we know, may find someone refusing to take responsibility for what he judges is truly good, good rather than pleasant or painful, satisfying or dissatisfying. Genuine authenticity demands free commitment to living a fully human life, taking responsibility for being authentic or inauthentic. Refusal to take this moral responsibility will inevitably affect our intellectual response to the God-question. Moral self-transcendence is a preliminary condition for engaging in any serious investigation of God's existence.

Bias

It follows that even before we undertake our intellectual investigation, we ask, "Have we attempted to face possible biases?" There is the general bias, one affecting everyone. At its core is reluctance to center our lives around intelligent living. Rather than face problems which require long-range solutions people concentrate on the immediate. Are we willing to face this tendency and insist on facing this fundamental question, "Is there a God?"

Supposing we have overcome the general bias, group bias is the most difficult to break free from. We all tend to live in accord with the significant "They" of our lives. "They" tell us what is important, what to think about, what to think about everything. "What the facts are" is passed around so that people accept everything without ever making any of it their own. We're encouraged to live with constant curiosity, eager to "see" the next thing but never tarrying to taste or wonder about anything. Far from acknowledging a sense of emptiness we tend to be convinced that living this way is truly living. Needless to say, one lives with profound ambiguity, not knowing what truly is real and what is hearsay.

The reality of dying can liberate from such group bias. Facing the prospect of one's own dying makes one starkly aware that "they" do not die; "I" die. Then it is about time to start living as "I," determining for myself what is true, what is real. Short of this radical method of liberation, one can become sensitive to views of conflicting groups, truly listen and form one's own judgment.

Finally, one must analyze her individual bias. Is she living under the drive of personal desires and fears? Does she let them override intelligence, sinning against the light when she discovers that fidelity to the demands of honest intelligence means self-abnegation and a transformation of a lifestyle fashioned under those desires and fears?

No one can seriously search to discover whether God exists without a moral conversion along these lines. It is, however, a *pre*condition for the search; it does not enter directly into the process as the intellectual conversion does.

RELIGIOUS CONVERSION

We've all learned the difference between knowing something and embracing what we know. How often have we been convinced we drink too much coffee, smoke too much, eat too many eggs and other rich foods - the list goes on - and neglected to do anything about it? Well, in our pursuit of an answer to the God-question, provided we've undergone intellectual conversion, it is possible to perceive the validity of the reasoning to God's existence without embracing that truth. Religious conversion concerns embracing the truth that reason discovers.

Gabriel Marcel works out the intellectual groping a person goes through in a search for God, reaching the critical point of free acceptance of the light, of grace.

> It is up to freedom, come to the point where it accedes to the greatest self-awareness, to liberate itself in some way from itself, I mean by this, from its perverse disposition to affirm its own self-sufficiency. And this liberation is none other than the act of humility by which it immolates itself before grace.
>
> One thus perceives how the calling into question or the interrogation of oneself changes at the extreme into a summons which is in fact the unique act of religious consciousness...This is what I have always called the invocation...: You who alone possess the secret of what I am and of what I am capable of becoming.
>
> But perhaps this ultimate transmutation is itself, in the last analysis, but the work of grace, provided that he who has felt its mysterious work taking place in him accepts to open himself to it. (*Problematic Man,* pp. 62-3)

In Marcel's analysis of the way a human person comes through reflection to open himself to the presence of God, both freedom and grace are involved.

Henri de Lubac, S.J. suggests a similar need for religious conversion.

> Reason may remain serene with its proofs untouched;...The theoretical problem may well have been solved in principle...but the practical question remains, the fundamental question about the use of the idea of God in the spiritual life.
>
> Then, to our astonishment, the Gift of God intervenes. It is the second gift, for the first is the gift of mind itself, of the affirmation. Then the *donum perfectum* (perfect gift) is grafted onto the *datum optimum* (the best thing given). It in no way adds to the force of the affirmation or to the value of its rational foundation. It in no way supplements the proof, nor does it offer

a substitute, which is not, in any case, required. Its action is of a different order: it comes to assure the spirit of the tranquil enjoyment of its object, without depriving it of its original impulse, and to restore peace to the mind.
(*The Discovery of God*, pp.110-111).

De Lubac captures precisely what constitutes the religious conversion. Intellectual conversion is intrinsically required in order that the reasoning be followed and recognized as valid. Moral and religious conversions are extrinsic to the reasoning process, but required if the person is to eliminate emotional obstacles and embrace what she's been able to know is true: Yes, there is a God.

That sounds neat and clean cut. But the three conversions are intimately interwoven, for indeed the human person is a harmonized unity. The insight about the three conversions is Bernard Lonergan's; he makes this inter-relationship clear. In the human process of self-transcendence one goes beyond experience to understanding and discovery of what is real -(Intellectual Conversion). But this invites us to act in accord with what we know, to embrace the truly good, to move toward authenticity - (Moral Conversion). This allows us to go beyond self to a total being-in-love as the efficacious ground of all self-transcendence, whether in the pursuit of truth, or in the realization of human values, or in the orientation the person adopts to the universe, its ground and its goal - (Religious Conversion). (*Method in Theology*, pp. 238-243)

How can these three distinguished authors be composed? Marcel and De Lubac are envisioning the experiences of people today as they struggle to break out of the chains of modern thinking to discover the ground of their very being. Lonergan, on the other hand, in a holistic view of the human person, recognizes that to be human involves a religious dimension.

Clearly, if there is a God, we human beings are related to God and the religious experiences people generally have enjoyed were valid, revealing this religious dimension. Furthermore, it is significant that historically, religious response to God preceded intellectual justification of God's existence. Long before theoretical thinking developed people related to God, established cults and codes. Only after theoretical thinking emerged among the Greeks in the West, were people equipped to assess reasonably the truth of the presuppositions of religious conduct.

The contemporary lack of religious experience reveals a dysfunctional state, harmful to human fulfillment. Perhaps today religious conversion is a question of unblocking the religious dimension, freeing people to embrace what intellectual reasoning leads to, God's existence.

Powerful religious experience, encounter with Jesus Christ through Scripture, or witness by loved devout believers may be what leads some people to affirm God's existence and to embrace some religious community. This, however, is not the religious conversion I am talking about. At some point most people today need assurance that it is intellectually responsible to affirm there is a God. The ability to embrace what cogent reasoning establishes about God's existence is the religious conversion I am referring to. Accepting the truth discovered will unblock the religious dimension structured into every human person.

Granted intellectual integrity, we may reasonably assume that some people will receive the grace for religious conversion so that they can embrace what their intelligence acknowledges to be true. They will recognize that their previous lack of religious experience marks a dysfunctional state. Grounded solidly on conviction, they will allow this dimension of themselves to become functional.

If what has been said about religious conversion is true, then believers can understand why reasoning alone can fail to lead a nonbeliever to acknowledge God's existence. Nonbelievers, on the other hand, are challenged to discern whether the reasoning is cogent even though they remain unable to embrace [accept, with consequent adjustments] the conclusion: God exists.

Needless to say, we are not proposing fideism, criticized earlier, for we insist that reason can establish there is a God. Still, reflection on the need for these three conversions should leave all people humble and modest. Believers, for example, must check whether they recognize the proof as intellectually convincing - as distinct from assenting by faith. At the same time they should respect those who deny that the reasoning is cogent, keeping in mind that nonbelievers might be expressing a feeling that the proof seems without "weight," or that the conclusion is one they prefer to ignore, certainly not one they are ready to embrace within their lives.

Nonbelievers, in view of the need for these conversions, should respect the sincerity of believers and their claim that they see the reasoning as valid. So detailed is the reasoning in Chapters 10 and 11 that we will be able to pinpoint precisely where they disagree with the reasoning and perhaps reach agreement. Otherwise there is question whether intellectual conversion has taken place, or question about possible obstacles that moral conversion is to handle or about their willingness to accept grace.

SUMMARY AND CONCLUSION

All knowing takes place by grasp of the virtually unconditioned. Intellectual conversion provides openness to any kind of reasoning that gives insight into the virtually unconditioned and clears away the most serious obstacle to genuine dialogue on God's existence. But because we are emotional, desiring beings as well as propositional-knowers, we must all attend to the biases and prejudices which could prevent integral search for the truth. Serious pursuit of truth in any area requires readiness to accept what is discovered, no matter the consequences. And affirmation or denial of God's existence can have so much impact on our lives that moral conversion may be necessary.

This moral attitude is important throughout the reasoning, but it is a *pre*condition, not something intrinsic to the reasoning process itself. Since any serious inquiry into God's existence is never merely an intellectual exercise, the objective is to incorporate the conclusion into one's lifestyle. The function of religious conversion bears precisely upon the ability to embrace what one has discovered to be true.

The attitudes arrived at by the three conversions are:
 openness to every and each way of thinking and reasoning
 which provides insight into the virtually unconditioned
 -- (intellectual conversion, intrinsically necessary)
and *freedom from bias and prejudice,*
 embracing of the truth concluded to
 -- (moral and religious conversions, extrinsically necessary).

If we possess these attitudes we are ready to face the question itself: "Is there a God?"

PART III

In an age of faith the burden of proof rests on the nonbeliever to demonstrate why people are deceived by believing in God. But today in an age centered not on faith but on human reason, the burden of proof must be shouldered by the believer.

For all the good achieved by reason we are very grateful: the material benefits, the growth in human dignity, the liberation from superstition. But truth and human happiness demand an expansion of reason, going beyond calculative thinking to include meditative, philosophical thinking - opening people to faith as well as reason.

After a eight-chapter effort to validate the God-question and to expand the understanding of reason, we are ready to demonstrate how reason can lead step by step to affirming, "Yes, indeed there is a God."

To determine just where a nonbeliever disagrees, the reasoning is given in multiple small steps. Progress from point to point is likened to a climb up a mountain passing through three plateaus and coming to rest on the fourth at the top. Read the page entitled "The Four Plateaus" from the bottom upward to see the stages of reasoning.

The development of the argument needs preliminary explanation. Because ascent to the Second Plateau requires rejection of Naturalism, a dilemma arises. Do I prove its two suppositions false before undertaking the argument? Or do I ask readers to grant - tentatively - that the suppositions are false, promising detailed refutation of them later? I chose the latter alternative. And readers have waited long enough for the promised argument; they want to see this philosophic reasoning. The earlier criticism of scientism and the explanation of intellectual conversion should allay any suspicion and dispose readers to grant tentatively rejection of the two suppositions of Naturalism. Readers can be assured that the conclusion will be clearly stated: "God exists - Yes" is conditional - conditioned upon successfully proving the suppositions false. And the Naturalist's position will be addressed in detail.

Here just brief intimation of the grounds for rejecting the suppositions can be given lest the force of the climb be lost. After the proof five chapters give detailed grounds for rejecting Naturalism.

After we have directly confronted and rejected Naturalism, only then can it be said we have established the existence of God.

Experience has convinced me that people interested in the God-issue are searching to find God; abstract reasoning will not satisfy them. Immediately after the quasi-empirical proof of Chapters Nine and Ten we shall identify the distinctive function of reasoning on the God-question: to demonstrate that it makes sense to interpret certain experiences as real encounters with God. For believers, religious experiences are the starting point; for nonbelievers, we shall unfold the experiences of knowing and loving as implicitly experiencing God. Then the final chapter will aim at leading nonbelievers to link the uncaused entity with their religious experience or their lived experience of truth and love. Ultimately this can lead them to religious union with God.

As for believers, this more empirical approach can deepen their conviction of God's existence; it can empower them to dialogue with friends who are puzzled about God's existence. They can communicate their belief in God in language nonbelievers understand.

A Glossary of significant terms is provided as an appendix for reader's use.

CHAPTER 9

CLIMBING THE MOUNTAIN: HALF-WAY

In the last scene of *Edmond,* the playwright, David Mamet, shows us Edmond and his prison cell-mate meditating on life. Edmond muses that a person can't control what he makes of his life; there is something that shapes our lives. And this something is beyond heredity or environment. It's "beyond those things we can know...If we knew it...we would be God...or some genius...or some philosopher..."

The God we are climbing toward in this work is one whose Providence guides all our lives, as Edmond was musing in the play.

It will not be an easy walk. Philosophy is very precise. It will help to keep in mind that the search begins with a rich experience interpreted as a religious encounter with God or - in the case of nonbelievers - with a rich experience of love (or truth) analyzed as an encounter with something or someone transcendent. At issue is whether it is reasonable to interpret those subjective experiences as encounters with God. If, during this climb up the mountain, intellectual honesty forces us to admit there is a God, then it is reasonable to think we encounter God in those experiences. What we're doing relates to this rich experience and will give it an even deeper dimension.

A QUASI-EMPIRICAL ARGUMENT FOR THE EXISTENCE OF AN UNCAUSED BEING

Presumably everything is in place for examination of a positive, quasi-empirical argument for God's existence. Each step in the argument is simple. But the many factors attended to, and the treatment of empirical factors in an abstract way, make the argument seem complex. A reader must focus on each step by itself.

The climb begins with the affirmation of a proposition which picks out a simple, undeniable state of affairs (a fact). On the last plateau we arrive at the affirmation of a proposition which picks out (presents, pro-poses) the existence of an uncaused entity. The ascent between these two points is long, but we take it by stages.

We begin with two maps. The first outlines the four Plateaus of the entire argument. The second has ten steps leading to the first Plateau. The significance of each step may be elusive now but each one will be explained. Just as in using a street map, directions have become much clearer by the time one reaches the point requiring decision. Both maps are to be read from the bottom up.

| THE FOUR PLATEAUS |

FOURTH PLATEAU

There exists an uncaused being, a necessary being, a being which cannot not be.

^^^^^

THIRD PLATEAU

There is an uncaused cause
which causes the network of interrelated causes to exist,
which in turn causes "Someone will read a sentence..." to occur.

^^^^^

SECOND PLATEAU

There must be an answer to "Why does the network of interrelated causes exist?" and since it cannot be found in itself, we must look for a cause outside it.

^^^^^

FIRST PLATEAU

There is a network of interrelated causes which causes "Someone will read a sentence..." to occur.

^^^^^

Starting Point
Someone will read a sentence...

GUIDE'S MAP
FOR
CLIMBING TO THE FIRST PLATEAU
There is a group of interrelated causes, which causes our example, "Someone will read a sentence..." to occur.

STEP 10. This group of interrelated causes causes "Someone will read a sentence..." to occur.

STEP 9. The group of related causes of "someone reading a sentence," identified by these criteria, includes all the conditions whatsoever required for that state of affairs to occur <u>unless</u> something is required which does not meet the second or the third criterion.

STEP 8. There are extrapropositional conditions of "someone reading a sentence" which fulfill three criteria:

1. They must each be satisfied for it to occur.

2. Each is a state of affairs which might or might not occur or exist.

3. Each occurs or exists only if further prerequisites, *not included in itself,* are satisfied.

STEP 7. Each of the obvious and immediate conditions prerequisite for the initial event to occur has its own prerequisites which might or might not be satisfied.

STEP 6. Therefore "Someone will read a sentence" cannot occur simply by itself.

STEP 5. If the proposition is true and the state of affairs of someone reading a sentence occurs, there will have to be fulfilled certain extrapropositional conditions prerequisite to it and not included in it.

STEP 4. This initial event is a contingent state of affairs.

STEP 3. The proposition picks out a future state of affairs, someone reading a sentence.

STEP 2. The proposition expressed by that sentence.

STEP 1. A sentence, "Someone will read a sentence in this book..."

TOWARD THE FIRST PLATEAU

Believers may wonder about the need for advancing in such small steps. Not unlike Moses they have been to the top of the mountain and know with lived experience that God is and is near. Still the detailed process assures them too that the attitude of a reasonable person is indeed belief in God, not disbelief.

There will be, I am sure, no disagreement in this first part of our climb. It is all empirical, straightforward common sense.

STEP 1. *Let's start with a sentence, something we can see or hear. "Someone will read a sentence in this book within a week."*

STEP 2. *Recall that sentences express propositions (pro-posals). Focus, then, on the interior act of knowing, which is the proposition expressed by the sentence above.*

STEP 3. *Recall also that propositions pick out (present, pro-pose) a state of affairs (a fact). Our proposition picks out a future state of affairs: within a week some person reading a sentence from this book. (Someone will read a sentence.)*

STEP 4. *Notice that the state of affairs picked out is a contingent state of affairs. [It might or might not occur.]*

Clearly it is not *necessary* that someone read a sentence of this book within a week. Conceivably it could be impossible. All copies of the book might be destroyed. A nuclear war could wipe out all human beings who read English. The event might or might not occur. Therefore if someone does read a sentence of this book, certain conditions will have to be fulfilled. Thus we begin with a contingent event, one which might or might not occur.

The proposition which picks out (proposes) the contingent state of affairs is itself contingent. Its contingency is evident since we can understand what it would be for the state of affairs picked out (Someone reading a sentence) to occur without knowing whether the state of affairs does occur or not. The use of the future reference emphasizes the contingent nature of the proposition and the state of affairs it picks out.

What is being said applies to any and every contingent state of affairs a person can experience. We could select sentences such as "Someone will drive a car on the Southeast Expressway tomorrow." "Someone will turn on a TV tomorrow." "Someone will prepare and eat breakfast tomorrow." We would then focus on the states of affairs (facts) which the propositions expressed by the sentences pick out and recognize that the states of affairs are contingent. If any one of them happens, it does not have to happen. If any of them happens, it will be because other states of affairs required for it to happen made it happen.

STEP 5. *If the proposition proves to be true and the state of affairs (fact) of someone reading a sentence occurs, then there will have to be fulfilled certain extrapropositional (outside the mind) conditions prerequisite to someone reading a sentence and not included in that state of affairs.*

We are merely spelling out what common sense takes for granted. It refers to the fact, for example, that light will be needed if someone is to read a sentence. Likewise it is obvious that there will have to be a human person alive, conscious, capable of, and inclined to, reading an English sentence. This book will have to have been printed and available. These conditions are all extrapropositional; they are existing conditions.

(These) "extrapropositional conditions (are) not included in the state of affairs" (picked out by our initial proposition).

Obviously the proposition which picked out the state of affairs of someone reading a sentence makes no reference to these conditions. Light could be provided by the sun, electric bulb, or candles. Any one of these would do, so the state of affairs picked out by the proposition does not include any of them. As for the need of a human person to do the reading, this involves physiological and neurological conditions and one could know that someone is reading a sentence without knowing biology or the other sciences. But one could not know that the state of affairs picked out occurs without knowing what is involved in the state of affairs of someone reading a sentence.

STEP 6. *Therefore the state of affairs of someone reading a sentence cannot occur simply by itself.*

One small step at a time! This obvious step does not advance much, if at all, beyond Step 4, for if a state of affairs is contingent something outside itself must exist and make the contingent state of affairs occur. Step 5 *implies* Step 6.

Nonetheless, Step 6 ought to be taken explicitly in preparation for later challenges. It is a logical articulation, drawn from Step 5, which explains the need of something other than the initial event to make it occur. At the First Plateau all the contingent causes of someone reading a sentence will be identified as constituting an interrelated group of causes.

The Naturalist normally assumes that is all there is. But the question, "Is that all there is?" is valid. Is this network of causes, even extended to include the entire material universe, adequate explanation of the *initial* event? We advanced to Steps 5 and 6 precisely because someone reading a sentence is a contingent event.

If the whole network of causes also is contingent, can that occur simply by itself? The challenge of Naturalism springs to life in the climb to the Second Plateau. One Naturalistic supposition claims that the network of causes does exist by itself, even though it is constituted by contingent things.

STEP 7. *Each of the obvious and immediate conditions prerequisite for the state of affairs of someone reading a sentence to occur has its own prerequisites which might not be satisfied.*

Again, I am merely using common sense and ordinary knowledge. Take the condition of light. If I consider the sun as the source, then the chemical conditions within the sun are required, as is the position of the earth and so forth. If I consider electricity as providing the light, there are required a bulb, electrical wires, and a source of the electricity. As for the human person as a condition, this requires countless physical, psychological, historical conditions. It is practically impossible to list all the conditions, and especially the conditions of these conditions, required for so simple a state of affairs as someone reading a sentence to occur. Enough to say that we know some extrapropositional conditions are required. And we can indicate the criteria of these conditions which are required.

STEP 8. *There are then extrapropositional conditions of someone reading a sentence which fulfill three criteria:*
1. They must each be satisfied for the state of affairs of someone reading a sentence to occur.
2. Each is a state of affairs which might or might not occur or exist.
3. Each occurs or exists only if further prerequisites not included in itself are satisfied.

Some steps are very important for later development of the argument. This is one. The criteria will be used to identify the group of interrelated contingent causes which Naturalism claims is sufficient and to show how the uncaused cause joins with these conditions we have been looking at and yet goes beyond them. The simplicity of the previous steps may have lulled a person but he will want to examine these criteria carefully lest he be taken by surprise in later steps. Every step must be consciously acknowledged.

The first criterion is obvious because there is no point to considering any extrapropositional state of affairs unless it is needed for our initial state of affairs to occur. The fact, for example, that water boils at a certain degree does not appear to be a condition required for the state of affairs of someone reading a sentence to occur. That Napoleon was Emperor of France likewise does not seem to enter into our state of affairs.

What about criterion number 2? First of all it is evident that each of the conditions I have looked at is a contingent state of affairs, one which might or might not occur. Is it logically permissible to *pre*suppose that *all* the unknown conditions required are such that they might or might not occur or exist? Not only do I not have to presuppose that, but the proof hinges on showing the presupposition is false. All we are acknowledging at the moment is that some conditions required for our initial state of affairs to occur might themselves exist or not exist.

Criterion number 3 spells out the contingency aspect stated in number 2. Each condition involved in the network of causes might or might not exist and so needs a prerequisite condition outside itself to exist. Also this third criterion simply registers the fact discovered about all the conditions which can be immediately known, namely that each does require something outside itself in order to occur or exist.

To guard against suspicions arising in this Step 8 consider how Steps 4, 5, and 6 are related.

Step 4 - The state of affairs picked out by our initial proposition is a contingent state of affairs. Step 5 merely spells out what common sense takes for granted: it points to extrapropositional conditions required for a contingent state of affairs to occur. Step 6 articulates the obvious, relating to Step 4 through Step 5: if a contingent state of affairs occurs, it cannot occur on its own power.

The third condition of Step 8 thus relates to the second condition just as Step 6 relates to Step 4. Condition 2 states that there are interrelated extrapropositional conditions required for the initial state of affairs to occur, all of which are contingent. It follows, as condition 3 expresses it, that each of these extrapropositional conditions requires other conditions not included in itself. In other words, as in Step 6, a contingent state of affairs cannot occur on its own power.

We are situating ourselves to confront Naturalism which assumes the group of interrelated contingent causes suffices to explain any event.

A red flag is waving here to warn that this criterion is crucial. Notice it states the need of further prerequisites *not included in itself*. For when we posit (declare to exist) an uncaused cause we shall point out that the prerequisite of being an uncaused cause, which as cause is contingent, is found not outside itself but *within the state of affairs of being an uncaused cause*, namely that there is an uncaused entity within the uncaused cause.

Step 9. A. *The group of related causes of someone reading a sentence, identified by these criteria, includes* all *the conditions whatsoever which the initial state of affairs requires to occur,*
   B. unless *something is required which does not meet the second or the third of these criteria for membership in this group of required conditions.*

"A. The group of related causes...includes all..."

Because it is impossible to know all the conditions of the conditions required for the initial state of affairs to occur, I refer to them in abstract terms and lump them together. They are all the conditions which meet those three criteria. It does not matter whether this group constitutes only part of the universe or whether it embraces the whole of the universe of contingent states of affairs. Any condition which meets all three criteria has to be a contingent state of affairs.

"B. *unless* the state of affairs...requires..."

Again a red flag is waved. This "unless" is the step which opens the way to posit the uncaused cause and then the uncaused entity. At this point in the argument it suffices to leave open the possibility that something beyond the set of contingent conditions may be required. In other words if the state of affairs of someone reading a sentence occurs, then everything that is required for it to occur must also occur or exist.

What is required for it to occur? At least all the conditions which I have lumped together as satisfying the three criteria. Is anything more required? At this point of the investigation we do not know.

To rule out any noncontingent condition is to close one's mind, to determine arbitrarily what one will accept as evidence and as truth. Thus, if intelligent reflection reveals that the group of contingent conditions lumped together is not sufficient to explain why the initial state of affairs occurs, intellectual honesty demands that we go beyond this group of contingent conditions. This is *not* saying we must go beyond contingent conditions or that there is a noncontingent cause. It is suggesting that this possibility not be excluded arbitrarily or by bias. It is waiting to see where honest reasoning leads us.

Why is the "something" which might be required designated as something which does not meet the second or third of the three criteria? First of all, if intellectual honesty compels one to go beyond the group of contingent conditions, the first criterion must be met. For there simply is no point to considering anything if it is not something which must be satisfied for the initial state of affairs to occur (the first criterion). On the other hand, if it fulfills both the second and the third criteria it will be included in the group of contingent conditions.

Therefore it *has* to be something that fails to fulfill one or other or both of these two criteria.

This type of detailed logical examination can "turn off" people unaccustomed to close philosophical reasoning. But the justification given above as to why anything required beyond the group of contingent conditions must *not* fulfill the second or the third criterion, this justification is essential for later development of the argument.

However, it suffices at present to leave undetermined whether the something which *might* be required fails to meet the second *or* the third criterion. How can anyone say which criterion until it is judged whether intellectual honesty demands that one go beyond the group of contingent conditions at all?

STEP 10. *This group of interrelated causes causes "someone reading a sentence" to occur.*

This network of causes is not merely a collection of different states of affairs (facts). Nor is it an arbitrarily constructed group. It is the set of the interrelated, extrapropositional conditions required for the state of affairs of someone reading a sentence to occur, conditions which meet the three criteria. We can identify some conditions required, but it suffices to specify all prerequisite conditions as those which meet the three criteria. Thus the states of affairs have this in common: each in its own way is an extrapropositional condition which must be satisfied for the state of affairs (fact) of someone reading a sentence to occur.

The fact that all these conditions are so interrelated as to provide what is required for the initial state of affairs to occur is also itself a state of affairs. Thus the network of causes is a state of affairs.

To articulate in detail the corresponding proposition, however, defies human knowledge and ingenuity. But to identify the proposition as that which picks out this interrelated group of contingent conditions is not arbitrary.

A cause in this argument, as explained in the Glossary, means a state of affairs, the extrapropositional prerequisite conditions, not included in another state of affairs--which must be satisfied for this latter state of affairs to occur or exist. This group of interrelated causes, then, causes the initial event to occur.

We have reached the First Plateau opening immediately onto the road to the Second Plateau, with a question leaping spontaneously to mind: Why does the series of interrelated causes exist?

REVIEW OF THE CLIMB TO THE FIRST PLATEAU

Before starting out on the climb to the Second Plateau I suggest rereading the schema and map of the climb to this First Plateau:

There is a group of interrelated causes, which causes "Someone will read a sentence..." to occur.

In summary, the initial state of affairs of someone reading a sentence in this book cannot occur without a whole group of conditions or causes causing it to occur. Surely, there is no difficulty with or objection to this First Plateau conclusion or to any of the steps. Something happens; it need not happen. Something causes it to happen. In fact many things are involved as causes. All these causes in turn have conditions or causes. Thus there is a series of causes which make the initial event happen.

As we continue our climb the reader is reminded to follow the Guide's Map from the bottom upward, # 1 to #6.

GUIDE'S MAP

CLIMBING TO THE SECOND PLATEAU

There must be an answer to "Why does the group of interrelated causes exist?" and since it cannot be found in the group itself we must look for a cause outside the group.

STEP 6. Therefore there must be an answer to "Why does the group of interrelated causes exist?" and since it cannot be found in the group itself we must look for a cause outside of the group.

STEP 5. The supposition that the group of interrelated causes (or the material universe as a whole) exists simply because it exists is false.

STEP 4. Therefore there is no answer in this group of causes itself or in its constituents to the question: "Why does it exist?"

STEP 3. Therefore the group of interrelated causes is a contingent state of affairs.

STEP 2. The supposition that the group is self-sufficient is false.

STEP1. Why does the group of interrelated causes exist?

TOWARD THE SECOND PLATEAU

Some readers may run over the steps leading to the First Plateau and be amazed that it took all that time to say so little. As they let the ten steps and explanation of each flash before their minds, they click and think, "Wow! You're saying that when something happens, something caused it to happen and a whole series of interrelated causes must be involved. Hardly news really!"

Articulating every step of the argument aims at identifying precisely where nonbelievers find that communication fails. And the most crucial steps requiring agreement occur beyond the First Plateau.

Climbing to the Second Plateau provides a precise challenge: Is there need to go beyond the network of contingent causes? This is head-on confrontation with Naturalism and its two presuppositions!

Five chapters will be devoted to proving these presuppositions false, thus showing why intellectual honesty demands we go beyond the network of contingent causes.

The climb to the Second Plateau requires six steps.

STEP 1. *So I ask why does the group of interrelated causes exist?*

STEP 2. *The supposition that the group of interrelated causes is self-sufficient is false.*

I shall use Chapters 13, 14, and 15 to prove this Step 2. Every argument for God's existence is a challenge to show why reasoning must go beyond the material universe. Consider the pivotal insights developed in those chapters.

Nonbelievers, I am sure, have been accustomed to assuming that the universe is limited to the sensible and quantifiable so they assume that the material universe is all there is. If so, they have felt, it *must somehow* explain all there is. Understandably then, the summary considerations offered here will not satisfy critical readers but should dispose them to grant *tentatively* the rejection of this presupposition of Naturalism. If this is granted then the entire argument can be laid out, identifying precisely where the issue of Naturalism is located.

The claim that the network of causes is self-sufficient, especially when extended to embrace the material universe as a whole, usually takes two specific forms: mutually supportive causes or an infinite series of causes. But mutually supportive causes is shown to be impossible because a circle of causal dependence requires that a thing both exist in order to cause and not exist in order to be caused. And an infinite series of mediating causes clearly is impossible. Without a first *non*-mediating cause, mediating causes mediate nothing.

What is important about these arguments refuting the specific forms this presupposition takes, is what follows from their success. Since these specific forms of the supposition assume that everything is contingent, once they are rejected the supposition of self-sufficiency does not make sense unless the material universe as a whole is noncontingent or includes a noncontingent factor.

At this point the going gets tough. But focus on the precise reason that the network of causes is *not* noncontingent. Because the universe is material, it is composed of matter and form and requires a cause to unite the diverse principles of matter and form. Because it is composed of matter and form it is likewise composed of essence and existence. Its existence cannot be identical with its essence, which, composed of matter and form, involves potency; the act of existence cannot be identical with potency. So composed, it needs a cause to unite the diverse principles of essence and existence. Thus the network of causes, however far extended, cannot be self-sufficient.

The radical reason, then, that the material universe cannot be noncontingent is that to be noncontingent the act of existence must be identical with its essence. Not only does this explain why the material universe (composed of matter and form in the order of essence and of essence and existence in the order of existence) cannot be identical in existence and essence, but it instructs us how to think about the noncontingent being we reach on the Fourth Plateau when we affirm the existence of an uncaused entity.

Finally, the vague suggestion that the material universe as a whole could be noncontingent because it contains a noncontingent factor will be shown to be futile. We could never know whether such a factor exists or not. Why? Because the only way to reach an uncaused entity is through reflection on an uncaused cause. But an uncaused cause is excluded from the network of causes causing the initial contingent event.

The reader is not expected to accept this syncopated summary of the rejection of the second supposition of Naturalism - other than as an intimation of how it will be proved false in later chapters. But provided readers tentatively grant that the supposition is to be rejected we can go on to Step 3, for then tentatively we can say, "The supposition that the group of interrelated causes is self-sufficient is false."

STEP 3. *Therefore the group of interrelated causes is a contingent state of affairs (fact).*

We stated in Step 10 of the climb to the First Plateau that all these causes taken together constitute a state of affairs. So if the supposition that the network of causes is self-sufficient is false then the network is a contingent state of affairs. It might or might not exist.

STEP 4. *Therefore there is no answer in the group of interrelated causes itself nor in its constituents to the question, "Why does it exist?"*

Innocuous as this statement seems, it intimates and denies the subtle, implicit assumption Naturalism requires: that the material universe as a whole must be so different from its contingent parts that it is noncontingent or that something within the material universe is noncontingent. Because of what we have just seen under Step 2 we deny this implicit assumption and affirm that there is no answer in the network of causes as a whole nor in its constituents to the question why it exists.

STEP 5. *The supposition that the group of interrelated causes extended to include the material universe as a whole exists simply because it exists is false.*

Step 5 might be mistaken as saying the same thing as Step 2. No trick is involved.

As we have repeatedly explained, there are two suppositions undergirding Naturalism:
    First, - the material universe as a whole exists simply because it exists, Second, - the material universe as a whole is self-sufficient.

Step 2 addresses the second supposition. Now in Step 5 we confront the first supposition. The first logically precedes the second, but in the quasi-empirical argument they emerge as challenges in the reverse order.

Naturalists appealing to this first supposition remain consistent; they maintain that the material universe is contingent. But they claim it is unreasonable to ask *why* it exists. The logic of explanation, they say, requires that one stop questioning at some point and accept something as matter of fact. Individual events can be explained by some causes and these by other causes, but ultimately reason must stop at the material universe as a whole, they say, taking it as matter of fact.

This supposition is treated extensively in Chapter 12. Very simply, isn't it ridiculous to insist that everything that happens in one's experience must have a cause, but then when it comes to explaining the *entire* universe it is all right to shrug, "It just happened - no cause!"

In Chapter 12 the issue is approached from three sides: traditional metaphysics, Lonergan's tour de force, and the limitation of scientism. In Chapter 16 the entire argument of these chapters is schematized, - laying bare the rationality norms which direct the pivotal Steps of the reasoned climb to the Fourth Plateau. As regards this supposition of Step 5, even though its proponents do not contradict themselves, they are shown to be irrational. (Irrational in a logically technical sense, not in a psychiatric sense.)

This brief indication of how the first supposition will be confronted allows readers to grant that Step 5 ought to be taken.

Obviously a crucial point in "Climbing the Mountain" has been reached. If it is reasonable to ask why the network of causes (extended to include the entire material universe) exists, granted we have shown (in Step 2) it is not self-sufficient, then intellectual honesty demands we seek a cause beyond, outside the material universe.

Notice the modesty of the next Step. The claim is that intellectual integrity compels us to search outside the material universe.

STEP 6. *Therefore there must be an answer to "Why does the group of interrelated causes exist?" and since it cannot be found in the group of causes itself we must look for a cause outside the group of causes.*

In other words we must go beyond the network of causes if we want to explain why the initial event occurs or exists. It may seem we have not climbed very high in mounting to this Second Plateau, but arrival at this point will allow us to ascend rapidly. For "if the group of interrelated causes does not exist because it exists" or because it is the state of affairs which it is, then intellectual honesty compels us to go beyond it and posit some cause outside it. And it is only a matter of unfolding the characteristics of this "something" to reach the conclusion: There is a God.

REVIEW OF THE CLIMB TO THE SECOND PLATEAU

Having established that there is a group of interrelated causes which causes the initial event of someone reading a sentence to occur, we face a question immediately. "Why does the group of interrelated causes exist?" And we acknowledge that the group may extend to include the entire material universe.

We outlined in some detail how we intend to reject Naturalism's second supposition (The material universe as a whole is self-sufficient). It follows tentatively that the group of interrelated causes is contingent and so cannot explain why it exists. Provisional granting rejection of the first supposition of Naturalism (The material universe as a whole exists simply because it exists) requires that we ask why this group of causes exists. We are forced, therefore, to go beyond these causes, beyond the material universe as a whole to a different kind of cause.

CHAPTER 10

CLIMBING THE MOUNTAIN: TO THE TOP

GUIDE'S MAP
FOR
CLIMBING TO THE THIRD PLATEAU

There is an uncaused cause which causes the group of interrelated causes to exist, which group causes "Someone will read a sentence." to occur.

STEP 3. *This cause of the group of interrelated causes is uncaused. Therefore there exists an uncaused cause which causes the group of interrelated causes to exist, which group causes "Someone will read a sentence..." to occur.*

STEP 2. *This further prerequisite is the cause of the group of interrelated causes.*

STEP 1. *Therefore there must be an extrapropositional prerequisite beyond the group of* interrelated causes for this group of causes to exist rather than not exist.

TOWARD THE THIRD PLATEAU

We'll ascend rapidly now, needing only three steps. The air, however, is getting rarified. Perseverance in one's intellectual conversion is essential; "knowing" is not sensing but grasping intellectually the virtually unconditioned. And all this refined speculation is anchored in experiences of something/someone transcendent. A successful climb aims at establishing that it is reasonable to interpret religious experience or experience of love as an encounter with God.

STEP 1. *Therefore there must be an extrapropositional prerequisite beyond the group of interrelated causes for this group of causes to exist rather than not exist.*

We begin our climb with the logical conclusion from what we reached on the Second Plateau. If there *must* be an answer as to why the network of causes exists, as claimed above, and if the reason it exists is not in the network itself, then there must be something in reality outside it which explains why it exists.

STEP 2. *This further prerequisite is the cause of the group of interrelated causes.*

Staying as close as possible to experience, I defined "cause" as an existing state of affairs, an extrapropositional condition, not included in another state of affairs, which must be satisfied in order that the latter state of affairs may occur or exist.

En route to the First Plateau in Step 10, I pointed out that the network of causes is a complex state of affairs consisting of all the contingent causes which together contribute to the initial state of affairs existing. Something, an extrapropositional state of affairs, *not included_in the group of causes* is required for it to exist and that clearly is what is meant by a cause. This extrapropositional state of affairs which is not included in the interrelated group of causes must exist in order for the interrelated causes to exist. This something causes the group of causes to exist.

STEP 3. *This cause of the group of interrelated causes is uncaused. Therefore there exists an uncaused cause which causes the group of interrelated causes to exist, which group causes "Someone will read a sentence..." to occur.*
This cause of the group of interrelated causes must be related to, yet distinct and different from, the group of causes. It is *related* to it because it causes it to exist, and also, since the group of causes is required for the initial event to occur or exist, then this newly discovered cause is required for someone reading a sentence to occur and so it joins with the group of causes in causing the initial event to occur. This newly discovered cause is *different* from the group of interrelated causes in that it does not fulfill *all* of the three criteria for membership in it.

It is essential to relate this Step to Step 8 and Step 9 of the climb to the First Plateau. I waved a red flag at that point to alert the reader about weighing the two Steps carefully; they're crucial for the Step we are taking in climbing to the Third Plateau.

As we investigated the causes of the initial contingent event of someone reading a sentence, we saw the interrelationships of the causes and of *their* causes was so widespread it was impossible to trace all of them individually. But we could specify them as fulfilling three criteria:

*[***STEP 8.** *There are then extrapropositional (outside the mind) conditions of someone reading a sentence which fulfill three criteria:*
1. They must each be satisfied for the state of affairs of someone reading a sentence to occur.
2. Each is a state of affairs which might or might not occur or exist.
3. Each occurs or exists only if further prerequisites not included in itself are satisfied.]

We moved on to Step 9 which explains exactly the relationship of this Step 3 on the way to the Third Plateau:

*[***STEP 9.** *A. The group of related causes of someone reading a sentence, identified by these criteria, includes all the conditions whatsoever which the initial state of affairs requires to occur,*
B. unless something is required which does not meet the second or the third of these criteria for membership in this group of required conditions.]

Again the red flag of warning waved at this "unless." "Unless" is the step which opens the way to affirm the existence of an uncaused cause and then the uncaused entity. An appeal was made for open-mindedness, that one not rule out arbitrarily any noncontingent condition, not arbitrarily determine what will be accepted as evidence. At that point it was asked only that such a cause or any possibility not be excluded arbitrarily or by bias.

Intellectual honesty demands we go beyond the interrelated group of contingent causes. In other words, the "unless" has been found fulfilled; something is required to explain why the initial event occurs which does not meet the second or the third of these criteria for membership in this group of required causes.

Still searching to explain why "Someone will read a sentence..." occurs means constantly relating every step of our ascent to this initial state of affairs. Thus the cause of the group of causes fulfills the first criterion of the causes which constitute the group of causes. ("1. It must be satisfied for 'Someone will read a sentence...' to occur.")

This cause of the group of causes simply cannot fulfill *both* the second *and* the third criteria, because then it would belong to the group, rather than be its cause.

This cause must fulfill the second criterion ("2. It is a state of affairs which might or might not exist.") This is an extremely subtle point. To prepare for it, consider this homespun example: the ceiling light in your living room. Sometimes it's on, sometimes not. What makes this so? Because the electricity is not always connected. Different members of the family turn on the switch or turn it off. The light might be on and might not be on, its being on a contingent fact. If, however, there were no light-switch in the room so that the electricity was always connected, then the light would have to be on. If, in other words, the *causing* of the electricity were always applied to the bulb, it could *not not* be lighted.

The example, as they say, limps. What about the bulb burning out, you say? Right. This is an attempt to find an example which may suggest a helpful image of a very mysterious relationship.

I am saying this cause of the group of interrelated causes "is a state of affairs which might or might not exist." Keep in mind that we are trying to explain why "Someone will read a sentence." occurs.

An explanation is needed precisely because the initial event is contingent, it might or might not occur. If the causing of this cause (if like the electricity, it were always causing) were noncontingent, it would cause the group noncontingently. That means the group of causes would cause the initial event noncontingently and someone reading a sentence would not be contingent. It would have to be.

I am straining to distinguish the "actual causing" of this cause of the group of causes from the "being of the cause." Back to the example. The electricity cannot *not* cause the bulb to light, *if* it is connected with the bulb. The light switch, sometimes turned on, sometimes not, makes the lighting contingent. So if the "actual causing" by this cause of the group of causes were noncontingent, the group of causes would exist noncontingently - and *precisely as causes, so that their causing* would be noncontingent. If the group of causes were actually causing noncontingently, then "Someone will read a sentence..." will *have* to occur, will occur *noncontingently.*

In other words, if the cause of all the contingent causes of someone reading a sentence were a necessary cause and so were necessitated to cause, the initial state of affairs would be a necessary state of affairs, not a contingent state of affairs. Clearly the cause of the group of interrelated causes must be a contingent state of affairs and thus it fulfills the second criterion of belonging to the group of causes of "Someone will read a sentence...".

Admittedly it sounds strange to say this cause of the group of causes is contingent, to say it might or might not be causing. The reasoning given above explains why it must be contingent. On the Fourth Plateau we shall establish that there is an uncaused *entity*. Obviously then it is essential to see the difference between an uncaused *entity in_itself* and that *entity inasmuch as it causes*. All we know about this cause or entity we reach by close theoretical reasoning.

Interestingly enough the problem arises most acutely in the minds of those who rush ahead and think of the uncaused cause as God. After all God cannot not exist. So how can the uncaused cause not exist? We shall ground the uncaused cause in the uncaused entity. So the uncaused entity cannot not exist. God is a necessary *being*; God's *causing* is contingent. In other words, God does not *have* to create. To claim God freely creates involves the insight that God's causing might or might not occur.

A person comfortable with the traditional understanding of God as uncaused cause need not be disturbed. I am not denying this. God indeed is the uncaused cause. The refinement between uncaused cause and uncaused entity is required for this particular way of proving God's existence. Traditional metaphysics definitely attended to the refinement, but discussed from a different perspective.

Therefore this cause of the group of interrelated causes is not subject to the third criterion ("3. It itself exists only if further prerequisites *not_included in itself* are satisfied.") This cause simply cannot meet all three criteria, for then it would be part of the group of interrelated causes. We have just seen that it meets the first two criteria; therefore it cannot meet the third. This cause does not require anything apart from itself in order to exist. Someone reading a sentence is related to the group of interrelated causes (It is caused by it); the group of causes is related to this newly discovered cause (It is caused by it). But this new cause is not related to anything in that way. Thus it is a cause, but it is uncaused. This cause of the group of causes is an uncaused cause. What grounds its existence is included within itself.

The reasoning here has been on a very abstract level and for a person accustomed to thinking scientifically, relating constantly to the sensible and the mathematical, this has demanded deep concentration. It is very easy to slide into expecting sensible or mathematical verification solely.

So when a person reads "what grounds its existence is included within itself" he tends to take this as spatial - and that makes no sense. So, confused, one wonders what "within itself" refers to. A spatial image is being employed non-spatially. Consider how we use the expression in other contexts. Ten contains within itself two fives. Love contains within itself commitment. So the reason this uncaused cause exists is found in itself.

During the climb to the First Plateau, at Step 8, the third criterion was noted as crucial. In fact "a red flag" waved warning that this requirement would allow us to establish the *uncaused* cause. In the group of interrelated contingent causes of someone reading a sentence each one "exists only if further prerequisites *not included in itself.* are satisfied." We have been logically forced to posit a cause of the group of causes, which cause, contingent as is its causing, does need a prerequisite to explain its existence as causing, but the prerequisite is *included within itself.* The cause of the group of causes is a *cause* since it is an extrapropositional state of affairs required for the group of causes to exist; but it is uncaused , since it has within itself what is required for it to exist.

To complete the discussion note that there is a proposition which picks out this uncaused cause: "There is an uncaused cause which causes the group of interrelated causes, which, in turn, is the cause of someone reading a sentence."

This remark about the proposition which picks out this uncaused cause need not be disconcerting. We reach the uncaused cause and the uncaused entity precisely by knowing that our propositions affirming the uncaused cause and the uncaused entity are true.

Recall that the function of the proposition is to pick out a state of affairs (a fact). In other words, in considering propositions we are considering what we think is real. When reflective insight leads us to the virtually unconditioned we attain truth and knowledge. We know what is the case; we know what is real. Because we know what is meant by the proposition that there exists an uncaused cause (and at the Fourth Plateau, an uncaused entity) and know that it is true, then we know there really is an uncaused cause (and an uncaused entity).

REVIEW: PROPOSITIONS INVOLVED IN CLIMBING TO THE THIRD PLATEAU

So now we stand on the Third Plateau: There is an uncaused cause. Three propositions mark the ascent. Each of these three propositions has been affirmed, for in each we have grasped the virtually unconditioned. This means that we know each is true.

First Proposition - Someone will read a sentence in this book within a week.

Second Proposition - Innumerable, interrelated causes cause the initial state of affairs to occur, each of which is characterized by three criteria.

Third Proposition - There is an uncaused cause which causes these interrelated causes to exist (which group of causes in turn causes "Someone will read a sentence..." to occur).

In the First Proposition we have treated the state of affairs of someone reading a sentence as a *future* event in order to emphasize that it is contingent. So the entire argument has been hypothetical. Later the opening proposition will be changed to an *actual past contingent* state of affairs, e.g. Someone wrote this book. The argument will then shift to an actual group of causes to catch the viewpoint of actually positing the uncaused cause.

The First Proposition, then, picks out a contingent state of affairs. If that state of affairs is to exist certain conditions outside of the initial state of affairs must be fulfilled.

The Second Proposition picks out all the contingent causes required for the initial event to occur.

Having shown that the group of interrelated causes cannot explain why it, as a group, exists and that an explanation is necessary, we pass swiftly to the Third Proposition.

This Third Proposition picks out that there is an uncaused cause which causes the group of interrelated causes to exist. Having grasped the virtually unconditioned, we know that there is an uncaused cause.

Many people would be satisfied that the existence of God has been established. They are correct in one sense, but only because they presuppose what remains to be proved. Logically, however, the mind can not stop there, for this uncaused cause, precisely as cause or in its causing, is contingent. It might or might not exist.

Have we met an impasse? The reason the uncaused cause exists cannot be "further prerequisites *not included in itself.*" We cannot explain why it exists as cause by appeal to something outside itself, for then it would not be an uncaused cause but a caused cause, and so belong to the group of interrelated causes. Yet in its causing it is contingent; it might or might not be!

So subtle is this point that the renowned British philosopher mentioned earlier missed it completely. If everything needs a cause and God is the first cause, then, he thought he had to ask, "What caused God?" He ceased to believe in God. But his question is meaningless - and it is not the same as the question I am raising. Why not? We have to climb to the Fourth Plateau to see.

GUIDE'S MAP
FOR
CLIMBING TO FOURTH PLATEAU

There exists an uncaused entity, a necessary being, a being which cannot not be.

STEP 7. *There exists an uncaused entity, a necessary being, a being which cannot not be.*

STEP 6. *I substitute the proposition: "Someone has written this book," for "Someone will read a sentence..."*

STEP 5. *We know that this proposition is true.*

STEP 4. *A proposition picks out this uncaused entity: "There is an uncaused entity."*

STEP 3. *We know very little about this uncaused entity.*

STEP 2. *This uncaused entity is self-sufficient. The group of interrelated   causes is not.*

STEP 1. *The reason the uncaused cause exists is the uncaused entity, an entity grounding but not causing the uncaused cause to exist precisely as causing .*

TOWARD THE FOURTH PLATEAU

Staying as close to experience as possible, we let the logic of explanation guide us from an experience of considering a contingent state of affairs, "Someone will read a sentence," to the causal explanation of that simple state of affairs. Intellectual honesty has forced us to declare there is an uncaused cause. Unlike Russell, the British philosopher referred to, we are not asking why an uncaused entity exists. We are asking why the causing by an uncaused cause (which causing might or might not exist or occur), - why this causing exists.

Only seven more steps to reach the top of the mountain where we shall "see" that there is indeed a necessary being.

STEP 1. *The reason the uncaused cause exists is the uncaused entity, an entity grounding, but not causing the uncaused cause to exist precisely as causing..*

Since the uncaused cause might or might not exist yet requires nothing *which is not included in itself* in order to exist, then it must include *within itself* a state of affairs which is noncontingent. This state of affairs exists simply because it is what it is. It requires nothing other than itself in order to exist and it explains why the uncaused cause exists.

Once again I speak of the uncaused entity being "within the uncaused cause." The image is spatial, but the intention is to insist that the reason the uncaused cause exists is found in itself, not in a state of affairs apart from it. The same point is being made when I claim the uncaused entity *grounds* but does not *cause* the uncaused cause to exist.

In Chapter Twelve the traditional metaphysical argument against Naturalism will distinguish the principle of sufficient reason (Whatever exists has whatever is necessary for it to exist) from the principle of causality (Whatever exists contingently has an efficient cause). This uncaused cause has what is necessary for it to exist - and what is necessary for it to exist is that it, as being, be an uncaused entity. An efficient cause must be different from its effect. Nothing can efficiently cause *itself* to be. It would have *to be* in order to cause: it would have to *not be* in order to be caused. Thus the uncaused cause we have reached is identical with the uncaused entity which provides the reason that it exists. There is, then, a distinction between the uncaused *entity* and the uncaused entity *causing.*

STEP 2. *The uncaused entity is self sufficient. The group of interrelated causes is not.*

Notice carefully how logical this is, but notice also how modest our claim is and how little we know about the uncaused entity. Once we climbed to the Second Plateau we found that intellectual honesty demanded that we go on to posit a theoretical state of affairs in order to explain why the group of contingent causes existed. This had to be a *cause*, but *uncaused*. We know, however, that the uncaused cause is in some respect contingent because the initial state of affairs (someone reading a sentence) is contingent. What is the connection? Because this uncaused cause does not cause the initial event *if the event does not occur*. And since "Someone will read a sentence..." is contingent, it *might* not occur. Thus the uncaused cause's causing might not occur. The uncaused entity which grounds the uncaused cause might not be causing.

Once again, the challenge: If we can stop our search with the uncaused entity, why could we not stop at the group of causes inasmuch as the entire material universe was involved? Such a challenge underscores the importance of the climb to the Second Plateau and how important it is to prove that the two suppositions of Naturalism are false. Precisely because the group of interrelated causes (even extended to include the entire material universe) is contingent, we are irrational not to continue to probe and to ask why it exists. And because the group of causes, indeed the material universe as a whole, can neither be noncontingent nor contain a noncontingent element, intellectual honesty pushes us to posit the uncaused cause. But this uncaused cause, while its causing is contingent, does identify with itself as noncontingent. The uncaused cause, inasmuch as it is a being, is an uncaused entity. Only inasmuch as it freely causes can we speak of the causing as contingent.

Thus this uncaused entity does not exist because of some other required condition nor does it exist simply because it exists (as the first supposition of Naturalism claims about the contingent material universe). This uncaused entity is posited as existing rather because of what it is. What the uncaused entity is, is the sole condition for it to exist. And since intellectual honesty demands that we posit it as existing, then this condition must be acknowledged to be fulfilled.

We do not understand directly what the uncaused entity is and so we do not explicitly know why being what it is necessitates that it be. But we do know *the fact that it must exist.* Why? Because we affirm that "Someone will read a sentence..." or any contingent event occurs. To affirm that such a contingent event occurs and to deny what is required for it to occur is a contradiction.

Supposing the validity of each step of our reasoning, we must acknowledge that the uncaused entity is required for someone reading a sentence to occur. Otherwise we equivalently affirm *and* deny it. It is like claiming to be an American while denying you were born in the United States or born of American parents or that you have been naturalized or any other way of being an American. You simply cannot be an American and not fulfill one or more of the requirements for citizenship. To affirm "Someone will read a sentence..." and deny what is required for it to occur is equally contradictory.

STEP 3. *We know very little about this uncaused entity.*

Years ago, in 1951, I climbed my first and only mountain. Outside of Innsbruck, Austria, there is a picture-book mountain, a sharp, triangular rocky peak. What a challenge to climb that sheer rock and what a thrill to stand on the top and see the world below! I did not climb that sheer rock. Like most people (including the middle-aged woman cook who climbed it the day before!) I mounted from the other side. I walked all day to the base of the mountain, to a small hotel where climbers stayed overnight. After a heavy breakfast I set out alone, an hour or more before anybody else. It was overcast and after walking two hours I reached a point where the climbing became sterner. Dark, threatening clouds overhead worried me. Is it dangerous to press on? Would experienced climbers stop? I had no idea. What helped me decide was the sight of a small party way behind me still coming on. Up I went. Finally after a few scares I reached the top.

So often as I had gazed up at Mt. Serlitz in the distance the wish rose in my heart, "Oh, to see the world from the top of that mountain!" Well, here I was on the top, panting from the climb. I rested and then standing on the peak I looked out. All was darkness. Black clouds shrouded everything. I could see nothing!

Step by step by step we have climbed to the top of the mountain and all I can offer is - not a vision of God - but the proposition: There is an uncaused entity! No wonder Thomas taught that we can only know what God is not, that we find God in darkness.

A ballad of the '60's took us through each stage of life from going to the circus for the first time, to first love, to marriage, to death - and after the account of each experience the lament was repeated, "Is that all there is ...?" Conceivably when some people discover what is learned on the top of the mountain they may be tempted to say, "Let's forget it, if that's all there is to a reasoned approach to God's existence."

Three things should be kept in mind. First, knowledge of the existence of an uncaused entity can save and fortify love. Second, the religious conversion required is what allows a person to embrace the conclusion fully. Presuming the good will of those who have followed the argument, it would be surprising if God did not offer the grace of religious conversion. And finally, the counter-culture revolution made clear that what we really desire is lifestyle, not mere theoretical thinking. Reasoning is a partial human response. It can provide only the foundation for the holistic response of religious lifestyle.

The darkness on the mountain top gives way ultimately to a joyous love and a religious lifestyle. And the religious person acquires the habit of "seeing" things, events, and persons "as" manifestations of God and God's presence. That person walks in God's presence.

So returning to Step 3, notice how little we know about the uncaused entity. The need is there of positing a theoretical state of affairs, an uncaused cause. All that is known about the uncaused cause is that it is, that it is a cause and yet different from any other cause because it is uncaused. And we know it does not depend on its causing in order to be. This uncaused *cause* exists because of something within it, an uncaused *entity*. Thus we reach the uncaused entity. We would not *know* it exists if we did not know some contingent state of affairs exists. But it *exists* because it is what it is. THE UNCAUSED ENTITY EXISTS, WHETHER WE KNOW IT OR NOT.

We know there is an uncaused entity, that it causes contingent states of affairs and that it has whatever is required to be such cause. Relating this uncaused entity with God as we understand God to be is a challenge to be faced later.

STEP 4. *A proposition picks out this uncaused entity: "There is an uncaused entity."*

The Third Proposition in the climb to the third plateau "There is an uncaused cause..." picks out the state of affairs of the uncaused cause. Similarly, this proposition picks out the state of affairs that there is an uncaused entity. Why introduce remarks about propositions? Step 5 will explain.

STEP 5. *We know that this proposition: "There is an uncaused entity" is true.*

The darkness at the top of the mountain seems even greater when we reach this step, because now it is revealed that what we know directly is our proposition that there is an uncaused entity. Only because we know that the proposition is true, do we know there is an uncaused entity.

As I was looking out my window just now I saw a car leave the parking lot. Seeing it I directly knew the car and knew it was moving. I was directly aware of the car being. A while later I talked by phone to my sister Mary in Wakefield, learned she was staying in this morning and that, yes, her car was fine. Do I know Mary's car is in her yard? Yes, but I am not directly aware of it. I am aware of my proposition: "Mary's car is in the yard," and I know the proposition is true. So I know her car being in the yard but without being directly aware of it.

What I directly know at the top of the mountain is my proposition, that there is an uncaused entity. The very meaning of the proposition is derived from knowing a contingent state of affairs and that for this to occur there is need for interrelated causes and, in addition, need for an uncaused cause, and that this uncaused cause exists because within the state of affairs of being an uncaused cause there is an uncaused entity. Thus the meaning of the proposition is acquired from the initial state of affairs and from the reasoning process. And we know the proposition is true from knowing that the *contingent event occurs* and that the *reasoning process* is *valid*. In this process a person is not *directly* aware of the uncaused entity.

Knowing as a distinct form of awareness should be linked with direct awareness of presence. Religious experience is an awareness of a transcendent presence. As it was developed for nonbelievers at the starting point of our reasoning process, experiences like love include awareness of something transcendent, absolute, and eternal. Reasoning, which is part of the complex knowing awareness, functions to establish that it is reasonable to interpret religious experience and other experiences like love, as encounters with this something/someone transcendent which will be shown to fulfill the agreed definition of God.

The seemingly cold direct knowledge of my proposition that there is an uncaused entity fuses with my religious experience and the other experiences mentioned, to provide a warm, human holistic response. My knowledge that my sister's car is in her yard lacks the direct sense awareness of her car being there. I can transform that knowing awareness into a fusion with sense awareness by traveling to Wakefield and standing beside that car. I do something similar by linking my rigorously reasoned conclusion with my lived experience of a transcendent other.

In the Bible Moses asks the Lord to show him the Lord's glory. The Lord replies, "Behold there is a place by me where you will stand upon the rock; and while my glory passes by I will put you in the cleft of the rock, and I will cover you with my hand until I have passed by; then I will take away my hand and you shall see my back, but my face shall not be seen." "You cannot see my face, for man shall not see me and live." (Ex.33)

It would be so satisfying, we feel, if at the top of the mountain we saw God face to face. That cannot be. We know the nonsensible by reason, not by sight. We know the uncaused entity only indirectly. We see, as it were, the back, not the face. Like Moses we are allowed in this life to catch sight of God as God has passed by, in and through what God does. In heaven we shall see God face to face, so Christian faith assures us.

Once again those three things must be kept in mind which I recalled under Step 3. Knowledge of the uncaused entity can save and fortify human love. A religious conversion is essential to your embracing wholeheartedly the reasoned conclusion. Only a holistic, religious response can satisfy us. Reasoning merely provides the basis of the religious lifestyle. No one seriously pursuing the God question will be satisfied with an abstract reasoning process to a conclusion that a necessary being exists. People seek communion with God. Reason can only lay the foundation for a religious lifestyle and it can remove the obstacle of thinking that belief is not intellectually respectable. Communion can come after that.

How do we know that the proposition picking out the uncaused entity is true? Assume, as we have generally been doing implicitly all along, that "Someone will read a sentence..." occurs or that its replacement, "Someone has written this book," (which I shall suggest in Step 6), exists. If, then, we understand the meaning of the proposition and recognize the validity of the reasoning, we know that the proposition is true. This proposition is an interior intellectual act, so that the state of affairs which it picks out is in the mind. Knowing that it is true, we know that the state of affairs picked out is also outside the mind, is extrapropositional. We are in touch with what is real. The initial contingent event cannot exist unless the uncaused entity exists.

Recall that a proposition has two principal parts, a name and a predicable. The name identifies what one is referring to and the predicable provides the sense, it says something about what is named. So in this proposition, the reference (an entity) and the sense (uncaused but known through its relation of causing the network of causes and thus the initial event) emerge from the argument itself. Thus we know the meaning and the truth of the proposition from the entire argument.

STEP 6. *I substitute the proposition:"Someone has written this book," for "Someone will read a sentence in this book."*

I started the mountain climb with a predicted state of affairs in order to emphasize its contingency, since we could not be certain that the state of affairs would occur and yet we could understand what it would be like for the state of affairs to occur, for someone actually to read a sentence in the book.

Now I substitute a contingent state of affairs (a fact) which actually does exist. I have written this book and I might not have written it. I ask the reader to adjust everything I have said about a future contingent state of affairs and apply it to this actual state of affairs. I suppose people have equivalently been doing that anyway, assuming that the predicted state of affairs actually did occur. The rest follows. All sorts of causes have joined together for this book to be written. The necessity of going beyond the network of causes pertains equally for the book and thus we reach the uncaused cause and uncaused entity.

STEP 7. *There exists an uncaused entity, a necessary being, a being which cannot not be.*

Intellectual honesty required us to posit a theoretical entity. Theoretical, note, does not mean hypothetical. Reason forces us to declare there must be something which is uncaused and so cannot not be. Since we reason to it without achieving any intuition of the being we call it theoretical.

This theoretical entity, the uncaused entity, is not a contingent state of affairs; it is not something that might or might not exist. It does exist although it is uncaused. A *non*contingent, *un*caused, *extra*propositional state of affairs is a *necessary being*. The proposition which picks out a necessary being is a necessary truth. We know that this proposition is true. So we know there is a necessary being.

REVIEW: KEY PROPOSITIONS OF THE ENTIRE CLIMB

Well, that's the technical argument. The climb progressed over three plateaus to the top of the mountain by establishing the *truth* of four propositions.

The four propositions and the state of affairs each picked out is as follows:

First Proposition: "Someone will read a sentence in this book within a week."

    State of affairs picked out: the fact of someone reading a sentence

Second Proposition: "Innumerable, interrelated causes cause the initial state of affairs to occur and they are characterized by three criteria...."

> **State of affairs picked out**: the group of interrelated causes on which the initial state of affairs depends

Third Proposition: "There is an uncaused cause which causes these interrelated causes to exist (which group of causes in turn causes 'Someone will read a sentence...' to occur)."

> **State of affairs picked out**: the uncaused cause which causes the group of interrelated causes to exist on which the initial state of affairs depends

Fourth Proposition: "There is an uncaused entity."

> **State of affairs picked out**: the uncaused entity which grounds but does not cause the uncaused cause existing precisely as causing.

The First Proposition I changed to "Someone has written this book." Clearly this proposition picks out a state of affairs equally as contingent as someone reading a sentence. Because the state of affairs picked out is contingent it raises the question why it occurred.

The Second Proposition picked out the group of interrelated contingent causes for the initial state of affairs.

That there are causes of the initial state of affairs is recognized as true because that state of affairs is contingent and since it exists it must have a cause. It is also true that we are able to identify many of the causes required for that state of affairs to exist. No one can doubt that we are able to specify (by means of the three criteria listed above) the other innumerable causes required for these causes to exist as well as any other causes needed for the initial state of affairs to exist. Therefore the Second Proposition is inescapably true.

This state of affairs, this interrelated set of contingent causes raises the same question as the initial state of affairs: since every cause in the group is contingent, why does the set of causes exist? Rejection of the two suppositions of naturalism is tentatively granted (with but intimations of proof to be later developed).

The Third Proposition picks out the existence of the uncaused cause.

exist? However, the uncaused cause is not a member of the group of causes precisely because the reason it exists is, and must be, in itself, not in another.

The Fourth Proposition picks out the uncaused entity.

The uncaused entity exists because it is what it is and grounds its own contingent causing. The meaning derived from the reasoning is clear, and intellectual honesty demands we declare the existence of the uncaused entity, the necessary being. This final proposition is also true.

CONCLUSION

Believers usually have no great difficulty positing an uncaused cause and then an uncaused entity. In fact they probably rush on to identify this with God. Nonbelievers may be intrigued at the logical laying out step-by-step of a process of reasoning to the existence of a transcendent uncaused entity.

Chapter 11 will explain that reasoning to God's existence grounds the interpretation that we definitely experience God. In the final chapter nonbelievers will be able to link the affirmation of the uncaused entity, the necessary being, with their lived experience of love. It seems eminently reasonable to interpret their experience with its implication of something eternal and absolute as an encounter with this uncaused entity. And this uncaused entity fulfills the agreed upon definition of God. But more about this later.

Some nonbelievers may be satisfied even at this point to identify this uncaused entity with God and acknowledge they encounter God in their love. Others remain reluctant to accept this uncaused entity. They have good reason for their reluctance. The very heart of the claim that intellectual honesty forces positing an uncaused cause involves proof that the two suppositions of Naturalism are false. And rigorous justification for their rejection has yet to be detailed.

What is at stake is clear. Proof that intellectual honesty demands we go beyond the group of contingent causes allows us to climb rapidly to the top of the mountain where we declare with confidence, "Yes, there does exist a necessary being." "Yes, God does exist." Although we are ready to confront Naturalism, it will help first to make manifest that we all experience God in our religious experiences or in our experience of truth and love.

After that comes the final challenge: I *EMBRACE* THE TRUTH THAT GOD DOES EXIST

CHAPTER 11

EXPERIENCE OF GOD AND FUNCTION OF REASONING

FUNCTION OF REASONING

Presuming agreement on the meaning of the term "God" and presuming that precise questions have been crystalized, we must now examine just how reasoning functions in answering our God-question.

The believer has experienced God; the nonbeliever counts on experiencing God if our investigation proves positive. Both may be disappointed unless they understand the function of the reasoning. It took years of teaching for me to catch sight of the problem. No one engaging in the question of God's existence will be satisfied with abstract, subtle, logical syllogisms. People want to know - to meet - God.

We "know" a person only by *experiencing* him/her. Clarence Thomas is at present a Supreme Court Judge. I only "know about" him. I "know" my sister Mary. I grew up with her. I have been closely in touch as she married and raised her children.

Since reasoning can lead only to "knowing about" God, there must be experience of God if our investigation of the God-issue is to be worthwhile. The function of reasoning is to demonstrate that it makes sense to interpret certain experiences as real encounters with God, that all along we have been "knowing" God.

RELIGIOUS EXPERIENCE OF BELIEVERS

Why we must identify the "experiences of God" from which we start will be evident. We begin with a Catholic's religious experience and the way it relates to reasoning about God's existence. Normally Catholics experience God at Mass and in reception of Holy Communion. When they pray, especially when they are just silent before God, they sense God's presence. Again God is real to them when they turn to God in earnest petition. They face God in making serious moral decisions and experience peace when they choose what they understand is good and experience guilt and remorse if they choose evil. Nature offers experience of God - looking at flowers, gazing at the sea, standing under the stars. Doesn't beauty open into a sense of God's presence? Many are convinced they meet God in others. Most sense God in a special way when they are in love.

Strands of faith and reason are interwoven in the common interpretation of such religious experience. In Mass and Holy Communion obviously Catholic faith is involved. In the other experiences mentioned, the understanding of who the God they experience is, likewise derives from faith. Catholics know it is God - and God as Father, God as the Blessed Trinity, whom they experience *because* the Church teaches them what and who God is. But belief in the Church *presupposes* belief that Jesus established the Church and gifted it with the charism of teaching the truth. But *that* has weight only because it *presupposes* belief that Jesus is God become man. And *that presupposes* there *is* a God who could become man. (The presupposing is logical, not psychological.)

We reach the question: Is it reasonable to affirm that God exists? For Catholic believers, clearly the question is linked with their lived experience of God. I shall not be leading them to *know* God; they already do. Once believers recognize that cogent reasoning demands they posit the existence of a necessary being, infinite and personal (a being which satisfies the meaning of God intellectually defined) it becomes utterly reasonable to acknowledge that they have been encountering God in their religious experiences.

Of course for adequate treatment we'd have to show the reasonableness of each of the steps outlined above. Granted we establish the reasonableness of affirming there is a God, we would have to show it is reasonable to make the extraordinary act of faith to acknowledge Jesus as divine. One would move on to show that Jesus

Experience of God and Function of Reasoning   161

established the Church and gifted it with the charism of teaching the truth. Finally, we'd show the Church teaches that the God present is the Blessed Trinity and is attainable in religious experience.

I limit our discussion to the question: Does God exist?--linking it as above to lived experience of meeting God in various religious experiences. Most people find little difficulty accepting the validity of the interpretation, granted proof of God's existence, without detailed treatment of the other presuppositions.

Readers who are Christians but not Catholic and non-Christian believers in God will describe their experience of God within their own religious structures. They can disentangle the strands involved in the interpretation and reach the challenge: Is there a God who could be so experienced? And at the end of the reasoning process, they link the conclusion with the initial experience.

What about nonbelievers who never have had religious experiences or at least do not now acknowledge any experiences as religious? My task is to call their attention to certain experiences they certainly have had and to unfold them in such a way that they can with integrity acknowledge that a *plausible* interpretation of them is that they have been meeting something beyond the immediate, something absolute and eternal. They are not admitting there is anything eternal and absolute. But if the reasoning of the climb up the mountain has struck them as valid and cogent, establishing the existence of a noncontingent being, an absolute and eternal, personal being, it will be evident how utterly reasonable they will be to interpret those experiences as encounters with God.

SIGNIFICANT EXPERIENCES OF NONBELIEVERS

I have always ardently desired to find some justification for the emotions inspired by certain things that seemed to stand outside human life and to deserve feelings of awe. I am thinking in part of very obvious things, such as the starry heavens and a stormy sea on a rocky coast; in part of the vastness of the scientific universe, both in space and time, as compared to the life of mankind; in part of the edifice of impersonal truth, especially truth which, like that of mathematics, does not merely describe the world that happens to exist.

The author observes that he cannot intellectually justify the implications of such emotional experiences. "And so my intellect goes with the humanists, though my emotions violently rebel." (B.

Russell, "My Mental Development," *The Philosophy of Bertrand Russell*)

A professed atheist, Russell acknowledges emotional experiences of "things that seemed to stand outside human life," so much so that his emotions rebelled violently against his intellectual stance.

J. J. C. Smart, a linguistic analyst, likewise acknowledges a distinctive experience of awe. In a very refined kind of thinking he dismisses the question, "Does God exist?" He finds it a meaningless question - the way "Do electrons exist?" can be a meaningless question. Why? Because, granted various experiments and scientific operations, the concept of the electron proves useful in physical theory. At that stage, the question "Do electrons exist?" no longer arises. In a similar way "Does God exist?" has no clear meaning for the nonbeliever and for the believer it does not arise.

Even while he rejects the cosmological argument for God's existence on grounds of linguistic analysis, Smart finds himself feeling a strange sense of awe. "The question, 'Does God exist?' does appeal [he admits] to something deep-seated in our natures." Seeking the explanation why a table, for example, exists, we can reach the question:

"Why should anything exist at all?" He states that the only logical reply is "Why shouldn't it?" Yet he finds he still wants to go on asking it. "My mind often seems to reel under the immense significance it seems to have for me. That anything should exist at all does seem to me a matter for the deepest awe." ("The Existence of God," *New Essays in Philosophical Theology*)

Russell cannot justify the emotional experiences which intimate something beyond the human. Smart can't explain the experience of awe before the question, "Why does anything exist?" I am convinced they are both encountering God in these experiences.

In my judgment, people constantly experience God - only it has not been customary to look upon experiences like those of Russell and Smart as God-experiences. Think of the times beauty in nature or art or a human face has communicated a sense of something beyond. How many times has the facing of serious moral decisions brought a sense of the absolute nature of obligation. The significance of such experiences is missed because they are not properly unfolded so they can be grasped as experiences of God.

Some thinkers are linking the thrusts of contemporary science with mystical contemplation. "The situation may be expressed by an image. Science without religion is lame, religion without science is blind." (Albert Einstein, quoted in I. O'Murchu, M.S.C., *Religious Life: A Prophetic Vision*, p. 230)

Because such experiences are not customarily considered related with God, they need proper unfolding. I shall limit myself to an analytic unfolding of the experiences of knowing and loving - suggesting how they involve a sense of the eternal and the absolute. In this way nonbelievers are able to share the same starting point as believers - experiences which conceivably can be interpreted as meeting God. If we establish the existence of a noncontingent being, personal, source of all things, it is reasonable to interpret these experiences as experiences of God.

EXPERIENCE OF KNOWING

Consider the numerous times a person reaches a serious judgment that "such and such" was the case.

"You can trust the person who loves you."
"Fighting for your country is worthwhile."
"Buying this house is a sound investment."

In the certainty of such judgments a person meant it was absolutely true, and not just at this time and for himself. He meant it was true for any person understanding things as he did; it would be true at any time, granted the same circumstances. He simply had to say, "Yes, that is so."

In all experiences like those, I believe one encounters in some way a transcendent something, an absolute, an eternal. When a person affirms that freedom and love are rich values, aren't such judgments intended to be true not just for him, but for every person - at all times and places? He intends to affirm them, I submit, as eternally true and absolutely true. Even in any simple affirmation: "I'm looking at the chair in front of me"--can I admit I could be wrong? Will it *ever* be the case that what I am now affirming is not, was not at this time, true?

All day long, then, we sense something absolute and eternal. But this insight needs considerable unfolding.

PHENOMENOLOGY OF KNOWING

At this point readers are invited to quiet themselves, close off the senses, go deep within themselves and attempt to experience what follows.

Sitting in front of me is a fan. I affirm, "The fan is on."
In this act of knowing I am aware of, I know, my act of knowing, as well as being aware of and knowing that the fan is on.

Reflecting on this experience, I notice my intellect has a natural appetite to know. I am dynamically ordered to knowing. I want to know. Granted my eyes are open and my mind alert, I cannot not know that the fan is on and know my act of knowing that fact. And that knowing is nothing forced on me. I want to know.

But notice, my wanting to know is not satisfied by this act of knowing. Once I know the fan is on, my mind moves on either to know more about the fan and its being on or to other objects of knowing.

By going beyond the fan being on and my awareness of and knowing my act of knowing I know them as limited, finite, and contingent. My appetite for knowing is never satisfied by any limited object of knowing. My intellect thrusts forward seeking to know everything, to know all that is knowable, to know something unlimited, infinite, noncontingent, or necessary.

Bear in mind I am not claiming there *is* anything unlimited, infinite and noncontingent. I am describing the thrust of my intellect in its knowing. Implicitly in all acts of knowing I refer to unlimited being.

Let me develop this insight from another perspective. Every object known and every act of knowing I know is "is." "The fan is on" - is part of reality. My knowing that knowing "is." But "is" extends beyond both - and beyond every limited object known. My intellect strives for a reality about which it can affirm, without restriction, "It is." But only about a being whose essence is to exist can be said, simply and exhaustively, "It is." All other, partial affirmations are anticipations of, intimations of, that final affirmation in which our intellect will finally meet a reality which exhausts its total capacity for affirmation.

Again, "Is" is. But, "The fan is on - is," "my awareness of, my knowing my act of knowing the fan is on - is" does not exhaust the "is." Yet I affirm each limited act of knowing and limited object as absolutely the case. Do I not add "a complement of intelligibility" which equates the object affirmed with the fullness of "is"? Every time I affirm something is, do I not intimate there is a being that is without limit, grounding the absolute, eternal sense connected with the limited "being"?

I am not claiming there *is* such a being. I am unfolding my experience of knowing in such a way as to suggest I am somehow, implicitly, affirming, indeed experiencing, an unlimited, infinite, necessary being.

Now if valid, cogent reasoning warrants my affirming that there exists a personal, noncontingent being, source of all things, won't it be reasonable to interpret the experience in all acts of knowing as indeed an encounter with that noncontingent personal being, source of all things? Such a being fits the definition of God.

All day long, then, people encounter something absolute and eternal in their acts of knowing. But another experience, love, may show more clearly that people do experience God - at least that they share an experience which, analyzed properly, shows it may be reasonable to interpret such an experience as an encounter with God.

EXPERIENCE OF LOVE

A few generations ago analysis of love would be less a problem. Sexual indulgence has trivialized sex and in the process trivialized love. Divorce has become so common that many question the possibility of committed love. This, I fear, has increasingly affected the children of divorced parents. A teenager whose father had left the family was comforted by a playmate, "You don't have it so bad. I don't even know who my natural father is." Will children of broken families, aware of how pervasive divorce is, be able to say [and mean] to a prospective spouse, "I love you - exclusively and forever?"

Look to our theater. A leading playwright, Sam Shepard, whose first play was produced in 1964, did not focus on a man-woman relationship until *Fool for Love* (1983), followed by *Lie of the Mind* (1986). In the first one a half-brother and sister fall passionately in love before they discover they have the same father. And this "love" clearly is a matter of compulsive need, not of cherishing and willing the happiness of the other. *Lie of the Mind* really is about lie and illusion rather than love, although the plot revolves around a demented, violently jealous husband and the woman whom he beat, whose brain he damaged.

Lanford Wilson's *Burn This* (1987) comes like a fresh breeze placing before us the budding love between Pale and Anna. And yet, the dawning awareness of their love evokes not "I love you," but "I don't want this." When the college students in my class were asked whether this love would develop and last, no one thought it would.

Nonetheless, even today hearts yearn for this exclusive permanent love. In spite of knowing the low statistical chances of their love lasting, most young brides and grooms believe their love will be different. They can sincerely and confidently pledge to love one another forever.

OTHER-CENTERED LOVE AND THE *UNCHOSEN* ABSOLUTE

A book published not long ago argues to the existence of God precisely from the reality of the experience of other-centered love. I offer a summary of the technical analysis of love, not as a proof of God's existence, but to show how that experience implies encounter with something (somebody) which (who) may be God.

Rigorous proof of the existence of an uncaused being may be linked with such experience, leading one to acknowledge it is reasonable to interpret one's experience of love as involving encounter with God.

Love As Chosen Absolute

The author focuses on other-centered love found ideally in mature conjugal love.

Genuine love reveals six characteristics. First, *perduring faithfulness*. Love involves self-giving, yet the lover cannot give the self all at once. Rather she keeps growing in her respect and understanding of the one loved, as well as in her capability to give. The intention, of course, is to love forever. The person loved, on the other hand, in the total acceptance of the lover's self-gift recognizes the "forever" quality of the gift, at least vaguely aware the lover will keep growing while experiencing confirmation of this "forever" quality in the countless manifestations of the commitment. Faithfulness forever, obviously, is based on well-grounded hope.

Second characteristic, *trustful intelligence*. The lover truly wants good for the one loved and so she intelligently assesses what is actually beneficial for this unique person. She does this with trust that the one loved will recognize her efforts to help intelligently. The one loved on the other hand, receives the loving gift not only gratefully, not only trustingly in appreciation of the value of the giving, but also intelligently creative in responding with gratitude.

Third, this love is also *expansive*. The lover has freely and intelligently risked total self-giving. But in the experience of total acceptance she feels confident and free to initiate other loves in harmony with this primary love. The one loved grows outwardly as well. The experience of receiving the self-gift and of totally accepting it makes him aware of his worth and opens him to engage in other loves, also harmonious with this primary love.

Fourth, in lover and the one loved there is a *liberation of the person*. This is not precisely the freedom to choose, but the harmony of person,
liberating all one's talents and inclinations to care for, to serve others.

Fifth, such a liberation blends into the *wholesome healing of this love*. "Wholesome" in the sense of healthy, full; it heals the many wounded areas we all suffer. "Wholesome" also in the sense of total love: giving of all one's self, with concern for all the weaknesses and needs in the one loved; total acceptance of the self the lover gives, warts and all, limitations and defects in the lover and her inherited family and community traits.

It should be obvious that such a liberating, wholesome healing associated with this love can only be achieved through *readiness to sacrifice self* (sixth) - readiness in lover and the one loved. Implicit in this other-centered love is the unspoken agreement that each is willing, if necessary, to suffer physical and psychological diminishment, even death for the liberation and wholesomeness of the other.

The special homily assigned in the old Catholic marriage ritual urges the couple to build their married lives on the principle of self-sacrifice. "Sacrifice is normally difficult, but love can make it bearable, perfect love can make it a joy."

Paradigmatically these characteristics are found in mature conjugal love. But they are likewise found in parental-filial love, in the love between other relatives, like grandmother and granddaughter, between devoted uncle and nephew. They describe the love of missionaries for their people, the love between one who works with the homeless and the homeless.

Furthermore, the six characteristics are intertwined; they really are facets of a single gem. Perduring faithfulness and self-sacrifice are the most striking facets. But the former is impossible without trust and wisdom. The natural fruits of faithfulness, impossible without self-sacrifice, are liberation and wholesome healing. No wonder this love turns one outward expansively to others.

Such an other-centered love is central in most people's lives. At times people feel as though they have no choice in such love. Obviously, powerful attraction is involved, but it is not really love unless one freely allows it to flourish. Thus love is *chosen*. And such love is absolute inasmuch as it is an ultimate value against which other values are measured and to which they yield when they conflict with it.

It is not surprising that people sense something absolute and eternal in the perduring faithfulness and self-sacrifice. Insight into the absolute and eternal in love crystalizes upon looking deeply at this beautiful gem, letting the six facets come alive as it turns slowly before one's inner eye.

Unchosen Absolute

Let me suggest the perspective needed to illuminate the experience of an absolute one does not so much choose but seems to discover.

Two things in the lived experience of *chosen* absolutes open into a sense of an *unchosen* absolute. First, the clearly experienced freedom to choose among candidates for the *chosen* absolute, even the freedom to change from one absolute to another. Second, the temporary dimension felt in any chosen absolute in contrast with the felt need of eternal fidelity in other-centered love.

FREEDOM TO CHOOSE *CHOSEN* ABSOLUTE

This subtle attraction of the absolute, operating *through* yet somehow *beyond* the beloved, becomes evident in the experience of selecting and establishing a *chosen* absolute in one's life. The child, unfree, has an instinctive absolute, its own immediate life of pleasure. Some years later an alternative *chosen* absolute emerges inviting the young person to embrace it in free choice: pleasure in an easy sex-life, perhaps as a college student, once-in-a-lifetime partner, a medical career, or finally perhaps celibate dedication to helping the poor. Clearly, one is also free to change from one of these absolutes to another.

Echoes of the "polytheism," and "henotheism" and "monotheism" of the first chapter can be heard in the listing of these absolutes. As the young person oscillates among these absolutes, there pulses the strange intimation that although no single one of them binds a person irretrievably to itself, still the absoluteness of each requires a commitment that is "forever." After all, how can a *chosen* absolute be the supreme value without demanding that a person submit all decisions to it and that the pursuit of it be forever? Anything less than "forever" submits this supposedly supreme value to the next value replacing it and so is not really supreme - unless, unless there is a value beyond every *chosen* absolute, yet operating through all such absolutes, which makes the person free to choose one absolute over the other.

Temporary Dimension in *Chosen* Absolute

The human heart definitely experiences a drive to promise eternal fidelity. This "forever" is not merely a certain indefinite time. In self-centered love the lover in his heart sets self-protective limits like "till you cease to excite me," "till I want my freedom again." But even self-centered lovers want to leave things indefinite; they do not want to say "I'll love you for a year, or seven years." The indefiniteness mimics the other-centered love's "forever." But other-centered differs from self-centered love precisely in truly intending commitment "forever."

This drive to promise the beloved a love faithful into eternity can be appreciated by observing the profound hurt, indeed trauma, felt in the lover cast off or betrayed. He or she must literally struggle to recapture some reason to go on living. The fear prospective spouses feel as they face marriage commitment is a comparable indication of this drive.

This promise to love "forever" is made with clear knowledge that marriages break down, careers founder, popularity and success change to oblivion and failure. So the absolute *chosen* is hardly worthy in itself of a "forever" commitment. On the other hand the lover feels less and less capable of guaranteeing fidelity for tomorrow, much less for twenty years, - or forever? Yet men and women feel the need to promise and try to give "forever" fidelity. Is it possible, then, that this "forever," always happening through the loved one, reaches beyond that person to a mysterious "more," totally worthy of the "forever"?

Is there a "more" always beckoning the lover on, always being more than the lover can comprehend; and this even in face of the reality that the beloved may psychologically break down, possibly betray, certainly physically corrupt and ultimately cease to exist (as he/she is now)?

Turning the gem of other-centered love around to let the light catch another aspect, we focus on self-sacrifice. Only three things limit the giving in other-centered love: the genuine needs of the one loved, the resources of the lover, and moral values. Within these limits other-centered love is a definite total self-giving.

Trust is unquestionably required. And growth brings wholesomeness and liberation to both people, allowing them to open themselves to love others. But none of this can happen without self-sacrifice; without self-sacrifice no love can be forever. Not only are lovers *ready* to die for the other, often dramatically rising to some sudden threat, but short of physically dying, those who love die regularly to self in living out their promised commitment. In such love one accepts willingly the diminishment of self when a loved one's needs requires this.

Examples: The mother who postpones her ambitions for a college education in order to support her husband and raise her family.

The husband who sells his business to care for his wife suffering from Alzheimer's disease.

The spouse willing to let his wife divorce him on advice of a therapist that this will help his wife get over a sense of guilt and the unwarranted feeling that he resents her because of the sacrifices he made during her nervous breakdown.

Doesn't it make sense to suggest that only the immanent presence of an unchosen absolute beyond all chosen absolutes can make deep sacrifice possible and endurable?

AFFIRMATION OF THE ABSOLUTE AND ETERNAL?

In these other-centered loves one not only experiences the absolute and the eternal, but implicitly *affirms* the absolute and the eternal. There are three possible attitudes a person can take toward this implicit affirmation. Having become aware of it one can deny there is anything absolute or eternal. But then that person ought, logically, to treat as illusion the thrust in his own heart to the absolute and eternal. Common sense directs such a person to protect himself against the illusion of love and center attention on oneself. Certainly one ought not be so unwise as to sacrifice in any serious way, never sacrifice one's life, for an illusion. A person can, of course, enjoy the romantic feelings experienced in "love" relationships, but carefully avoid getting involved and simply use the other as long as that other arouses these enjoyable feelings. A colleague once called my attention to the fact that Sartre, pretty much alone among thinkers, consistently denied the existence of God *and* the possibility of genuine other-centered love.

The second attitude a person can take, and probably the most common, is to ignore the link between the experience of love and the absolute/eternal, and just go on loving. Atheists, whether militant communists or secular humanists, do love. But they do so by being logically inconsistent. Thank God they are. The lives of most of us are not fully consistent with our beliefs either! The Christian who is not saintly in loving and caring for others is not logically consistent with his belief that we're all one in Jesus Christ.

Thirdly, one can acknowledge God as the absolute, the eternal, and relate to the loved one as sacred. The believer, bringing his belief consciously to the experience, lets the heart go to the loved one, but at the same time lets the heart go to God, too. Within the lived experience the lover does not attend to the different objects of love. To the extent believing lovers reflect about the two loves, there is the sense that they love one another in God, are grateful to God for the love, that somehow they give the heart in love *because* it is God's will that they do. All these perspectives provide motives for commitment in complete trust. In the pain of loss by death, resentment toward God may spring up in the heart, but more normally the bereaved lover may draw comfort from conviction that it was right to love with utter commitment, that this loss and pain are also within the providence of a loving God, that the loved one is happily with God and they'll be together again, reunited forever.

It seems clear to me that human love can flourish best within the framework of belief in God. The reflective atheist ought logically to arrest any impulse to other-centered love. Love without attention to the implicit affirmation of God as the absolute and the eternal is possible and can flourish. But love takes on a richer dimension when two people love within love of God.

Experience of something absolute and eternal, even implicit affirmation of it, does not constitute proof that there *is* something absolute and eternal. Aggressive atheists would admit some people have subjective experiences they interpret to be experiences of God. Conceivably, love and life and reality are all absurd. I'll propose an argument to move from any sensibly experienced happening to the necessity of positing the existence of an uncaused cause. If a person can accept the argument as valid, then it's reasonable to interpret the experience of something absolute and eternal in love as an experience of an uncaused cause, or God. This should help in recognizing the sacred in love and help in cultivating the sense of God in all parts of life. Prayer is the way to further nurturing the union with God.

Starting Point for Nonbelievers

Believers needed to uncover presuppositions within their religious experiences and thus identify just how the question of God's existence relates to the experiences. But nonbelievers normally do not interpret any experiences as experiences of God. It no doubt comes as a surprise to have anyone suggest they have been encountering God all along, in spite of their unbelief. They may feel intrigued at my efforts to unfold their experiences of knowing and loving as experiences of encountering God.

Assuming they have responded favorably to the challenge that the question of God's existence warrants serious investigation, then it suffices (1) that they acknowledge this unfolding of their experiences is at least plausible and (2) that they understand how reasoning to God's existence functions.

If the reasoning is shown to be valid, they will be able to change plausibility into conviction that indeed they have been encountering God.

SUMMARY AND CONCLUSION

The function of reasoning in our God-question is to establish that it makes sense to interpret certain experiences as encounters with God. Believers point to religious experiences. Nonbelievers have discovered that certain of their experiences, for example knowing and loving, can at least be unfolded in such a way that they *could* be understood as experiences of God, *if* reason can establish that there is a God, an eternal, absolute being.

Readers who have found the quasi-empirical argument convincing and sufficient can link their lived experiences with the uncaused entity, confident they "know" God, that they have been in touch with God all along. Readers still sensitive that they had been asked to grant *tentatively* that the two presuppositions of Naturalism are false withhold their assent to the existence of an uncaused entity. Before they consider associating their experiences of the eternal and absolute with the uncaused entity, they expect the promise to be kept: the detailed proof that the presuppositions are indeed false. We proceed to do just that.

PART IV

Promises are to be kept. In this case unless they are kept we have no proof of an uncaused cause and uncaused entity. In order to climb beyond the network of interdependent contingent causes to an uncaused cause, readers were asked to grant, tentatively, rejection of the two suppositions of Naturalism - with a promise to confront those suppositions in detail. Besides fulfilling the promise, confronting Naturalism head-on constitutes another proof of God's existence as developed in Chapters Twelve through Sixteen.

Some readers may prefer to skim or skip these chapters explicitly confronting Naturalism. Perhaps they have found sufficient proof in the earlier criticism of scientism which grounds Naturalism, in the explanation of intellectual conversion, together with the synopsis of the arguments which were given to encourage tentative rejection of each of the suppositions. Chapter 16 summarizes the sweep of the entire climb, laying bare how "rationality norms" demand each step be taken. The rest of this introduction to Part IV may help them decide whether to go immediately to Chapter17 or to confront Naturalism more thoroughly.

After defining Naturalism the argument against the first of its two suppositions is presented: No question about the material universe as a whole need nor may be asked.

Three chapters are devoted to refuting the more profound challenge of the second supposition. The claim that the material universe as a whole is self-sufficient takes two specific forms: mutually dependent causes or an infinite series of causes.

Refutation of the latter specific form allows us to treat the traditional approach of subordinated series of causes.

Implicitly as the matter above reveals, Naturalism is claiming that the material universe as self-sufficient is noncontingent. Herein lies the heart of the God-issue. Every argument for God's existence must establish that the material universe cannot be noncontingent. In order to be noncontingent, the essence of the noncontingent being must be identical with its existence. But the essence of any and all material beings cannot be identical with its existence. Of course, using these Aristotelian-Thomistic categories requires explanation of act and potency, matter and form, as well as essence and existence.

Finally, we prepare to link the uncaused entity of the Fourth Plateau with the definition of God and personal experience, by review of the entire argument including rejection of the two suppositions using "rationality norms."

CHAPTER 12

NATURALISM: FIRST SUPPOSITION

People who unquestioningly buy "the whole nine yards" of contemporary mainstream consciousness live as though there were no God - as though beyond the material universe there were nothing. Some ask, "In the search for the very first cause of reality, what difference does it make whether you stop at the material universe as a whole or stop at God?" Or, "If reason demands a necessary being, why can't the material universe be that being?" These two questions spring from the two suppositions of Naturalism.

First Supposition: The material universe as a whole exists simply because it exists.

Second Supposition: The material universe as a whole is self-sufficient.

NATURALISM DEFINED

The significance and pertinence of those suppositions becomes clear once Naturalism is understood.

Naturalism holds that the spatial-temporal universe is all there is and the method of solving all problems, small and particular, or large and universal, is the natural method: common sense and/or the scientific method. An erroneous assumption here is that science is the extension of common sense. Naturalism is the atheistic consequence of scientism. What is true about the world or any part of it is what the science of the time tells us is true. The universe is intelligible in its parts inasmuch as each part can be explained, but not as a whole, for as a whole it must be taken as mere matter of fact. Lonergan's argument will attempt to undercut this claim.

Negatively, then, Naturalism denies the following dualisms: between sense and intellect, between body and soul, between earth and heaven, between the material universe and God. In other words, there is no knowledge other than sense knowledge, there is no soul, no God. The denials are based first of all on arguments to show the error or inadequacy of any attempt to posit a dualism. Then one explains away beliefs in each of the dualisms. For example, Freud holds that belief in God originates in wishful thinking; Feuerbach explains that God is simply the projection of characteristics that belong to the people. What it means positively is getting on with the problems of the world, employing the natural and social science without wasting energy on religion.

So many in our culture implicitly live Naturalism! Indeed, every atheist implicitly or explicitly affirms Naturalism, no matter what the route to atheism and no matter what form the atheism takes. To live without God presupposes Naturalism.

After the emergence of the natural sciences in the 16th century, for two centuries more thinkers failed to recognize the revolutionary method of reasoning these sciences are. Their success and increased prestige prompted the cultural option to identify reasoning with scientific reasoning. When science came to be distinguished from philosophy naturalists took the stand that every particular event can indeed be explained, but that the universe as a whole can not, need not, be explained.

Interestingly, during the first two centuries of the scientific era, outstanding "scientists" (the term was not coined until 1840!) considered themselves "philosophers" and felt obliged to use the new ways of thinking to justify belief in God and to defend religion. Isaac Newton and Robert Boyle illustrate that fact.

Earlier chapters reported the development of scientism and Naturalism with specific treatment of the mistaken use of science in defense of religion.

By the early 19th century the validity of these physico-theological arguments for God's existence was generally denied. Hegel observed that with Diderot, d'Holbach and their circle of Enlightenment thinkers "This philosophy has developed into atheism, and has defined matter, nature, etc. as that which is to be taken as ultimate." (Michael

J. Buckley, S.J., "Newtonian Settlement and Atheism," *Physics, Philosophy and Theology* p.96).

Naturalism, then, maintains two pivotal positions: "1) The scientific method is the only reliable path to knowledge; 2) Matter (or matter and energy) is the fundamental reality in the universe." (Ian G. Barbour, "Ways of Relating Science and Theology," *Physics, Philosophy, and Theology* p.22) Accordingly, only the beings and causes with which science deals are real and science alone can disclose the nature of the real.

Many proponents of this scientific materialism assume certain forms of reductionism. Epistemologically, they claim that the laws and theories of all the sciences are in principle reducible to the laws of physics and chemistry. Metaphysically, they claim that the most fundamental reality of any system is constituted by its component parts. Hence all phenomena can be explained, but the claim is that the universe as a whole cannot, need not be explained.

Carl Sagan epitomizes scientism in popular form. Although his TV series and his book, *Cosmos*, are devoted to brilliant presentation of the discoveries of modern astronomy, he does not hesitate to interject his philosophical position: "The Cosmos is all that is or ever was or ever will be." For him the scientific method is "universally applicable." So he attacks Christian ideas of God, arguing that mystical and authoritarian claims threaten the ultimacy of the scientific method.

One rarely finds any serious attempt to provide philosophical arguments to justify the naturalistic enterprise. I know of no solid argument which positively establishes Naturalism. Naturalists assume that Hume and Kant have sufficiently eliminated philosophical insight into reality. They took Kant's thesis that there is no speculative knowledge of God as definitive, ignoring his argument that practical reason posits the existence of God. Recent authors do directly address the issue of God's existence but for the most part their approach is to attack as invalid all efforts to prove the existence of God.

In fairness it must be admitted that in the present academic climate of opinion atheism is in force and it is the responsibility of believers to prove that something more than matter in motion is needed to explain the universe. Admittedly, it is very difficult to prove a negative, i.e., that there is no God. So the tactic of attempting to invalidate arguments for God's existence is reasonable. But undergirding their attempts at invalidation are their theories of knowledge and of metaphysics. Naturalism is especially weak in positive philosophical justification of these theories.

The heart of Naturalism lies in its two suppositions. And here is how those suppositions emerge. In every reasoned approach to God's existence there is introduced a unique step in the argumentation. It takes the form of - "There is no *infinite* regress in causes and so there must be a *first* uncaused cause or there must be a necessary being." Or after identifying the cause of some being or some event one argues, "But there can be no *adequate* explanation of why this being exists or this event happens unless there is a first uncaused cause or a necessary being." Thus the step is taken *beyond* this material universe.

Naturalists deny any such step is necessary. They claim either that no question should be asked about the material universe as a whole or that the material universe is self-sufficient. Intellectual honesty requires taking that step beyond.

We are ready to address the first Naturalistic supposition.

NATURALISM'S FIRST SUPPOSITION: THE MATERIAL UNIVERSE EXISTS *SIMPLY BECAUSE* IT EXISTS.

The claim that the universe as a whole must be taken as just matter of fact is, they argue, inescapable, due to the logic of explanation. For every explanation must take something as matter of fact and the ultimate explanation of anything must take the whole universe as mere matter of fact.

What is meant by "matter of fact" and "logic of explanation"? Matter of fact means what is taken for granted, what is *not questioned*. Just what "matter of fact" is varies according to circumstances. For years it has been taken for granted that people were free to smoke at their work, in airplanes and in restaurants. No longer true! For years it has been taken for granted that only men are top executives. It was just a matter of fact that all top positions in business were to be held by men. No longer true!

In every field of knowledge, every science, every political system, every code of morality, certain things are so immediately evident or so firmly established and generally accepted as true that in any explanation or argument they are taken for granted. They are considered facts, not to be questioned. Some of the presumed "truths" are later discovered to be errors. But while they are accepted as truths, they are taken for granted.

So the "logic of explanation" means that whenever you set out to explain anything or argue a point, it is necessary to take something as matter of fact, something which is taken for granted and not questioned. A young couple, for example, have been looking for an apartment and in an attractive one the wife wonders about the discoloration of the wall behind the stove. The husband explains, "Oh, that's because of steam from a kettle." If the wife takes that as sufficient explanation, she takes as matter of fact that steam affects the paint on walls that way. But if she is not satisfied she pushes further, "But why does steam affect the wall that way?" The landlord proceeds to explain the molecular interaction of heated vapors on certain kinds of paint. If she takes such interaction as matter of fact, she finds the explanation satisfactory. She can continue to ask for further explanation and ultimately she will reach the molecular structure of matter, which she will have to take as matter of fact. Otherwise she challenges what is universally accepted among scientists as the ultimate constitution of matter. (And the marriage may get off to a rocky start.)

SITUATING THE PROBLEM

The detailed argument in Chapter 10 started with a conditional, empirical fact picked out by a proposition like "Someone will read a sentence in this book..." "Someone will turn on a TV tomorrow." Or "Someone will prepare breakfast here tomorrow." The future emphasizes the contingency of the event, for though we understand what is meant, we cannot know with certainty that it will take place. (Will a nuclear war destroy us all?)

It was easy to see that for that event to take place certain causes or conditions are required. There must be this book and some light, a person able to read English, and so forth. Because each of these causes/conditions requires other causes/conditions in extremely complex interrelationships, I lump them together by identifying appropriate characteristics needed in order to be a member of the group of causes bringing about the initial state of affairs.

Everything hinges on proving that we can and ought to ask why the network of interrelated causes, including perhaps even the material universe as a whole, exists.

Naturalism insists there is no need nor possibility of going beyond the material universe. The material universe *happens* to be. We take it as it is. We can logically ask why particular contingent states of affairs occur, but we simply have to take the contingent universe as a whole as the ultimate. No intellectual need to go beyond the universe as a whole. In fact it is logically nonsense to try. "The world [is] believed to be wholly intelligible without the adoption of a theistic hypothesis." (*Critiques of God*)

TWO CHALLENGES FOR THE FIRST SUPPOSITION

It is not hard to imagine some readers thinking to themselves:

> You claim you have to posit an uncaused cause to explain why things exist. But why does the uncaused cause exist? You answer, 'Because the uncaused cause contains an uncaused entity.' Well, what's the difference between the material universe and the uncaused entity? After all you have to take as ultimate this uncaused entity. Then why not accept the whole material universe as ultimate? You cannot explain why the uncaused entity is as it is. You seem satisfied to take the uncaused entity for granted. What's so different about the uncaused entity and the entire material universe as a whole? It is what it is. It is, *simply because* it is.

A well known atheist enunciates that precise challenge.

> It is surely incongruous to postulate a first cause as way of escaping from the coils of an infinite series. For if everything must have a cause, why does not God require one for His own existence? The standard answer is that He does not need any, because He is self-caused. But if God can be self-caused, why cannot the world itself be self-caused? (*Critiques of God*, E. Nagel)

The words put in the mouth of the reader are more accurate than this atheist's argument. For it is not claimed that "*everything* must have a cause" and "the standard answer" is *not* that God is self-caused. Such a notion is contradictory nonsense: to cause, a thing must exist; to be caused it must not exist. Nothing, not even God, can simultaneously exist and not exist. Rather, God is a necessary being and so cannot not be. And since the world is a contingent being, not a necessary one, it needs to be caused to exist.

A reader might urge a further objection:

> You start out with an ordinary state of affairs, you say, like someone reading a sentence in this book. You offer an *explanation* why that state of affairs occurs by pointing out extrapropositional states of affairs, like a human person, light,

and so forth which cause it to occur. I understand what you mean by *explanation*. The causes or conditions are things subject to experience. When you arrive fundamentally at a network of causes subject to experience you insist it too must be explained. But now you appeal not to a cause subject to experience, but to a theoretical entity which we cannot experience. You change the meaning of *explanation*.

I am comfortable with the reasoning up to the complexus of contingent causes. The way beyond this becomes another ballgame. I truly believe you have no grounds for going beyond this material universe. In trying to, it seems to me, you get into babbling nonsense.

So forceful an attack is to be applauded. I'd reply:

You recognize that this is the heart of the issue. You have to insist that the material universe exists simply because it exists or, if the second supposition - that the material universe is self-sufficient - is shown to be false, you have to affirm that God exists.

This entire section will be devoted to those vigorous challenges. The first and central one will be confronted explicitly in the two traditional solutions. As for the charge that I have changed the meaning of explanation, the objector is forgetting the need for intellectual conversion. In fact, what is at issue is precisely whether or not explanation must be limited to *scientific* explanation. We have seen that "knowing" consists in grasping the virtually unconditioned. Intellectual honesty demands one be ready to go where the virtually unconditioned leads, even if it leads beyond the quantitative and sensible, the contingent and temporal.

THREE SOLUTIONS

Why then is it not true that the material universe as a whole exists simply because it exists? The first two approaches within a more or less traditional framework prove that this first supposition of Naturalism is false.

First: Metaphysics and Naturalism

The first approach attacks head-on the Naturalist's charge that theism has to take God as mere matter of fact in exactly the same way

Naturalism: First Supposition

Naturalism takes the material universe with the fundamental laws of matter and energy as mere matter of fact. It has always amazed me that a famous British Empiricist acknowledged that he gave up belief in God when it dawned on him to ask, "If the world needs God because everything needs a cause, what caused God?"

> I believed in God until I was just eighteen, when I found in Mill's *Autobiography* the sentence: 'My father taught me that the question "Who made me?" cannot be answered, since it immediately suggests the further question, "Who made God?" In that moment I decided that the First Cause argument is fallacious. (B. Russell, "My Mental Development," *The Philosophy of Bertrand Russell.*)

Let's start with the first metaphysical principle, the principle of noncontradiction: A thing cannot be and not be at the same time and under the same aspect. It corresponds to the first logical principle: Nothing can be affirmed and denied of the same thing at the same time. So if we start with an existing thing, like yourself, we know you cannot simultaneously exist and not exist.

The next principle clearly follows, though it is not identical nor is it derived by way of deduction: Whatever exists has whatever is necessary for it to exist. Otherwise it would be because it exists - but it could not be, since it would lack what is necessary for it to be. That we refer to as the metaphysical principle of sufficient reason.

We advance to a third fundamental principle: Whatever exists contingently has an efficient cause. That means that whatever exists but is possible not to exist, whatever exists but does not have to exist, must get what is necessary for it to exist from another. An efficient cause is that which positively influences the being or existence of another by its action. It is the agent causing a contingent thing to exist.

Where are we? We have the metaphysical principles which explain the difference between taking the whole material universe as the explanation of everything that is ---and--- taking God as that explanation. The material universe is nothing other than all the individual beings composing it and since every individual material being is contingent, so the material universe as a whole is contingent.

Naturalists do not describe the universe as a whole in those terms, but plainly that is what is meant.

> Naturalism...is a species of philosophical monism according to which whatever exists or happens is 'natural' in the sense of being susceptible to explanation through methods which... [are]

paradigmatically exemplified in the natural sciences...Nature...is not simply a collection of all the natural objects but a system of all natural processes...Nature is in principle intelligible in all its parts, but it cannot be explained as a whole. For this would presumably require reference to a natural cause, and outside nature as a whole there are not natural causes to be found.
(*The Encyclopedia of Philosophy,* s.v.""Naturalism," by Arthur C. Danto)

Faced with the question, "Why should anything (the universe) exist at all?" a famous retort by a Naturalist was, "Why shouldn't it?" In other words there is no need, it is illogical, to ask why the universe as a whole exists.

In confronting this first supposition I take Naturalists at their word that everything is contingent and apply the three metaphysical principles. Whatever exists has what is necessary for it to exist. Since the universe is contingent it does not have *in itself* what is necessary for it to exist; therefore it, the universe, finds what is necessary to exist, in another. Consequently, the material universe has an efficient cause. God, on the other hand, reached by reasoning to an uncaused cause, is not contingent, is necessary. The uncaused cause cannot not be. This uncaused cause has *in itself* what is necessary for it to be.

To rephrase--yes, one has to stop somewhere in any proof; you must take something for granted, as matter of fact. The theist stops with the uncaused cause, for the uncaused cause has within itself whatever is necessary for it to exist, so the mind can stop at it; its being can be taken as matter of fact.

The Naturalist stops with the material universe as matter of fact, but since the material universe is contingent it does not have in itself what is necessary for it to exist. To stop at the material universe is to stop not at matter of fact, but at mere matter of fact. "Matter of fact" in this expression means that we stop at the fact that the material universe is; "mere matter of fact" means it is, but there is no necessity that it be. To stop here marks a loss of intellectual courage. To take the material universe for granted is to give up the search for explanations; it is to abandon intelligence, fearful of going beyond the sensible. We have the exact same question to ask of the material universe as a whole which we asked at the beginning: If a thing does not *have* to be, why *does* it exist?

Two examples illustrate this difference. A series of freight cars is being pushed uphill. Each freight car requires something to keep it moving. Whether there are two or a billion, none has in itself what is necessary for it to be moving. To stop at the engine in the search to understand how they are moving is like stopping with God as the uncaused cause. Both have what is necessary for them to be, the engine as source of its own moving and the moving of the freight cars; God as the ground of God's own being and the source of the universe's being. The Naturalist's position is like imagining the universe is an infinite series of freight cars any engine. None of them and not all together have in themselves *without* what is necessary for them to be moving.

Another example--a chandelier hangs suspended from a chain of metal links, each link supported by the preceding link. But the top link is fastened to a beam on top of pillars. In our search to explain things and happenings in the world around us, to stop at the uncaused cause is like stopping at the well-supported beam. We get outside the series of dependent metal links. The beam on its pillars has what is necessary to be where it is and explains why the chandelier hangs as it does. The Naturalist, as it were, wants to pretend there is some sort of infinite chain of links without anything like a supporting beam, none of which, nor all together, has in itself what is necessary to provide the support of the chandelier.

Second: Lonergan's Philosophy and Naturalism

In the second approach Bernard Lonergan's insight actually makes the same point as the traditional metaphysics, but does it in a striking way. Rather than start with things, Lonergan starts with knowing. He defines "being" in terms of knowing: being is that which is subject to intelligent grasp and reasonable affirmation. This pen I am using is being for it can be intelligently grasped as being a pen and reasonably affirmed to be and to be as a pen.

It follows that that which is not subject to intelligent grasp and reasonable affirmation is not being. This does not mean that what I do not know does not exist. Whether I know a thing or not, it remains something subject to intelligent grasp and reasonable affirmation. Neither does this mean that if I do not understand something it does not exist. Lonergan is directing our attention to a way of understanding what the term "being" means. Carried to the ultimate, his perspective lets us recognize that things exist because God knows them. All that is is intelligently grasped and reasonably affirmed by God-(as well as willed).

All right then, being is that which is intelligently grasped and reasonably affirmed. Proportionate being adds to those two characteristics "subject to sensible experience." The world with which we are immediately familiar, the material universe, is proportionate being.

Naturalism claims that the material universe is intelligible (i.e. subject to intelligent grasp and reasonable affirmation) in its parts, but not intelligible as a whole. It holds being is limited to proportionate being. Any effort to push to an ultimate explanation of any part of the universe must end with (and one must be satisfied with) proportionate being as mere matter of fact.

We have seen that "matter of fact" means that which is taken for granted. And the logic of explanation does require that something be taken for granted. But mere matter of fact implies that the ultimate something taken for granted is something about which no questions can be asked. There is nothing to be intelligently grasped in response to any question, nothing reasonably affirmed.

Well, then, the ultimate explanation and ground of any part of the universe is nothing, non-being. That which is not subject to intelligent grasp and reasonable affirmation is outside of being and to be outside of being is to be nothing. The material universe as a whole, Naturalists maintain, must be taken as mere matter of fact. The material universe as a whole is not subject to any questions, is not subject to being intelligently grasped and reasonably affirmed.

Accordingly, in this perspective the contradiction inherent in Naturalism is arrived at by two routes. The material universe as a whole is affirmed to exist as proportionate being - but is also affirmed not to exist since, as a whole, it is not subject to intelligent grasp and reasonable affirmation. And what is not subject to intelligent grasp and reasonable affirmation is outside of being. The Naturalist thus holds that the material universe exists and does not exist.

To affirm that a contingent state of affairs occurs is implicitly to affirm that it has whatever is required for it to occur. To affirm it occurs and to deny that there exists what is required for it to occur is equivalent to saying it simultaneously occurs and does not occur. To say that someone won a blue ribbon for steeple-chase performance but that she has never ridden a horse is equivalently to affirm and deny the same thing. To affirm that some initial state of affairs, like "Someone will read a sentence in this book" occurs and as contingent rests upon a series of contingent causes, each of which rests upon other contingent causes, but that the ultimate causes are contingent although they rest on nothing is to be contradictory. The contingent state of affairs occurs *but what is required for it to occur does not exist*. The network of causes is admittedly contingent and therefore requires something to ground it in being. This something is the

material universe as a whole. But the universe as a whole is non-being because it is not subject to intelligent grasp and reasonable affirmation. *The network of causes, consequently, is grounded in being and is not grounded in being.*
Back to the starting point. "Someone will read a sentence" requires a cause precisely because it is contingent. It may or may not be. Since the series of causes is also contingent, the series needs a cause as much as the initial event does. To deny the series has a cause is to deny the initial event has a cause. Thus one affirms that someone will read a sentence in this book (and that as contingent it needs a cause) and one denies it occurs (because one denies that the cause it must have exists).

This seems harsh, but it is rigorously logical, a *tour de force* disproof of Naturalism. To take the material universe for granted, claiming no further questions can be asked, differs radically from taking God for granted, understood as uncaused cause and necessary being. In one sense there are no further questions *to be asked* about the necessary being; it cannot not be. You can, of course, ask questions, but answers are forthcoming. As that which cannot not be, the uncaused cause is intelligently grasped and reasonably affirmed. The material universe is proportionate being and only arbitrarily does the Naturalist stop asking questions. In fact, there is the identical reason to ask why the material universe as a whole exists as to ask why any particular thing or event exists. It, too, is proportionate being and contingent.

Third: Rejection of Scientism and Naturalism

For readers trained in science perhaps direct confrontation with scientism may be more convincing than traditional ways of rejecting Naturalism.

Should not the material universe as a whole be taken as matter of fact? It is simply a fact that the whole is greater than and different from its parts. Electrons, for example, behave differently in a whole thing than they do in separation. And any attempt to explain the human person by reducing the person to chemical elements will fail, for in his knowledge, love, and religion the person poses problems the natural sciences cannot answer. But the radical reason for omitting such attempts at reductionism is that our question is not even faced here. Whatever the reality reached as ultimate, is it self-sufficient or does it require further explanation?

Science certainly has been extremely successful in pushing back the horizons of knowledge, making technology possible and thus bringing marvelous and tangible benefits to us all. But sophisticated readers will acknowledge that there is no "science" of the whole. Their confidence, however, they'll say, is in the scientific *method*. But scientific method simply will not suffice to explain the universe as a whole. We have already seen the limitations and inadequacy of science and the scientific method. We clearly identified the areas and problems which science does not and cannot deal with. But the heart of the issue is that the scientific method is abstractive and selective. It excludes the individuality of things and the subjectivity of human persons.

Thus, apart from the inability of any science or the scientific method to satisfy the human subject's search for meaning and commitment in an individual's life, the abstractive nature of the scientific method makes it inadequate to explain the universe as a whole. The extrapolation of the scientific method as an explanation of the universe as a whole is self-contradictory. In other words, since science studies only parts of reality it cannot explain the whole.

Ian Barbour puts the same point very trenchantly.

> The astronomer, Arthur Eddington, once told a delightful parable about a man studying deep-sea life, using a net with a three-inch mesh. After bringing up repeated samples, the man concluded that there are no deep-sea fish less than three inches in length. Our methods of fishing, Eddington suggests, determine what we can catch. If science is selective, it cannot claim that its picture of reality is complete. ("Ways of Relating Science and Theology," *Physics, Philosophy and Theology*, 1988 p. 32)

Again, this is not attacking or denigrating science. It is a claim that the extrapolation of science and the scientific method to embrace and explain the whole of reality is unwarranted. The following syllogism clarifies it irrefutably.

Every (any) method capable of explaining the whole of reality
is
equipped to study the whole of reality.
++++++++++++++
But the scientific method
is not
equipped to study the whole of reality.

(Proof: The scientific method and the complexus of methods of the different sciences are by nature abstractive. [They abstract and deal with only certain aspects of what they study.] Therefore it [the method] is partial in its explanatory power. It does not encompass the whole of reality.)

Therefore the scientific method
is not
capable of explaining the whole of reality.

Euler's circles make the rigor and validity of this reasoning starkly clear.

"Equipped to study the whole of reality" is the middle term, **M**.

"Capable of explaining the whole of reality" is the predicate, **P**.

"The scientific method" is the subject, **S**. Thus:

P ("capable of explaining) is found to be within M ("equipped to study")

S ("The scientific method") is found to be outside M.

Since P is within M, with compelling logic S ("scientific method") is found to be outside P ("capable of explaining...")

[The various forms of scientism] seem to have assumed that there is only one acceptable type of explanation, so that explanation in terms of astronomical origins, or biochemical mechanisms, or evolutionary development, excludes any other kind of explanation. Particular scientific concepts have been extended and extrapolated beyond their scientific use; they have been inflated into comprehensive naturalistic philosophies. Scientific concepts and theories have been taken to provide an exhaustive description of reality, and the abstractive and selective character of science has been ignored. Whitehead calls this 'the fallacy of misplaced concreteness.' It can also be described as 'making a metaphysics out of a method.' But because scientific materialism starts from scientific ideas, it carries considerable influence in an age that respects science.

(Ian G. Barbour, "Ways of Relating Science and Theology," *Physics, Philosophy, and Theology* p. 25)

But isn't it the nature of science, the nature of all fields of knowledge, to be abstractive? Metaphysics, the philosophical science of being, includes all aspects of being precisely as being. It excludes nothing! Metaphysics is a field of knowledge, traditionally called a science, though a philosophical science, which does encompass the whole of reality - and alone is able to offer some explanation of the whole of reality, of reality as a whole.

Thus Naturalism as the correlate of scientism is unjustified. Science and the sciences are very trustworthy and invaluable. But to slip from that position to scientism [*only* science and the scientific method can give us truth] is unwarranted. And so the supposition that the material universe as a whole is all there is can not be justified by science or scientism.

SUMMARY AND CONCLUSION

Essential to the quasi-empirical argument to God's existence is the demonstration that it is necessary to go beyond the network of contingent causes of any particular contingent event. Naturalists maintain the material universe as a whole exists simply because it exists. There is no need to ask whether reason justifies going beyond the network of contingent causes.

We have offered three different ways of showing why this first supposition of Naturalism is false. Many may find these arguments sufficient grounds for belief in God. Our principal objective, however, has been to remove this supposition as an obstacle in our quasi-empirical argument for God's existence to pass beyond the network of contingent causes to the second plateau, there exists an uncaused cause.

Granted, then, that it is not true that the material universe exists simply because it exists, is it possible that the material universe is self-sufficient? We are ready to confront Naturalism's second supposition.

CHAPTER 13

NATURALISM: SECOND SUPPOSITION

THE MATERIAL UNIVERSE IS SELF-SUFFICIENT

The insight in the God-issue is simple. Articulating the evidence for the insight is most difficult. Everything hinges on seeing the need to go beyond the contingent material universe to a different kind of being, an immaterial, noncontingent being. The articulation hinges on proof that the two suppositions put forward by Naturalism are false.

"The material universe as a whole is self-sufficient." The confrontation begins by demonstrating that the two specific forms this supposition takes are impossible. These two forms seem to assume that everything is contingent and yet that the whole constituted by all these contingent things is self-sufficient. What seems to be operating is the assumption that the universe as a whole is different from the sum of its parts; that the material universe, composed of contingent causes, does not labor under the same requirements as its parts. Normally Naturalists ignore the implication that for this move to succeed, the reason the universe as a whole is different must be that it is noncontingent. In other words, this second supposition makes sense only if "self-sufficient" means noncontingent.

Thus proof that both specific forms of the second supposition are false forces to the surface the implication that to claim that the series of causes is self-sufficient must intend to claim that the material universe as a whole differs from its parts because it is noncontingent or because it contains something noncontingent.

This claim once realized forces one to face the question: Is it *possible* for the material universe to be noncontingent? The question cuts to the heart of every proof of God's existence. Actually, the material universe is not noncontingent nor does it contain something noncontingent. The analysis above dictates the strategy: (1) to address the two specific forms of the supposition and (2) to confront the implicit and radical claim which follows- that the material universe is noncontingent (in Chapters Fourteen and Fifteen).

REFUTATION OF SPECIFIC FORMS OF THE SUPPOSITION

FIRST SPECIFIC FORM
An Immense Happening Machine

[A Circle of Happenings]

The first specific form holds that the material universe is self-sufficient because the contingent causes mutually cause themselves to exist.

As long as a person does not think concretely of the causes involved, this claim of mutual causing may seem plausible. But it really involves impossible circular causing. It is like saying:

Bill exists because Abel begot him.
Charles exists because Bill begot him.

Abel exists because Charles begot him.

Abel has to <u>exist</u> in order to beget Bill. But he has to *not exist* in order for Charles, son of Bill, to beget him. Thus mutually satisfying conditions, each contingent, cannot explain why the group of conditions or causes lumped together exists.

Another example of what is being assumed. Four men, arms linked, are suspended in a circle two feet above the ground. To explain how they are so suspended each of the four men points to one on either side of him and says, "They hold me up." Granted a partial answer in such support, why all four are suspended in the air simply is unanswered.

Notice the difference between this example and that suggested by Paul Edwards, an articulate Naturalist. Edwards asks why five Eskimos have come to New York. One comes to avoid the extreme cold in the polar region; her husband comes to be near her. In similar fashion he provides an explicit reason for the presence of each of the others. Then he asks, "Is it not absurd to ask why the group as a whole are in New York?"

Actually, it would be reasonable to pursue that question in terms of socio-economic or political reasons. But the significant point to be made is that these five Eskimos are not mutually affecting any one action. In the previous example the four men are supporting one another two feet above the ground. Something more is needed to explain that action, something like a magnet or some form of propulsion.

It seems obvious that a circle of causes cannot explain why anything exists. Why then are some people satisfied to stop the investigation at a set of conditions all of which are contingent? There are two reasons. First, everyone recognizes the interlocking necessity of conditional propositions. For example, if I have $100,000 and you have $50,000, then I *necessarily* have twice as much as you. But that necessary relationship says nothing about whether I or you actually have that amount of money. It is easy to pass from the insight that things *have to be such and such* (I have to have twice as much as you) to things *have to be* (I have to have $100,000 and you have to have $50,000).

Thinking along the same lines, Naturalists (challenging the quasi-empirical argument which seeks to explain why "Someone will read a sentence...") recognize the conditional truth that *if* all the required conditions included in the series of interrelated causes exist, then someone has actually read a sentence in this book. Right, but the conditional knowledge does not let them know whether either the series of causes or the initial event *actually* does exist.

They are lured into this mistake by knowing that, granted "Someone actually reads a sentence...," then all the causes required for this to happen, must exist. Thus, if the initial event occurs, *at least* all the causes in the interrelated series of its causes occur. I underscore "at least" because Naturalists fail to keep in mind that the basic question is: What causes must exist in order for the initial, contingent event to occur? Is the series of contingent causes sufficient to explain why the initial event occurs? Not if the series of causes is contingent!

This leads to the second reason people tend to stop the investigation at the group of contingent causes. The fact is that each of these required conditions actually does contribute to the initial state of affairs being investigated. For example, a person capable of reading definitely is involved in causing the state of affairs of "someone reading a sentence" to occur. So if you take for granted that each of these causes exists, that the world exists, then it can seem enough to appeal to the interlocked group of causes which contribute to the fact of "someone reading a sentence." But what explains the existence of the world? If the reason the initial state of affairs requires conditions outside itself is that the state of affairs is contingent, then a world composed of contingent states of affairs, a world that is contingent, likewise requires something to make it exist.

SECOND SPECIFIC FORM

An Infinite Series of Causes
[Infinite Series of Railroad Cars with No Locomotive]

Tackling this form of the second supposition involves the meaning of cause, series of causes, and infinite series.

Science reasons causally, but a cause, for science, means being an appropriate antecedent from which an effect regularly follows. Philosophy based on Aristotle and Thomas looks to the *dependence* of effect on cause. Cause then for our discussion is defined as that which positively influences the being of another thing. For full appreciation of the reasoned approach to God's existence, cause must be seen as that which positively influences the being of another thing.

When multiple causes influence the same effect, they must somehow be subordinated one to the other. It has long been recognized that causes can be subordinated in three kinds of series: a series of causes subordinated directly in the actual causing (a mediating series), or causes subordinated as a confluent series, or finally a series of causes subordinated but not in their actual causing.

Can any of these three kinds of series of causes be infinite? By an infinite series people often just mean that there are a lot of causes, too many to investigate, and they assume appeal to the series makes sense as the explanation of the thing or happening. They know it has to make sense since the effect actually exists. The appeal to an infinite series of causes may only refer to a large number of causes with the presumption that there is a first cause on which the rest depend. But if there is a first cause, the series is not infinite.

On the other hand it may intend to claim that the series is somehow noncontingent. And I shall demonstrate later that no series of contingent causes, even taken as a whole, can be noncontingent.

Just what does infinite mean? The word is made up of two Latin words, "finis" which means end or limit and "in" used for negation. So according to the origin of the word, infinite means having no end or limit. How did the idea of infinite ever arise? Everything we see is definite and limited. We get intimations of the infinite in many situations. We wonder, for example, how far the horizon of the universe stretches. The horizon we see always has something beyond it. Stars are billions of light years away. Is that infinite? The sea looks as though one could never reach the other side. How many drops of water are in the ocean? How many grains of sand on the shore? How many stars in the heavens? Intimations, yes, but since everything we see or imagine is limited and finite, the very idea of infinite must originate in the intellect, not in the imagination. The idea of infinite arises naturally with regard to size and number. Hence the negative is privative, i.e., the negative of a limit in something naturally limited.

Every bodily thing we know has a determined figure. There can be no actually infinite body. If there were, there could be no local motion of such a solid body from place to place. There would be no space or place for it to move in or to. Besides, no matter how much or how often you add to a body, even in imagination, it is always a definite magnitude, a definite size. We can, however, think of dividing it an unlimited number of times. Consider dividing any body in half and that in half and so forth. You would never reach the end (provided of course this were physically possible). So with regard to magnitude there can be a *potential* but not an *actual* infinite, provided we think of the infinite through division, not by addition.

Can there be an infinite number? There can only be a *potential infinite* in number, for to be a number is to be a definite number. One can always add to any number and so number is potentially infinite. Not actually infinite, because whenever you add a number the result is a finite, definite number.

When we ask whether there can be an infinite series of causes clearly we refer to an infinite *number* of causes . Since no actual number can be infinite, we are asking whether the causes in a series might be *potentially* infinite in number.

Reflection on a series of causes subordinated in any of the above three ways can bring about the insight that eventually there must be a cause which exists, in such a way that it cannot not be. The obvious consequence is that there cannot be an infinite series of causes. So this specific form of the second supposition is false.

Each series, however, generates that insight in a different way. We begin with the paradigm series of causes, the mediating series. It clearly leads to a *first* cause.

Mediating Causes

To be a mediating cause is to cause something to be but at the same time to be dependent in its very causing upon a preceding cause. It becomes a channel for the influx of a preceding cause. For a subordinated series of mediating causes there has to be a first cause which is not mediating, a cause outside the order of mediating causes.

A series of *instrumental* causes can illustrate the series of mediating causes. Consider the writing I am doing at this moment. I caused the writing of that sentence by the instrumental causes of arm muscles, hand and finger movements, and the movement of the pen. The pen is the immediate cause but dependent upon the causing of the fingers and hand which were dependent upon the causing of the arm muscles which were dependent upon my willing to write that sentence. Each cause in its actual causing is directly subordinated to the preceding cause. There has to be a first cause outside the series of instrumental causes and in this example *I* am the first cause, a person willing that that sentence be written. Those mediating, instrumental causes required a noninstrumental cause, me.

To hold there is no need of a first cause is to assume an infinite series of causes, which is impossible in this kind of series of causes. An infinite series is a series without a first cause, since there would always be potentially one more cause in the infinite series and so it renders all the imagined causing impossible. Take, for example, three causes subordinated directly in their causing. No.3 is the cause immediately producing the effect, x. Subordinated in its causing to No.2, No.3 will not produce x unless No.2 is actually causing, transmitting the power to produce x. But No.2 cannot actually cause, actually transmit power to No.3 unless No.1 is actually causing, transmitting power to No.2. Whether the series has three or a million causes, remove No.1 and no subordinate cause will be able to cause. To imagine there might be an infinite number of causes subordinated this way is just that, vague imagining. For without a first in the series, there will be no second and no effect.

A learned Naturalist denies this analysis and his reasoning reveals he misses two essential points. First, the fact that any numerable series of objects can be infinite only potentially. Second, that to explain the effectiveness of a series of causes producing a present reality or event, the causes must be operating simultaneously.

In his example there is a book 100 miles up in the air supported by another book and it by another. If the series comes to a first book, not resting on another book or in some way supported, the whole collection, he says, would crash. "What we seem to need is a first member of the series, a first support (such as the earth) which does not need another member as *its* support, which in other words is 'self-supporting.'" Why, otherwise, would the stack of books crash? In a *finite* series the first or lowest member would not have a predecessor as support. *But*, he argues:

[I]n an infinite series every member would have a predecessor as support. In other words, a finite series with a first book supported *or* an infinite series can justify such a stack of books. [Paul Edwards, "The Cosmological Argument," *Critiques of God* (Peter Angeles, ed.) p. 49]

The stack of books, however, rather than come crashing down, obviously could never have been found! In that sense his example is utterly unreal. But suppose we are in an aircraft and spy a stack of books 10 miles up in the air. What we know and, in principle, can verify is that there will be, there must be a first book supported by a "self-supporting" thing like the earth. Any actual number of books *has* to be a definite number and there will be a first, indeed a first outside the series. Conceptually the series can be infinite potentially - one more can be added. But if we seek to understand how a book *can actually be* 10 miles up in the air, we know the series of books must be a definite number, there must be a first - or we are faced with this Naturalist's conceptual series of books without a first which he imagines would crash. But clearly it could never have been constructed.

Since these are mediating causes, there would be no *source* of what the mediating causes would be doing or passing on. Supposing number 2,590,767 is the book supporting the top book, if there is no number one - supported by a self-supporting something, number 2,590,767 will be unable to support the top book.

Another example: I give you $100. When you thank me, I say, "Don't thank me. I'm just a messenger, a channel, a mediator. I'm just passing on what Suzanne gave me to give you." You turn to thank Suzanne, but she interrupts you: "Don't thank me. Where would I get $100? I'm just passing on what was given to me for you." Unless there is someone like Uncle Ron, the actual benefactor, starting the whole chain, Suzanne will have nothing to pass on, nor will I.

If we discover any series of causes subordinated in their causing, it is logically necessary to admit that there is a first cause, different from all the subordinated causes. The first cause cannot be a mediating cause. It must be nonmediating; it must be transcendent and originative.

If Naturalists think they can claim the interrelated series of causes of someone reading a sentence is self-sufficient by appeal to an infinite series of dependent causes, they are clearly wrong because such a series is impossible! Intellectual honesty demands we go beyond this thought to a different kind of cause - as we must go beyond railroad cars to a locomotive and beyond a succession of messengers bringing $100 to a benefactor providing the $100, beyond a series of ordinary books to an extraordinary self-supporting book or something like the earth which is self-supporting and supportive of the series of books.

Confluent Causes

The paradigm case, just outlined, presents evidence that there must be a first cause. In that first kind of series, a series of causes subordinated directly in their actual causing, the causes subordinate to the first cause are mediating causes and so are dependent in their causing. This second kind of series, confluent causes, allows us to recognize that (and why) certain causes are dependent in their causing. Thus reflection on a confluent series of causes leads into the pattern of causes subordinated [because dependent] in their causing. It disposes the mind only indirectly for the essential insight that a transcendent nonsubordinated cause is also involved.

To explain the series of confluent causes, consider the example of an annual flower blooming. Why does it exist as blooming? What caused it to be? There was need of a seed. But a seed without earth (or the equivalent in proper chemicals) will not grow and bloom. Water is also needed, sunlight as well (or its equivalent). No matter how many more contributing causes there may be, obviously there cannot be an infinite number of causes. In other words, the number has to be limited. Otherwise the causing agent would never be completed and so there would be no blooming plant. Since we start from an actual plant blooming we know the complexus of causes had to have been completed.

As we catch the insight of a circle resulting eventually when a person thinks of an increasing number of sides of a polygon, so we catch the insight of the need for a necessary, self-sufficient being by reflecting on a confluent series of causes each incomplete as cause and each having an existence which is only possible-to-be.

As for appeal to a confluent series of causes of the initial state of affairs of "someone reading a sentence in this book," the series necessarily will be complete if anyone does read a sentence in this book. There cannot be an infinite confluent series of causes of this or any effect which actually exists.

We are asking why this series of interrelated causes exists. Pointing out that the series cannot be infinite only re-emphasizes the issue: Why does the series exist? Naturalists claim that the series is self-sufficient. But the Naturalists must hold that the confluent series, which cannot be infinite, either is a series of mutually supporting causes (and we have seen why that is impossible) or is somehow noncontingent. But if every cause in the series is contingent, the series as a whole must be contingent. That seems so conclusive that there emerges a new realization: the Naturalist must implicitly assume that the series of causes (extended to the entire material universe as a whole) differs from its parts - and differs precisely by being somehow noncontingent. This point will be taken up in detail in the general argument.

Causes, Subordinated But Not in Their Causing

This third way in which causes can be subordinated differs significantly from the first two. Pivotal in those two series is the logical impossibility that the series be infinite. But for the series of causes, subordinated but not in their causing, an *infinite* series cannot be ruled out. Supposing an eternal world, in principle there could always be another cause involved.

Consider your existence. All your ancestors--your grandparents, their grandparents, all the way back--certainly contributed to your existence. Each set of parents in the series is genuinely and directly a cause of their child. And if any one of them had not existed and given life to a child, you would not have been born. If your grandmother had not existed, your mother would not have existed. All your ancestors constitute a subordinated series of causes contributing to your existence.

This series is characterized as causes subordinated but not in their causing because, for example, no ancestor was directly involved in the causing by which your parents gave you life. Each set of parents is directly the cause of their child. To that extent these parents contributed to their child bringing new life to the world. Thus they are related to their child's direct causing of his/her child, but not directly. Your two sets of grandparents explain why your parents came into existence. They do not explain or contribute directly to your parents' conceiving you and bringing you to birth. They all could have died before your parents even married.

How many ancestors could there be? An infinite number? The simple fact that you actually exist does not require any limit, for none of the ancestors affects your parents' actual causing you to be. This works both ways: in principle your parents could have been the first human beings and although many of your physiological and personality aspects might be different, your existing could be explained by your parents without any dependence on ancestors. On the other hand your actual existence does not rule out the possibility of an infinite series of ancestors, again because no ancestor directly influenced the causing by which your parents gave you life and so the *number* is irrelevant.

Reasoning to a nondependent cause and necessary being takes a very different route when this sort of series is involved. The dependence of your existence on your ancestors is merely illustrative. Everything in the present world depends on a similar regression in causes. Remember too that each of the causes in these series of causes begins and ends, so each is a *possible* kind of existence. But whatever is possible-to-be and not-to-be, at some time, is not or was not or will not be! If *all* things are "possible-to-be and not-to-be," at one time there was nothing in reality. If there was nothing in reality, it is impossible that anything should *begin* to exist or be.

To see the point, time must be considered. To say a thing is possible-to-be and not-to-be is meaningless, unless there is a time beyond which it is impossible for the thing to be. An annual flower lasts a few weeks or months. It does not last years. A person lives - what, 80, 90, 120 years? Not 300. To say a thing is possible-to-be and not-to-be but that it endures forever is contradictory.

Obviously, then, if the time of duration of a thing that is possible-to-be and not-to-be is limited (i.e. with a beginning and an end), and if absolutely everything in the universe were possible-to-be and not-to-be, there would have to be some point at which there is nothing in reality. If at some point absolutely nothing exists, there could be nothing existing now! How could anything begin to exist? Surely, then, not everything in the universe can be possible-to-be *and* not-to-be. There must be something which cannot not be.

The primary intention in treating the series of causes subordinated but not in their causing was to provoke the insight that there must be a necessary being. So striking is the force of that "must" that implicitly Naturalists have to be operating with such an assumption, perhaps not appreciating all that is involved. They must be assuming that the material universe is a necessary being. Our general argument underscores precisely why this cannot be.

SUMMARY AND CONCLUSION

The efforts of Naturalism to insist that the interrelated series of contingent causes, when extended to the material universe as a whole, suffices to explain why any contingent event happens seem to take either the form of a circle of causes or the form of an infinite series of causes--both of which are impossible. The specific forms of the supposition that the material universe is self-sufficient therefore fail and the failure suggests that implicitly the Naturalist is assuming the series of causes as a whole is self-sufficient because it is somehow noncontingent. We face that implicit and radical position in the general argument of the next chapter.

CHAPTER 14

SECOND SUPPOSITION: PRELUDE TO GENERAL ARGUMENT

THE MATERIAL UNIVERSE AS A WHOLE IS SELF-SUFFICIENT

We are at the heart of the God-question. Implicitly, by "self-sufficient" Naturalists mean that the material universe is non-contingent or includes in itself something noncontingent. Although this implicit assumption really denies Naturalism's fundamental claim that everything is contingent, occasionally one actually finds the claim made explicitly. Paul Edwards, a professed atheist, reports:

> It is sometimes maintained in this connection that in order to reach a 'self-existing' entity it is not necessary to go beyond the universe: the universe itself...is 'self-existing.' And this in turn is sometimes expanded into the statement that while all individual things "within" the universe are caused, the universe itself is uncaused. Statements of this kind are found in Buichnes, Bradlaugh, Haeckel, and other freethinkers of the nineteenth and early twentieth century. Sometimes the assertion that the universe is 'self-existing' is elaborated to mean that *it* is the "necessary being." Some eighteenth-century unbelievers, apparently accepting the view that there is a necessary being, asked why Nature or the material universe

could not fill the bill as well as or better than God. (Paul Edwards, "The Cosmological Argument," *Critiques of God*)

As early as the eighteenth century one finds Hume asking, "Why may the material universe not be the necessarily existent Being?" Whether explicit or implicit this crucial objection to proof of God's existence must be faced.

Those who argue Naturalism on the basis of the first supposition remain consistent, claiming that everything is contingent, but they are, as I shall explain in Chapter Sixteen, "irrational" in demanding that the existence of the material universe, contingent though it is, must be just taken as matter of fact. It is presumably by refutation of the two specific forms the second supposition of Naturalism takes that committed Naturalists might realize the implicit challenge they are posing: Why can't the material universe be noncontingent or contain something noncontingent? Thus they really acknowledge that not everything is contingent.

RESULT OF IMAGINATION AND CONTEMPORARY CONSCIOUSNESS

In one sense this assumption that the material universe is noncontingent is based on imagination rather than thought. In another sense it reflects the contemporary consciousness. But in a third sense [and be on guard] it goes to the heart of the matter.

To escape the demand of reason to go beyond a network of contingent causes to an uncaused cause, the objection slides into a vague assumption that the material universe is a massive whole different from the individual causes composing it. The objector abandons intellect and imagines a vast, self-sustaining universe as a whole.

The Naturalist may not recognize he is having recourse to imagination for it is clear that the whole is different from and greater than its parts. Within the molecule electrons act differently than in isolation. A man feels incomplete without a woman and the woman feels incomplete without a man. But together they can feel complete. Individual persons cannot repel an enemy force, but united as an army they can. So why is it not possible for the material universe, composed of contingent parts, to be self-sustaining as a whole? Supported by such reflections Naturalists can vaguely imagine the material universe is self-sustaining. Thus, why can't the network of causes be ultimately sustained by the whole of the material universe? Granted that the individual things and causes are contingent, that they might or might not occur or exist, why can they not, within the whole, be different? As long as the objection remains vague it is understandable as the logical stance of the dominant mainstream consciousness. For this consciousness is characterized as assuming that everything is contingent, relative, and temporal. Surrounded, as we are, by the contingent, people shaped by this dominant mainstream consciousness would easily slip into the assumption that the material universe is the ultimate ground of all that is. And since their consciousness conditions them to count only on contingent things, their solution is left vague, thus avoiding explicit contradiction. The material universe must "somehow" be self-sufficient. But since they are implicitly holding that the universe as a whole is noncontingent, they im̲plicitly contradict what they e̲xplicitly hold.

The third characteristic of the consciousness, namely that everything is temporal, nothing eternal, encourages the same assumption. An outlook which envisions only contingent and temporal things naturally leads people to expect the explanation of every happening to be found in the material universe as a whole.

The second characteristic of the consciousness likewise encourages such loose thinking. For if everything is relative, and nothing absolute, then truth is unattainable. So what's a little implicit contradiction among friends!

The uncritical acceptance of the contemporary consciousness allows, even generates the implicit and contradictory assumption that the material universe as a whole is noncontingent. Contemporary consciousness with its characteristics makes evident that the issue of a necessary being should be debated.

INDIRECT REFUTATION

So we are almost ready to come to grips with the Naturalist assumption inasmuch as it *goes to the heart of the matter*. But before we do some simple reflections on the implications of there being a necessary being may dispose us to resolve the challenge.

How does the very idea of a necessary being emerge? Search for a causal explanation of things and events concludes to a being which cannot not be (a necessary being), a being which grounds the being of all other things. That much human reason can be certain of, but the nature of this being remains shrouded in mystery.

Nonetheless, reflection on the reason for positing a necessary being allows analogous insight into what this mystery must be like. It must have whatever is essential to its being the source of everything in the universe. Since "nothing can give what it does not have," this ultimate being must be intelligent and must be possessed of will for it made - created - intelligent, willing beings. Of course, intelligence and will in the necessary being cannot be limited powers as they are in human beings. Again, utterly mysterious.

Furthermore, since contingent beings might or might not exist, that they do depends on this noncontingent necessary being. This suggests that the necessary being freely chooses to create, much as things we freely choose to bring about might or might not exist. But to act through free choice presupposes intelligence and purpose. One, therefore, can reasonably think of this ultimate source of the universe as an intelligently purposeful agent - a person.

Not only can one argue that intelligence and will are immaterial powers, but more can be asserted about this necessary being. Since it is inconceivable that anything can act without intending (in some sense) a good or a purpose, and since a necessary being is infinite and so needs nothing, the necessary being must have intended to communicate good, not receive or achieve it. An infinite personal being willing good to others loves those others, for love means to will good to another.

The conclusion is obvious: the *material* universe in no way can be considered *immaterial*, or personal, knowing, and loving.

Two further facts could call into question any assumption or claim that the material universe is ultimate and they would dispose a person to follow sympathetically the radical, though sophisticated and subtle, refutation of the implicit claim that the material universe is somehow noncontingent. Just consider two truths which materialism denies: free will and the spirituality of the soul.

There can be no free will in the Naturalist's material and deterministic world. Yet most people believe they are free and that others are free and responsible for their actions. Without free choice there is no love. Naturalists have to blind themselves to the freedom and love they experience and attempt sophisticated arguments for the determinism their material universe demands.

A definitive argument against determinism has been developed. Every viable argument proposed by determinists must appeal to the exercise of free choice, so they falsify themselves. In one form or another such arguments insist that one ought to be reasonable enough to accept the argument. If one "ought to" do something, one is able not to; one is free to do it or not.

The dignity of free, loving individuals is based on their spiritual souls. A detailed, metaphysical argument can be proposed to show the spirituality of the human soul. By analyzing the process of intellection one can grasp the immateriality of the soul, principle or agent of intellectual knowledge, because of the total reflection involved and because of its universal ideas.

If it is true that we possess freedom of self-determination and that the human soul is spiritual, the material universe does not constitute the whole of reality and cannot be the ultimate explanation why any contingent state of affairs exists. Each step of the above presupposes significant development, but even the schematic outline may prepare for the subtle reasoning of the general argument.

THE HEART OF THE ISSUE

Notice was given above that the Naturalist objection [the material universe as a whole is noncontingent] goes to the *heart of the God-issue*. It is time to meet the radical challenge head-on.

THE SOLUTION, BRIEFLY

Let me first state the solution and then try to explain. On so subtle and radical a point one simply has to speak (and think) in terms of a definite philosophic system, in this case, Aristotelian-Thomism. Readers who share that background will see the significance and validity of the analysis. For those who do not share the background, the central insights required are presented.

The ultimate explanation of why contingent things and events exist compels us to posit the existence of a noncontingent being as source of all. **The essence and the act of existence of this noncontingent being must be identical.**

Why? Because otherwise its existence must result either from the principles of its essence or from something apart from itself. The former alternative is impossible, for essence would simultaneously exist (as source of its existence) and not exist (to be constituted existing by the act of existence). The latter is likewise impossible because a noncontingent being does not have a cause.

Can the essence of a material being be identical with its existence? No. Why? Because the essence of a material being involves potency. Existence is act. Act cannot be identical with potency.

That is the heart of the issue and the heart of the solution. To prove something, is always to prove it *to someone*. The first and the most important person to whom one tries to prove something is oneself. I had to convince myself that the material universe simply cannot ultimately justify the existence of any contingent event. I now feel comfortable with the proof for myself. I have reservations whether many others will be able to follow and accept this ultimate reason for rejecting Naturalism. They may find themselves more satisfied with the reasoning proposed to reject the specific forms of Naturalistic justification of the material universe as self-sufficient.

What prompts concern about understanding of the general argument is awareness of how difficult it is to enter into a different philosophical system, to come to think in an unfamiliar set of categories. And this is not the place for an extended introduction to Aristotelian-Thomistic philosophy, which structures the general argument. Still, I shall set out the central insights required if one is to follow the general argument in the next chapter.

ARISTOTELIAN-THOMISTIC CATEGORIES

To explain the solution we must deal with the composition of essence and existence. But the distinction between act and potency, as well as the composition of matter and form, prepares for that.

Change and Being in Potency

Two steps were involved in Aristotle's development of the categories of act and potency: (1) the insight that besides being and nothing there is being-in-potency -- and (2) the insight that material things are composed of act and potency.

The catalyst for Aristotle's insights was the problem of change. How is change possible since the opposite of being, the real, is nothing? Thinkers before him had found a chasm between the two. Some understood being as that-which-is-what-it-is. In order to change, it would seem, being, that-which-is-what-it-is, would have both to be what-it-is (by definition) and simultaneously to be what-it-is-not (on the supposition that it changes). On the other hand, others held that being really is change, that everything is in flux, nothing is permanent in being. For the former the chasm could be closed by denying change, maintaining that change is illusion; for the latter by denying being as anything permanent.

Aristotle accepted both being and change. Take a seed which grows or changes into a tree. There is something that continues through the entire process of growth. This something at the beginning is actually in the shape of a seed. At the conclusion this identical something is in the shape of a tree. Consider the *process* of seed growing into a fully developed tree in contrast to a succession of totally different things. After planting a seed someone, impatient, roots it up and substitutes a seedling developed from a different seed altogether; then still impatient he later substitutes a scrub tree developed from a different seedling and finally, tearing up the scrub tree, he substitutes a fully grown tree. Such a succession can give only the illusion of growth and change. In growth, however, one and the same thing develops under the identical genetic code through different stages of growth. In the contrasting case there are four successive things, each different and each having its own genetic code.

The planted seed is in a very real sense the tree, but in its initial stage. A stone, similar in size and shape, in no way is a tree. The seed, actually a tree in its initial state, is potentially a fully developed tree. After the process of growth, of change, the identical something is actually a fully developed tree. The apparent chasm between being and change is bridged by being-in-potency. For the grown tree did not come from absolute non-being, but from being-in-potency, the seed potentially a developed tree.

Matter - Form

The solution to the problem of change also reveals that things which change are composite beings. The *something common* throughout the change has to be composed with the special and real differences of the initial and terminal stages. First there is composition of the *common something* with the *form* of a tree in its initial stage as a seed, though ordered *potentially* to being under the *form* of a fully developed tree. And then there is composition of the *common something* with the *form* of the tree developed. (More precisely, the form is a "tree-form" in the state of being a seed developing the composite into being a full blown tree, so that at the point in the process of being developed we have the tree, composed of matter and form from beginning to end.)

To understand the use and meaning of the terms, "matter" and "form," know that Aristotle took the word "hule," originally meaning "wood," to stand for "matter." His position is called hylomorphism: hylo (hule=matter); morphism (morphe=form). Imagine a boy sitting on a porch whittling. One piece of wood he shapes into the figure of his father, another the same size, into the figure of his mother. The wood is exactly the same, the shape is different. Think of the wood as *matter*, that which is potentially the figure of his father or of his mother. The shape is *form*. The statues are composed of matter and form.

In this example the matter is solid, visible, and tangible. The form is visible and tangible as well. Notice that each statue is a unity. Neither the matter nor the form exists separately. Yet they are really distinct. One is not the other. After all the wood (matter) could be carved into a different figure (form) - or the figure of father or mother (form) could be in clay (matter).

The general definition of matter and form can be derived from this example. *Matter* is a *subject of change* capable of taking on new forms. It is a potency, a capacity. *Form* is the *complement or the actuation of matter*. In our example the shape is an accidental form and makes its matter, the wood, to be qualified as the figure of the father or that of the mother. *Form is act.*

The categories of matter and form having been introduced, we can turn to things which are subject to *substantial change*. Take living things. They live, they die. A dog, for example, has a specific nature evidenced by ability to perform certain kinds of activities. The dead body of a dog is simply incapable of those activities and so is specifically different from the live dog. At death *substantial* change takes place. Or take nourishment,--the dog eats a steak. The nonliving meat is absorbed into the living cells of the dog. It is transformed into the dog. *Substantial* change occurs. What was inanimate beef now exists as part of the living dog.

In the case of death a living substance changes to non-living substances (actually to a number of chemical substances accidentally and temporarily united). In nourishment the nonliving substance(s) uniting with a living substance changes to one living substance. The initial and terminal stages involve substantial change: a living thing becomes a nonliving thing or vice versa. A dog in death becomes a collection of different chemicals. Aristotle explains substantial changes by means of two intrinsic principles. One is called *substantial form*, that principle by which a substance is of a definite kind: living, nonliving, dog, cat, etc. The other co-principle of substantial change is called *prime matter*.

While the form whittled out of the piece of wood is visible and tangible, *substantial* form is *not sensible* at all; it is *intelligible* only. The intellect, not the senses, apprise us of its being. You can understand that there is something which makes the living dog a dog - which is absent immediately when it dies, even though it looks almost the same. We grasp the *meaning* of substantial form by thinking of the function of the shape of a statue and linking this with the *reasoning* which demands that there be something which once made that decaying flesh a living dog but which is absent when the dog dies.

The same procedure provides the meaning of substantial form when we try to understand how what once was an inanimate piece of steak is absorbed by a dog and comes to exist in the living dog. What was nonliving now is living. Again take the example of the shape of the statue as form and link its function with the reasoning which demands that there be something which made that accidentally organized nonliving steak now exist as living flesh.

Since we are talking about *change*, and not about substitution of one thing for another, then something must be common throughout these substantial changes. The substantial forms relate to that common something. In the example of the wood-carving the wood is a thing, a complete thing which is modified by the new, accidental form of father or mother. But when the steak becomes living flesh the substantial form of dog does not join with the inanimate steak; it transforms it. So that which in substantial changes corresponds to the wood in the whittling is called *primary or prime matter*. It is not matter in the ordinary sense of a material thing, but a protomatter devoid of specific characteristics. Aristotle defined it as the "primary substratum of each thing, from which the thing comes to be without qualification, and which persists in the result."

"Secondary matter" refers to something existing, like the wood which undergoes accidental change by being whittled or like an infant which grows. The prime matter, however, is united with the substantial form of wood or with the substantial form of a human infant. Secondary matter is potential, for example, to new size or shape, yet it possesses an actuality of its own insofar, for example, as it is a piece of wood or an infant.

In substantial change, since it *is change*, something common perdures. When a dog dies, something present in the dog perdures in the decaying flesh, in the resulting chemicals. When the steak is assimilated by a dog, something present in the coordinated chemicals of the steak perdures in the dog's living flesh.

The living dog is a substantial unity: it is one thing, one dog. At death the substantial form ceases to be and the one dog becomes an accidental unity of many different chemical substances. What perdures in the change is *prime matter*. The reverse occurs when the steak becomes living flesh; the common something within the multiple chemicals accidentally coordinated in the steak is united with the one substantial form of the living dog.

It is critical to underscore the fact that the substantial form and prime matter are not perceivable by any of the senses. They are intelligible only, understood by the intellect. The intellect posits them or declares them to be as it analyzes substantial change.

Notice that prime matter and substantial form are not individual "beings" but *principles* of beings. A principle is that from which anything proceeds. In this case we are talking about real principles, something in the real order, from which a complete being proceeds or results. These co-principles are really distinct, though not separate. In the whittled statues the accidental form is really distinct from, but not separate from, the wood. So the substantial form of dog is distinct from, though not separate from, the prime matter.

It should be evident that the distinctness of substantial form and prime matter means that form is not, cannot be, matter. Form is act and matter is potency. Act is not and cannot be potency.

This insight leads to understanding why essence and existence cannot be identical in the material universe.

Act - Potency

The prime matter of material things is the potential co-principle, passively ordered to receive a specific form which is act.

Act and potency are correlative. We are interested in what is called "passive potency," that which merely receives an act or perfection (not in "active" potency like potency of closed eyes to actually seeing). The pieces of wood were in potency to receive the form whittled out. The piece of steak was in potency to become part of a living thing. Prime matter is pure potency, lacking any act but capable of receiving many substantial forms (in proper conditions, of course). Prime matter, it should be noted, is not absolutely nothing. It is, under its substantial form, that which limits the form.

And we always know act and potency together. Prime matter is never found alone. Always prime matter is actualized under some form. Act and potency are learned together and are *really distinct* from one another. The things we experience are all composed of act and potency. *Material things* are all *composed* of matter and form.

Essence - Existence

One important composition Aristotle never realized. In his search to understand what being is, what it is for anything to be, he realized that to be primarily refers to substance rather than accidents, to be a dog or human being rather than a brown dog or a tall human being. And pushing further he discovered that within substance, being refers primarily to form: being primarily means to be what a thing is.

In the thirteenth century Thomas being very conscious of creation, of initial existence, because of his Judaic-Christian background, pushed the inquiry further and discovered the act of existence. He thus conceived the act of an act, an idea Aristotle never entertained. For Aristotle an individual is because it is a definite kind of being and is such because of the substantial form, because of *act in the order of essence* correlative to prime matter as potency. Thomas asked, "Why does an individual exist?" and discovered the *act of existence correlative* to the composite *essence* itself as *potency*.

To ask what a thing is and to ask whether it is, is to ask two different questions. Clearly also the act of existing is not a further determination of what a thing is. In knowing what a thing is we identify the essence, the substance resulting from, for example, the human soul and prime matter, together with all the accidents further individuating a person. These are the principles by which the being is what it is, by which it is limited, and is capable of change in various ways. The act of existence actualizes that essence. To be a unity and capable of change is thus the correlative opposite of the act of being, the act of existence.

Take any person you know, a young girl for example. Her specific essence, which she shares with all human persons, is a substantial unity of body and soul. All her life that unity of body and soul has been individualized and changing - in size, in her intellectual, emotional, and spiritual development. Possessing the specific perfection of being a woman she lacks what makes a man a man. Limitation on the level of existing being relates directly to essence. At her present age she is not, but is capable of becoming, highly skilled as a horsewoman, a mother, and so many things. Her existence does not specify or determine her in some other way; existence makes all the above actual.

The *principles of limitation and change* cannot as such also play the role of *intrinsic actualization*. It is the *act of existing* which makes a being be.

No person is identical with his/her human nature or with his/her act of existence. If the young girl in the example above were identical with human nature there would be no other human beings. If she were identical with her existence she would have to exist, she couldn't *not* exist.

SUMMARY AND CONCLUSION

We are ready, I believe, to show precisely why the noncontingent being needed to explain why anything exists or happens cannot be the material universe. This chapter prepared us to do just that.

Is the material universe self-sufficient as the second supposition of Naturalism claims? Refutation of the two specific forms the supposition takes revealed the assumption implicit in the claim of "self-sufficiency": the material universe as a whole differs from its parts because as a whole it is noncontingent or because it contains something noncontingent. This claim was seen to be based on imagination and contemporary consciousness - yet in another sense it goes to the very heart of the issue.

The general argument confronts this radical challenge. Because it is subtle, sophisticated, and difficult to follow, an effort was made to dispose readers properly. First the characteristics of the noncontingent ultimate cause were unfolded: intelligent, volitional, and therefore a personal loving being. Hardly qualities associated with the material universe as a whole. Then human freedom and human spirituality (which Naturalists deny) certainly belie materialistic determinism.

These efforts to dispose readers properly supply supporting but indirect refutation of this second supposition. It is the general argument which is counted on to satisfy readers. But that required a schematic summary of Aristotelian-Thomistic categories of act and potency, matter and form, essence and existence.

In spending so much time explaining the meaning of these categories the objective has been to help readers grasp the significance of the radical reason that the material universe cannot be noncontingent, why it cannot be the ultimate explanation of any state of affairs.

Now we apply the categories to the issue: Why cannot the material universe as a whole be noncontingent?

So - to Chapte 15 and the general argument.

CHAPTER 15

THE MATERIAL UNIVERSE CANNOT BE NONCONTINGENT

Now to expand "The Solution, Briefly" offered in Chapter 14 to answer the radical challenge, "Why cannot the material universe as a whole be noncontingent?" Preparation for this general argument has been sophisticated. The very concept of principles of being, the insight that matter and form are not two beings, but two principles of being constituting one being, is subtle. If, however, a person has some inkling of matter and form, act and potency, as diverse principles of being so that matter is not form, act is not potency, one will follow more easily the reasoning I am about to lay out. Even those who feel unable to assess the validity of the reasoning will know the issue has been faced.

The Material Universe As a Whole

In Chapter 11 we claimed that the network of contingent causes - even extended to include the material universe as a whole - did not suffice to explain why the initial event ("Someone will read a sentence...") occurred. Accordingly, the implicit assumption undergirding the second supposition involves "the material universe as a whole."

What can "material universe as a whole" refer to? Three interpretations are possible. First, it refers to all the contingent individual things somehow united as a whole inasmuch as they are ordered to one another, mutually supportive of one another in relationships of cause and effect.

So understood, the material universe surely cannot be noncontingent because in such a view the whole is nothing other than the interrelated contingent individuals either mutually causing one another or an infinite series of mediating causes. We have already shown the impossibility of these two specific forms the second supposition takes.

A second meaning of "the material universe as a whole" might be that there is only one material substance, all apparently individual things being merely accidental forms this one substance takes. Such an understanding of the universe is clearly unacceptable. Living things, plants, and animals are individual things, beginning, ending, and with proper individual histories, and beyond question individual persons exercising their freedom of self-determination are individual substances with definite histories. All persons with their friends and families are separate, individual substances, unique in their histories with corresponding responsibility and accountability proper to each person.

But *if, if* one "imagines" the material universe as one substance, could it be noncontingent? The third very vague way of understanding the universe makes it impossible to conceive what its form might be. But it differs from the first interpretation by assuming that the network of contingent causes extended to include the entire universe somehow is radically different from the contingent causes themselves. What is insisted upon, however, is that the universe as a whole is still material.

Of course, "imagining" the material universe as a whole to be one substance may camouflage an assumption that the material universe as a whole, filled obviously with multiple things composed of matter and form, in some mysterious way contains a noncontingent factor. This differs from the implicit claim that the material universe as a whole itself is noncontingent, and will be addressed.

EXISTENCE IDENTICAL WITH ESSENCE

In the third understanding of "material universe as a whole" we come full circle to the solution stated in the last chapter under the heading, "The Solution, Briefly." The ultimate reason that the material universe as a whole cannot be noncontingent is that the noncontingent source of all that is and happens must be such that its act of existence is identical with its essence. This simply cannot be true of the material universe as a whole. In this step we not only reach the radical reason for rejecting Naturalism, but also suggest how to think about this ultimate source of all that is.

Why must the essence of the noncontingent ultimate be identical with its existence? Because there are two and only two alternatives, each of which is false, indeed impossible: its existence would have to result either from the principles of the essence or from something apart from itself. No other alternatives are possible.

But the principles of the essence cannot cause existence, for in that case the essence would have to exist and at the same time not exist.

No not-existing thing can cause anything. So the essence would have to exist, if it is to be the source of existence. But that by which an essence exists is an act of existence. Therefore the essence would have *not* to exist, in order to be constituted existing by its act of existence. Thus to be the cause of its existence the essence would have to exist before it exists.

Because the necessary being is absolutely independent it has no cause. Consequently its existence cannot result from something apart from itself.

Therefore the essence of the noncontingent being must be identical with its existence. The very awkwardness of this reasoning provides insight into the meaning of identity of essence and existence and suggests how to think about the source of all things.

Earlier we described the quasi-map of all possible knowledge about God. Since human knowledge is rooted in sense experience, we can know only as far as sensible things can lead us. But sensible things, clearly not effects exhaustive of God's power, can not give us knowledge of the divine essence. Grasped as effects causally dependent though, they can lead us to know that there is an ultimate ground of all things - also to know what has to be true about this being precisely as the first cause of all things, surpassing all things caused. Consequently, human knowing of this ultimate being must employ a threefold way of predication. By way of causality we must affirm certain perfections of this being. But immediately we must pass to the way of negation and deny the perfection is applicable. Then we must reaffirm it of the ultimate being but in a supereminent way. Voila! We end in mystery.

Even the affirmation of existence demands this threefold way of predication. The ultimate being *is* (as intelligible source of all things) - but it *is not* - (like any contingent being) - still it is *in a supereminent way* - (its existence is identical with its essence).

MATERIAL BEING CANNOT BE IDENTICAL IN ESSENCE AND EXISTENCE

And here is the precise point. A material being cannot be identical in essence and existence. Why? The essence of a material being is composed of act and potency. Existence is act. Act cannot be identical with potency. As explained earlier the essence of a material thing is composed of potency (matter) and act (form). Consequently it is impossible that the act of existence of the material universe be identical with its essence inasmuch as the composed essence includes potency.

This insight can be reached by various approaches. In whatever way we conceive "as a whole," the material universe obviously has to be composed of matter and form.

But whatever is composed of matter and form must also be composed of essence and existence. Why? Because composition of matter and form relates to what a thing is, not to the fact that it is. Anything composed of essence and existence is subject to non-being. Thus the material universe, composed of matter and form, must be contingent: it can be and not be, and so if it exists, it is caused to exist. Its essence cannot be identical with its existence.

To claim that the material universe as a whole is the ultimate cause of everything that is, is contradictory. For whatever is composed of diverse principles requires something else to bring them together into one being. Thus the material universe, composed of matter and form, requires an efficient cause to unite its matter and form.

If one objects, "But the material universe, composed of matter and form, just is and is from eternity," one is reverting to the first supposition. In Chapter 12 we demonstrated that it is unreasonable to quit questioning once we reach the material universe as a whole, to claim that the material universe is just because it is. Granted the validity of asking why the material universe as a whole exists, we confront the issue above and must acknowledge that because it is composed, it must have an efficient cause.

We have been working with three possible meanings of "the material universe as a whole." There is a fourth possible interpretation. Perhaps all it refers to is the infinite duration of the material universe undergoing an infinite series of changes. Assuming an eternal universe there would indeed be something necessary, something which could not not be - prime matter which would be required for this infinite series of changes.

Prime matter, pure potency, conceivably could be of infinite duration- assuming an eternal universe. But first of all, passive potency cannot function as efficient cause. To explain why things come into existence and events occur, efficient causes are required. Second, prime matter never exists alone, but is always united with substantial forms. The explanation above, why things composed of matter and form are contingent, suffices to underscore that even in this fourth interpretation the material universe as a whole is still contingent and so eternally would be a caused, a dependent universe.

In contemporary terms a Naturalist may think that the material universe consists of matter changing into energy and energy into matter in an infinite duration of the universe. But reinterpreted and expressed in Aristotelian-Thomistic terms this view repeats either the claim just refuted- infinite duration of the material universe undergoing an infinite series of changes, presupposing prime matter as something necessary or noncontingent, - or it repeats the first specific form of the second supposition of Naturalism - mutually supporting causes. Both of these attempts have been shown to be false.

Coming to grips with what is at the very heart of the God question required speaking within the context of a particular philosophy, here that of Aristotle and Thomas. Technical concepts are necessary. And it is impossible to follow a technical argument without understanding the technical concepts. For this reason I chose to show the necessity of going beyond the network of contingent causes by rejecting the specific forms the first supposition must take, a circle of causes or an infinite series of causes. Still, the heart of Naturalism demands that the issue be faced on the level of existence, the level of being. This we have done; the material universe is composed of matter and form, essence and existence. Its existence is not identical with its essence. The material universe cannot be noncontingent.

THE MATERIAL UNIVERSE DOES NOT INCLUDE ANY NONCONTINGENT FACTOR

Human intelligence can leap swiftly over such detailed, logical analysis to the essential insights (which actually guide examination of details) and grasp the conclusion: there must be an uncaused cause of the material universe. On the other hand some people may be encouraged to entertain the critical insight precisely because of the detailed analysis. While they may not feel comfortable enough with the Aristotelian-Thomistic perspective to agree the arguments are valid, yet they can hardly refuse to acknowledge that the radical Naturalistic position has been straightforwardly confronted. For them, perhaps the arguments for rejecting the specific forms which this second supposition takes provide the essential insight.

In any event, it is time to deal with the alternative way of understanding that the material universe as a whole is self-sufficient; it *includes* something noncontingent.

How could there be a noncontingent factor in the material universe? First of all, this noncontingent factor itself would have to be some state of affairs within the material universe which state of affairs exists simply by being the state of affairs it is, an uncaused entity.

Second, either this uncaused entity is within a state of affairs which is an *uncaused cause* or within a state of affairs which is *not an uncaused cause*. No escaping that dichotomy!

At this point we reverse the reasoning in Chapter 11 where we affirmed the existence of an uncaused cause. There the starting contingent event is dependent upon a network of causes. The network is identified as all those causes required for "someone to read a sentence... "*unless* something other than such causes is found to be needed." Members of this network fulfill three criteria, the third of which is, "Each exists only if further prerequisites *not included in itself* are satisfied." This network of causes itself requires a cause, but one which is uncaused and thus not fulfilling this third criterion. Gradually there was unfolded the need of an uncaused entity within the uncaused cause.

In refuting the claim that there may be a noncontingent factor within the material universe it is clear that the noncontingent factor must be an uncaused entity. There are only two ways in which an uncaused entity could be in the material universe: either as an uncaused cause or not as uncaused cause.

But an uncaused entity *within an uncaused cause* cannot be included in the network of causes because the third of the three criteria for membership in the network of causes excludes an uncaused cause. Every member of the network of causes "exists only if further prerequisites *not included in itself* are satisfied." An uncaused cause exists of itself. It needs no prerequisites not included in itself. Thus an uncaused cause is excluded from the network of causes by definition.

Well, could the uncaused entity be in the network of causes extended to embrace the entire material universe but *not within a state of affairs of an uncaused cause*? No one could ever know! For this sort of uncaused entity would be inaccessible to human inquiry beginning from a contingent state of affairs.

To claim there is an uncaused entity within the material universe without being within a state of affairs of an uncaused cause is a *meaningless* postulate and posits an *unknowable* entity. Reasoning to an uncaused *entity* within an uncaused *cause* in Chapter 11, we saw that the theoretical entity is a necessary being and its *meaning* emerges from the reasoning. Thus the argument in Chapter Eleven does not propose a meaningless postulate nor does it posit an unknowable entity.

It can be said very confidently that the material universe is not self-sufficient. It neither is noncontingent nor includes anything noncontingent. This second alternative is so farfetched it could have been ignored. But it is one way Naturalists might go. That it is impossible seems evident

SUMMARY AND CONCLUSION

Once it was shown in Chapter 13 that the network of contingent causes even extended to the material universe as a whole cannot be a circle of mutually supportive causes or an infinite series of causes, it became evident that Naturalists are forced to assume implicitly that the material universe as a whole is noncontingent or contains a noncontingent factor. This discovery crystallized the heart of the God-issue. Why can't the material universe be self-sustaining and noncontingent? Subtle, metaphysical reasoning met the challenge head-on. In the ultimate being which grounds all that is, essence must be identical with existence. The material universe cannot meet this requirement, for its essence involves composition of matter and form and its being involves composition, not identity, of essence and existence.

Appeal to a noncontingent factor within the material universe was seen to be futile. It would have to be linked with an uncaused cause or not linked with an uncaused cause. The former is impossible because an uncaused cause is excluded from the network of causes by the third criterion of membership. And without a relationship with an uncaused cause the uncaused entity is unknowable, a meaningless postulate.

Confronting Naturalism head-on may have provoked the needed insight that there has to be a transcendent necessary being. Certainly this was a desired objective. But the detailed treatment of Naturalism's two suppositions was primarily to fulfill a promise. The critical step in the quasi-empirical argument was to acknowledge the need to go beyond the network of contingent causes, thus opening the way to an uncaused cause and then to an uncaused being.

In order to make this critical step valid the two Naturalistic suppositions had to be known to be false. Readers were asked to grant tentatively that the suppositions are false; full treatment was promised. The promise fulfilled, the conclusion ceases to be tentative; there is an uncaused cause.

To capture the force and sweep of the entire argument in "Climbing the Mountain," the next move is identification of the "rationality norms" operative in mounting step by step to the summit statement: "Indeed there exists an uncaused entity." In the final chapter, the uncaused entity will be linked with our agreed-upon definition of God.

CHAPTER 16

QUASI-EMPIRICAL ARGUMENT, NATURALISM, RATIONALITY NORMS

Confronting the two suppositions of Naturalism fulfilled the promise made in the ascent to the Third Plateau and at the same time offered another proof that a transcendent necessary being exists, a proof geared in some ways to contemporary consciousness.

We still must examine whether this uncaused entity, this necessary being, fulfills the definition of God we agreed upon. Then, most importantly, we must link all this with the lived experience of God in prayer or with the something absolute and eternal experienced in love.

To prepare for these two remaining challenges we shall lay bare the force and sweep of the entire argument in "Climbing the Mountain" under the guidance of the rationality norms operative in every step of the reasoning.

SOLUTION BY APPEAL TO RATIONALITY NORMS

To begin this sophisticated approach return to the description of "knowing awareness." Involved throughout the process of knowing is a proposition which picks out a state of affairs. People take different attitudes toward the same proposition. Regarding the proposition,

"God exists," a mind can take one of three different attitudes. Obviously one person may adopt an attitude of questioning toward that proposition and it becomes "God exists.-Yes or no?" Another takes the attitude of denial, "God exists.-No." Billions of other people take the affirmative attitude, "God exists.-Yes."

The attitude one adopts toward a proposition is distinct from the proposition itself. Two different acts are involved: 1) the proposition or picking out the state of affairs and 2) the attitude of questioning, of investigating, affirming, or denying the proposition.

Formal logic traditionally concerns itself with the propositions, their content, and provides rules to guide our thinking, especially our reasoning. Basically, logic enables us to be consistent in our thinking, to avoid contradiction and so to be coherent. For example, logic shows that to hold that all animals are mortal and yet that some animals (human beings who are acknowledged to be animals) are not mortal is contradictory.

Only in recent years, however, do we find authors dealing with the norms which direct *acts* involved in attitudes taken toward propositions.

Such norms are called rationality norms and they ensure that we adopt reasonable attitudes toward propositions and reasoning. If we fail to follow these norms we do not fall into *contradiction* or *incoherence*. We *act unreasonably*.

Just as people think logically with or without an explicit knowledge of logic, so people think and reason rationally with or without an explicit understanding of rationality norms. But explicit knowledge of traditional logic enables a person to think more accurately and to detect and avoid errors in reasoning. Reflective understanding of rationality norms ensures rational and honest thinking, with ability to detect and avoid unreasonable moves.

RATIONALITY NORMS

A norm is a binding directive. *Moral* norms direct human behavior so that people know what they *should do* in order to be fulfilled as human persons. *Intellectual* norms, on the other hand, are directives of unconditional obligation for anyone committed to the pursuit and acceptance of truth. For example, a definitive argument for free choice has shown that Determinism cannot be argued without falsifying itself because it has to appeal to the unconditional obligation in certain rationality norms. Such norms, like moral norms, do not describe what people do, but state what people *ought* to do (in pursuing truth).

What is the source of the "binding" force of norms? Both moral and intellectual norms are related to the pursuit of "good." Everything we choose can be reduced to eight basic human *goods*, such as life, play, friendship, and integrity. These are known precisely as desirable and as goods which are to be pursued. Among these basic human goods is knowledge or truth. Every human person naturally desires to know. Pursuit of none of these goods, including knowledge and truth, is unconditional. For all the goods are equal in one sense or other. Thus, for example, the scientist may well interrupt and put aside her pursuit of truth in favor of pursuing the good of friendship.

Moral obligation is concerned with pursuing a good in such a way that all the goods are respected. It rises to consciousness when the goods are in conflict. The scientist is *morally* obliged not to harm life [a good] directly and deliberately, even if doing so might provide valuable knowledge. *Intellectual* norms come into play once one chooses to seek knowledge. The scientist, for example, does not have to pursue knowledge rather than the good of friendship. But granted he chooses to pursue knowledge [a good] to find the answer to some question, he is unconditionally obliged to follow certain norms, the canons of research proper to the particular science. Commitment to truth and intellectual honesty demand this, just as commitment to all the human goods and to being good at being a human person demand observance of moral obligation.

Why are they called "rationality" norms? In general, because they determine whether one pursues truth *reasonably* or not. But also because these norms apply especially to the class of affirmations which can be called "rational," a technical classification.

There are three kinds of well-grounded affirmations. First, there are propositions for which a person has direct, sensible evidence ("The sun is shining"). Second, propositions for which one has logically compelling evidence (13 + 2 = 25 - 10). In both kinds it is not only reasonable to affirm the propositions, but it seems impossible to deny a proposition for which one has such evidence. All other affirmations of propositions which are more reasonable to affirm than their contradictory are "rational" affirmations. Thus affirmations which govern daily living are "rational" - like "Shopping for meat is best at such and such a market." Historical and sociological propositions fall into this class. That God exists is another such proposition, for obviously it is not so evident as "The sun is shining," or "13+2=25-10." The rationality norms are especially needed in reaching affirmation or denial of such propositions.

These norms identify what intellectual honesty demands in pursuit of truth. Finally, rationality norms have objective normativity.

Although they are not descriptive or factually objective, they are objective and obliging. They provide directives, guides to straight thinking - guides to asking legitimate questions, developing sound arguments, and making critical judgments.

Four rationality norms operate in the argument for the existence of God. They reveal the reasons why one <u>ought</u> to take the pivotal steps from the initial experience of a contingent state of affairs to the affirmation of an uncaused entity, a necessary being. No one, I believe, can honestly find fault with these four norms. Open discussion of them should lead a person to agree that each step is reasonable and should provide the stimulus to take the metaphysical leap, to go beyond the material universe, and affirm the uncaused entity.

NORM 1

If a question arises and one sees no good reason not to ask it, one should ask it.

This is the source of daily inquiries as well as of everything in science. You notice, for example, a dent in your car. A question arises: How did that happen? or Who did that? or How am I going to pay to have that repaired? Immediately the search for answers is on. Many scientific breakthroughs start with a novel question. The scientist is intrigued and sets out to find the answer. George Stevens, for example, invented the steam engine as the result of asking, "Why does the lid on Mother's kettle keep rising when she boils water for tea?"

In some situations there is good reason *not* to ask the question that comes to mind. A person wonders what the doctor told his friend after her battery of tests. Then he realizes it's none of his business, that she will tell him if she wants him to know. Again, in researching a project, a person puts aside questions which would only distract. At times one ignores a question because a good other than truth becomes involved. For example, at the same time the dent in his car is evoking questions, a man notices a child in danger.

Assuming such built-in exceptions, the norm obviously undergirds all pursuit of truth. But it takes on more and more the character of obligation as one commits oneself to the pursuit of some truth. It particularly "forbids" arbitrarily walking away from a question because one does not like the answer which may be found. This norm seems utterly reasonable and very definitely has bearing on the questions arising about *why* any contingent event occurs. Why does it occur, since it does not have to occur? Why does the network of interdependent causes exist? Can there be an infinite series of causes?

NORM 2

If a question of a certain form has been asked and answered, one can and should expect another question of the same general form to be answerable if it is asked.

The child asks, "Where do baby chicks come from?" and is told, "From mother and father chickens." It is natural for the child to have confidence in proceeding to ask, "Where do baby boys and girls come from?" Nor will she hesitate to extend the same form of question to artificial things. A more sophisticated example is, "Why does anyone get AIDS?" - since it is of the same form as "Why does anyone get hepatitis?" And we do know its answer.

Again, I presume no fault will be found with this norm.

NORM 3

If one asks a question, one ought to suppose that things are as they must be if the question is to be answered.

This norm is obvious. We employ it regularly. And yet fundamentally it is very sophisticated. Why does AIDS exist? Studies besides linking the disease most directly with gay sexual activity, use of infected needles by drug addicts, and infection through transfusion of blood obtained from people with AIDS (or HIV), have also determined it is related to a virus in the blood which destroys the immune system. Here is a very serious question and there is no good reason not to ask it. So Norm 1 is operating. Since it is similar to the questions about hepatitis which also involves a virus in the blood and one which can lie dormant, and for which treatment has been discovered which can keep it under control, following Norm 2 we ought to expect it can be answered. And now according to Norm 3 one ought to suppose things are as they must be if the question is to be answered. This only means that things must be such that there must be a *cause* of AIDS, that at least in principle there is an explanation to be found for the disease. There is no guarantee that things are such that a *cure* can be found. This we can hope and this hope keeps people researching.

Behind the accepted, regular application of this norm is a sophisticated understanding of reality. We seldom attend to this because in our highly developed civilization and culture so much is taken for granted. "One ought to suppose that things are as they must be if the question is to be answered," means fundamentally that we live in an ordered rather than capricious universe and that spirits do not arbitrarily intrude into the workings of the universe.

The flourishing of the natural sciences has made us take this for granted. But the natural sciences emerged and flourished in the West because Christianity generated the mindset that the universe as God's creation is intelligible, ordered, and worthy of profound study. When superstition was replaced by Christian belief in an orderly universe subject to its own natural and scientific laws, people searched for the laws of nature.

Lest this idea of an "orderly, intelligible universe" seem too abstract or remote, consider this example. Your car just won't start. The mechanic "supposes things are as they must be if the question (Why won't it start?) is to be answered." He supposes the world is such that provided the electrical and mechanical parts of the car are functioning, and provided there is fuel, the car will start. If he finds a part out of order and repairs or replaces it, it is supposed that the car will run well. The mechanic does not face the problem with a supposition that it is all a matter of chance or that possibly evil spirits are interfering.

APPLYING NORMS 1, 2, AND 3

Here is how those indubitably true norms operate in the quasi-empirical argument for God's existence developed in Chapters 8 and 9.

The proof starts with an empirical fact: "Someone will read a sentence..." (Which could just as well be, "Someone will turn on a TV tomorrow.")

Precisely because "Someone will read a sentence..." might or might not happen, the question, "Why *does* it occur?" is raised. A reasonable question and there seems no good reason not to ask it (Norm 1). Little thought is required to recognize both that something causes the event to occur and that the reason something must cause it to occur is precisely because the event is contingent; it does not have to occur.

Following Norm 3 (If one asks a question, one ought to suppose that things are as they must be if the question is to be answered), one supposes that things are such that something can ground a person's reading a sentence. The immediate extrapropositional conditions prerequired for it to occur are quickly recognized. There must be a person, a person able to read English, light, and this book available. These conditions are equally contingent and, guided by Norm 2 (If a question of a certain form has been asked and answered, one can and should expect another question of the same general form to be answerable if it is asked), one asks the same question that was asked about the initial event: Why does each of these conditions occur or exist? Since it is practically impossible to identify in detail all the conditions involved, they are gathered into one category: conditions which fulfill these three criteria:

1) Each is needed for the initial event to occur.
2) Each is a state of affairs which might or might not occur.
3) Each itself occurs only if further prerequisites not included in itself are satisfied.

Then why does this interdependent series of causes exist or occur? Applying Norm 1 (If a question arises... no good reason not to ask it, should ask it), there is no good reason not to ask this question. After all, each cause in the network of causes is contingent and occurs because of something outside it. This is a question of the same form as "Why does 'Someone will read a sentence...' occur?" and it is grounded on the same reason: the initial event is contingent and needs something outside it to occur. Norm 2 (If a question of a certain form one can and should expect another ...of...same...form...answerable...) directs a person to expect an answer for this question about the series of causes, for he has found at least a partial answer to why the reading occurs by identifying the network of causes.

Caution and honesty are needed at this point, dealing with the two suppositions of Naturalism. Why do some people insist there is good reason not to ask why the network of causes occurs? Is it the *assumption* that everything existing is sensible and contingent? But is that not precisely what is at stake? What about the question whether there may be something *besides* the sensible and the contingent? Does not commitment to truth and intellectual honesty demand *this* question be asked?

It may be countered, there is very good reason not to ask about the set of interdependent causes, granted it is extended to include the material universe as a whole. It is simply the nature of explanation to take something as matter of fact. And taking the uncaused entity as matter of fact is no different from taking the material universe as matter of fact.

Chapter 12 rejected this attempt to justify the first supposition of Naturalism. But to reply in the context of the rationality norms, there *is good reason not to ask* why the uncaused entity exists, because it is noncontingent and so it cannot *not* be. One is free, of course, to ask the question, but upon reflection he is forced to acknowledge there is no good reason to do so precisely because the noncontingent cannot *not* be. The uncaused entity is subject to intelligent grasp and reasonable affirmation; it is a being which cannot not be. There is, however, *no good reason not to ask* the question: Why does the network of causes (extended to embrace the entire material universe) exist? - Because it is contingent. It might or might not exist.

Within the context of these rationality norms how can an intellectually honest person avoid the question? If people refuse to accept these norms, they do not contradict themselves, as they would if they were to admit that all animals are mortal yet deny that human beings are mortal. They do *act irrationally* without becoming incoherent as in contradiction.

One final thought about this first supposition: Why might an intellectually honest person not follow Norm 2 and ask the question about the network of contingent causes? Is not the only reason fear of what Norm 3 will then demand? Fear that, since it is obvious that reality may have to include something noncontingent, one may have to go beyond the material universe to answer the question? But to refuse to ask why it exists is to abandon one's intelligence, to refuse to follow where the question leads; it is to be intellectually dishonest.

Naturalists who appeal to the second supposition acknowledge it is appropriate to ask the question and propose an answer: the material universe as a whole is self-sufficient. This universe is noncontingent or contains something noncontingent. They are ready to follow Norms 1 and 2. We devoted the previous three chapters to confronting this answer and established that the answer is false.

To follow these three norms in the process of the quasi-empirical argument for God's existence requires intellectual conversion.

Knowing is not taking a look, but insight into the virtually unconditioned. Knowing is not limited to what senses perceive or to what the natural sciences prove. These rationality norms specify the reasons for rejecting the two naturalistic suppositions and their false understanding of knowing.

If, then, we are obliged to ask why the network of interdependent causes - even extended to include the entire material universe - exists, and if the answer is not to be found in the material universe itself, we are obliged to go *beyond* the material universe. That step involves the fourth rationality norm.

NORM 4

If one can provide a partial answer to a theoretical question by positing a theoretical entity, and if doing so opens the way to further questions which, if answered, promise a satisfying answer to the initial question, then one ought to posit such a theoretical entity.

This norm is critical. As will be clear, this is the norm which allows affirming the existence of an uncaused cause and a necessary being. What has to be shown is that it is a norm compatible with common sense reasoning and with the natural sciences.

The reference to a "theoretical entity" may cause a few raised eyebrows. All it means is something which theoretical or speculative reasoning seems to demand in order to explain certain phenomena. One has no experience of the something before and frequently not even after judging it must exist. The idea is not far-fetched.

Ancient Greek astronomers asked how the stars were able to hang up there in the sky? Supposing things are as they must be for the question to be answered, they posited solid crystal spheres. These were theoretical entities; reasoning seemed to demand such things even though they could not be detected. They were conceived to be solid but transparent spheres in which the stars and planets were thought to be embedded. Thus they explained why stars and planets stay up in the sky. The spheres allowed further questions about the different positions of the stars and planets and their relationships with the sun and the earth. Positing the theoretical spheres made sense of what they knew already about the stars and planets and allowed further discoveries to be made.

Is this not one of the steps modern sciences employ to advance knowledge? Germs, carriers of disease, were posited as theoretical entities; their very existence was scoffed at when first proposed. Astronomical discoveries verified predictions of Einstein who had posited, without visible evidence, theoretical entities to explain certain phenomena within his physical theory. Again there is the case of a companion star being postulated to explain the strange motion of a visible star - which postulated star was later discovered. Astronomers continue to search for a 10th planet in our solar system because of certain perturbations which otherwise cannot be explained. They even have a name prepared for it, Vulcan.

Here is a technical description of this move.

> Oftentimes, in discussing the methods of science, people accentuate the two processes of deduction and induction. But...there is a much more important and powerful general method which is commonly employed in science. That is what has been called retroduction, in which one argues from an observed effect - or an observed congeries of effects - to their cause. That cause may be observable or unobservable in practice, observable or unobservable in principle. If it is known to be observable in practice, it falls within the competency of the sciences, strictly speaking. If it is, instead, unobservable in practice and in principle, it does not. If it is unobservable in practice but observable in principle, it may be considered to fall within the realm of the sciences. In the second case the consideration belongs, rather, to philosophy, though not necessarily so. It may, as a matter of fact, fall outside the competency of every discipline.
> (William R. Stoeger, S.J., "Contemporary Cosmology and Its Implications for the Science-Religion Dialogue," *Physics, Philosophy and Theology*, p.227

Such a norm then is reasonable and is regularly invoked in the sciences. But it likewise is basically the way crimes are solved. Consider this home-spun mystery. Liquor keeps disappearing from a cabinet. The question is raised, "Why is the bottle of wine found half emptied more or less regularly each morning?" Amateur detectives run through the list of everyone who has access to the cabinet. Imagination develops the picture. It is someone who... (and suitable characteristics are listed). Thus a "theoretical entity" is posited as the culprit. Later, however, it is discovered that the pet chimpanzee in that household has learned how to get out of his cage, open the bottle and drink. A member of the household as the "theoretical entity" proved to be an erroneous starting point. But the procedure to posit or postulate a theoretical entity was indeed correct.

Let me just sketch how this norm functions in our technical argument. Three conditions are incorporated in it. The theoretical entity ought to be posited if (a) positing it can provide a partial answer to a theoretical question; and (b) so doing opens the way to further questions; and (c) which, if answered, promises satisfying answers to the initial question.

APPLYING NORM 4

Norm 4 is clearly operative in the argument of Chapters 10 and 11 directing progress in "Climbing the Mountain." To explain why "Someone will read a sentence" occurs, we point to an interrelated series of causes even extending the series to include the material universe as a whole. As we have just seen, Norm 1 (If question...and no good reason not ask it ...ask it) and Norm 2 (If a question of a certain form... one can and should expect another question of same form...to be answerable) rule out Naturalism's first supposition, so that we ought to ask why the material universe exists. It seems then that

1) the material universe exists necessarily or
2) it exists because it includes a factor in itself which exists necessarily or
3) it exists because something else causes it to exist.

No other alternatives are possible.

In Chapters 13, 14, and 15 we ruled out the first two alternatives by rejecting the second supposition (The material universe exists because it is self-sufficient). It seems then that the third alternative follows with logical necessity, unless the process of positing a theoretical entity counts against positing it. The process is simply following Norm 4 which is in accord with the accepted procedure in the sciences and in common sense solutions to problems. So we posit an uncaused cause. We know what is meant because we know from personal experience what a being is and what a cause is. Under the guidance of reason directing us to posit it, we extrapolate from understanding of experienced being to a cause accounting for the fact that someone will read a sentence, yet which has to be uncaused.

Positing the uncaused cause provides only a partial answer for the initial question since one must still try to understand why the uncaused cause exists, still needs to know how the contingent causes function. The theoretical entity can be said to promise satisfying answers to the initial question inasmuch as it permits the inquiring mind to be honestly satisfied that it has discovered the *ultimate* reason why the initial event occurs. The uncaused cause causes the network of causes to exist and this causes "Someone (to read) a sentence...". And the reason the uncaused cause exists in its causing is within the uncaused cause itself, an uncaused entity.

IS THERE REALLY AN UNCAUSED ENTITY?

Naturally, many committed atheists will be slow to capitulate, ready to challenge with the question: How is it possible to know whether the theoretical entity actually exists? Granted an entity may make the theory plausible, but is the claim true? Perhaps the Greeks were reasonable and creative, but we know they were wrong. The stars and planets are not imbedded in solid crystalline spheres. Even in the example of the amateur detectives trying to detect the wine-thief, the theoretical entity posited was proved wrong. Moreover, were the scientific postulates mentioned above *known* to be true until experience verified them? Have not other theoretical entities been abandoned, proof provided that they do not exist?

Error occurs, I believe, not in positing a theoretical entity, but in going beyond the evidence in specifying the entity. The Greeks knew that the stars and planets were in the sky and were in different positions at different times. To theorize that the stars and planets were imbedded in solid crystalline spheres was a reasonable theory which has proved erroneous. And certainly astronomy and all sciences have to make bold, specific theories in order to advance human knowledge of the material universe. We can analyze what the Greeks did and recognize that the approach was correct, but that they went beyond the evidence in specifying the entity required to explain the data. It would have been more accurate to theorize that the stars and planets require *something*, whether it be a solid or some attractive force or speed or whatever to keep them in the sky and able to move. Restricting themselves this way might not have allowed science of the time to advance rapidly enough, yet on the other hand it might have opened up greater and more numerous possibilities.

Similarly in the case of the missing wine, the "detectives" leaped over the evidence too quickly to assume involvement of human beings. What they knew was that wine was regularly missing. Ruling out leakage or evaporation, what the evidence really permitted positing was an "entity" capable of opening the cabinet and the bottle. This analysis reminds one of the game, Twenty Questions. One wisely begins by identifying the secret referent as mineral, vegetable, animal, human, or artifact.

Certainly it seems reasonable to posit a theoretical entity as something required to explain why someone reads a sentence yet which does not fulfill all the criteria of the causes in the series of interrelated, contingent causes. If it were to fulfill all the criteria, it would itself be a member of the series, not its cause. The only claim being made here about this theoretical entity is that it is something, some sort of cause which is uncaused, and that it has whatever is necessary for itself to be and to be this cause. This obviously is not a claim to have established with this step the existence of God as infinite, immutable, the one encountered in prayer, and so forth. Ultimately all that *can* be shown, but at this point the claim is simply that it is reasonable to posit a theoretical entity understood as uncaused cause and implicitly that this uncaused cause possesses whatever is necessary in order to be the cause and ultimately that within this uncaused cause is an uncaused entity.

Norm 4 directs making this affirmation. Not only is it reasonable to do so, but intellectual honesty compels it; not doing so is unreasonable. Some readers may feel squeamish about taking this leap. They are accustomed to depend on sensible verification or mathematical evidence. In the case of science postulating a theoretical entity they are willing to grant it as an hypothesis for which only later scientific verification warrants acceptance as truth. Here they are asked to take a metaphysical leap and accept as true the claim that there is an uncaused entity: there is no further direct verification.

Clearly then, rationality norms guided each step of the reasoning in Chapters 10 and 11. Intrinsic to the reasoning process is intellectual conversion: to know is to grasp the virtually unconditioned and to examine things and events on the level of being. After all, even when a person is just looking at a dear friend, it is his *intelligence* which lets him know it really is a loved one before him. The mind clicks that, granted the experience of seeing and touching the other, he could not be mistaken. The friend is known to be there because the fact is grasped as virtually unconditioned. In the quasi-empirical argument to God's existence, without the satisfaction of sense verification the challenge is to trust information provided by the intelligence, not by the senses. Every step of the reasoning was openly discussed. To go where reason leads takes courage. It takes "nerve" to trust and leap to the affirmation of a being totally different from one's experience. This explanation of rationality norms and their application in the proof justifies making that climb up the mountain to the uncaused entity.

SUMMARY AND CONCLUSION

We have climbed the mountain on the other side, this time under guidance of the rationality norms, firmly rejecting Naturalism's two suppositions. Intellectual integrity requires affirmation that there exists an uncaused entity. Looking out from the top of the mountain all is dark. No additional experience - just awareness of the proposition: an uncaused entity exists, and conviction that this proposition is true.

But is the uncaused entity God? And do I experience this God? Our last chapter, addressing these two questions, may be the most important.

Lily Tomlin, in her one woman show, *The Search for Signs of Intelligent Life in the Universe*, muses about things that worry her but she finds, "One thing I have no worry about is whether God exists." She later reports:

> On the way to the play, we stopped to look at the stars
> and as usual
> I felt in awe.
> And then I felt even deeper in awe
> at the capacity we have
> to be in awe about something.
> ...
> My space chums got a word for it:
> 'Awe infinitum.'
> ...
> Suddenly I burst into song:
> 'Awe,
> sweet mystery of life,
> at last I've found thee.'
> And I felt so good inside
> and my heart felt so full,
> I decided I would set time aside each day to do
> awe-robics.

CHAPTER 17

FINISHING THE JOURNEY

The journey is not over. We have climbed the mountain, gazed into the darkness knowing only that the proposition, "There exists an uncaused entity" is true. So? Is this entity "God"?

UNCAUSED ENTITY IS GOD

We agreed in Chapter 7 that the existence of God would be established if we established the existence of "something entirely different from anything else, cause of contingent things, possessing whatever is necessary in order to cause contingent things to exist - and so, not contingent but necessary." One can hardly doubt that "uncaused entity" fulfills that definition. This uncaused entity grounds the existence of any and all contingent things and as uncaused it must exist necessarily. (Recall its essence is identical with its existence.) Thus, obviously it is different from anything else.

We could perhaps make it more apparent that we have established the existence of God by unraveling the implications of positing an uncaused being and show that such a being is infinite, all powerful, immutable, and intimately present. Far from suggesting we have a neat, compelling understanding of God, such conceptualization should alert us that we end in mystery. Recall St. Thomas's teaching that the way we know about God is through sensible things and that we can know about God only as much as sensible things can lead us to know.

But they can lead us only to know God exists, as cause, and that God has whatever is necessary to be cause of all things. Thomas recognized that in predicating anything about God, existence included, we must follow a threefold way of predication. One must begin by affirming, for example, that God is, but one must immediately deny that God is - in the way anything else exists. Then one must reaffirm that God exists in some mysterious, superior way. Thomas insists on an agnosticism about what God is. We know God only in darkness and mystery.

In the Bible Elijah's experience hints at this. He fled for his life and was hiding in a cave when "The word of the Lord came to him...'Go forth and stand upon the mount before the Lord.' And, behold, the Lord passed by." Hurricane winds rent the mountains - "but the Lord was not in the wind." An earthquake shook the earth, "but the Lord was not in the earthquake." A fire burst out, "but the Lord was not in the fire." Finally "after the fire a still small voice. And when Elijah heard it, he wrapped his face in his mantle...and stood at the entrance of the cave. And behold there came a voice to him..." (1 Kings 19)]

We ask, "Is there a God?" and climb laboriously to the top of the mountain expecting bright vision and sweeping vistas. Instead, in the darkness our intelligence whispers, "Voila, there exists an uncaused entity." God is most mysterious and the important role God plays in lives involves far more than reasoning.

RELIGIOUS CONVERSION: EMBRACING THE CONCLUSION

It is one thing to recognize the cogency of the reasoning, another to acknowledge that knowing a necessary being exists is knowing the necessary being is God. It is still another thing beyond that to embrace what one knows. Without religious conversion (as explained in Chapter 9) two things can happen. Either people blot out the full weight of the reasoning process, "Yes, that's an interesting, rigorous proof. I'll have to reflect on it some more and see whether I have considered all aspects of the issue. I'll get back to you." And they busy themselves with "important" things like their careers. Or they follow the reasoning to the end, posit the existence of a necessary being, but give no significant *must-follow-through* to such positing. "Yes," they say, "the reasoning is cogent. I see the logical need to posit the necessary being. But somehow it doesn't seem to mean much to me." Conceivably there can even be deep regret that they feel unable to respond to the truth which they see.

Arthur Kopit's *End of the World with Discussion to Follow* centers exactly on this psychological problem: personal response to what one actually knows. In Kopit's script a playwright turns detective to uncover the actual situation on nuclear deterrence. Trent, the playwright, hears from experts in Washington these bewildering contradictions:

- We need nuclear weapons in order to avoid nuclear warfare.
- Preëmptive strikes are defensive, not first strike offensive, actions.
- Anticipatory retaliation is not the same as first strike.
- Fear is what prevents nuclear war, and fear is what could trigger nuclear war.
- We need more nuclear weapons to prevent use of those stockpiled.

And in the light of the overwhelming capacity to destroy civilization, a key character in American strategy, a United States General, reveals the real issue: "We do not believe what we know." Trent's agent illustrates the identical response when she hears what Trent has uncovered. "That is not the world I believe in. Nor the world I want to live in. So don't tell me any more about it. I think I'll take a stroll through the meadow. It's such a beautiful day. It would be a shame to waste it."

Without religious conversion, nonbelievers--like the general--can find themselves in the psychological state of simply not believing what they have come to know. On the other hand, granted grace and conversion, their minds are open to pursue the question of what they are to do with this knowledge. Conceivably an areligious nonbeliever may push ahead, acknowledge that God exists, and be concerned about relating to God. A man who has lost his faith probably might be tempted to do the same. After all only one insight is required and we've presented the grounds for that insight over and over again: things and events we experience cannot be explained unless there is a necessary being. But a person who once lived with that assumed insight and had come to reject it will be slow to re-admit it and restructure his life in accord with it. Besides, clear thinking tells you that a desire to know whether there is a God is not satisfied by "an uncaused, necessary being."

Personal Experiences Interpreted As Encounters with God

Religious conversion enabling a person to embrace what she knows is more likely to happen if the abstract reasoning is linked with concrete experience. People genuinely engaged in the question of God's existence really want to "know" God, not "know about" God. One knows God, as one knows anybody, by experience; the function of reasoning in the God-question is to establish that it is reasonable to interpret certain experiences as encounters with God.

In a previous chapter we identified the pertinent experiences of non-believers and of believers desiring to engage in the God-question. Believers intellectually convinced that an uncaused necessary being exists should find it eminently reasonable to link their rich experiences in prayer, in worship, in the sacraments, especially in Holy Communion, with the reasoned conclusion and feel satisfied they have been experiencing God in these experiences. Their habitual interpretation of personal encounter with God is confirmed. In fact they probably experience a new sense of the reality of God inviting them to a more total commitment. Grace and "religious conversion" in this context can change the believer's life.

Nonbelievers raised in an areligious home and those raised, for example, as Christians but who ceased to believe lack religious experience. But they do, as developed in detail in Chapter Seven, sense something absolute and eternal in their lives, especially in love. By absolute I mean the sense of something unconditioned: a person commits himself to the other without conditions. He feels ready to die for the other. By eternal I mean she senses her love is without end, not just for a long time. In fact people tend to say, "I shall love you forever." Obviously the sense of the absolute and eternal is only implicit; they do not think about it in loving. But they also implicitly affirm that there is something absolute and eternal. For if they were to deny there is anything absolute and eternal they would logically be forced to acknowledge the sense of the absolute and eternal in love is an illusion and that a person ought to resist giving himself in love. Logically each of them would affirm that a person should take care of "number one," enjoy the feelings but check any inclination to commitment.

A couple of logical steps lead to recognizing that an uncaused necessary being is absolute and eternal. The use of "absolute" may be more familiar in relation to truth. "That is absolutely true." In this sense it is opposed to relative truth and refers to objective truth which is undeniable. I am using "absolute" in reference to reality, something which is of itself unconditioned. The uncaused being, then, is unconditioned, not dependent on anything. And this is what is meant by "absolute." As uncaused it is a necessary being; it cannot not be. But to be and in such a way that it cannot not be is to be eternal, a being without beginning or end (and totally without change or time).

Doesn't the interpretation seem reasonable, then, that the absolute and eternal you implicitly affirm as you experience your love really is this uncaused being? The abstract metaphysical reasoning can thus be anchored in lived experience and generate a sense of *knowing*, not just *knowing about* this uncaused necessary being. In and through love, people experience God. Granted the reasonableness of this interpretation, the relationship discovered by metaphysical reasoning becomes a living encounter with God. For nonbelievers this means a discovery that all along they have been experiencing God.

A Personal God: Cause of Love, Cause of Oneself

This understanding can be considerably enriched. Reflect on the difference between "what your love is" and "that it is." People tend to repress any idea that their love might cease. But in cold fact they know that a number of their friends have broken up, their love gone. There could come a time when their own love would not exist.

Face the fact that *loving one another* is a contingent state of affairs; *that it is* is not due to *what it is*. At one time it was not. At least conceivably at another time it could cease to be. Because one's love is contingent it requires many conditions or causes for it to exist. Each of the two has to be, to be alive, to have the personalities and characters they do have which fuse together so beautifully. But this contingent state of affairs, *loving one another*, like any contingent state of affairs, ultimately *requires* an *uncaused necessary being* which causes those contingent causes to exist and occur and so causes one's own love to exist. The uncaused being is involved in everyone's love itself. Their love could not possibly exist without the influence of the uncaused being. From this perspective not only can people say that it is the uncaused being they sense in their love, but that their love itself is a precious gift from God.

Those who accept the argument as valid and reflect that the uncaused entity is influencing their love, can let their love flow and grow, grateful for the love, trusting in the love and really trusting in this strange uncaused being.

Trust, indeed union with God can grow with realizing one's complete dependence on this being and with awareness that this being is personal.

Let the reader zero in on his or her own existence. Try to taste the reality that you exist. Start by realizing that you *happen* to exist. You did not always exist. And as soon as you began to be in your mother's womb you were old enough to die. You simply cannot escape the possibility, which everyone must make actual, the possibility of not being. Obviously you exist contingently. The reason you exist is *not what* or *who you are*. Although psychologically you cannot imagine or experience your own non-being, you know *definitely* that at one time you did not exist and that in the not too distant future you will not exist.

Why then do you exist? You can easily pick out states of affairs which contribute to your existing: air, food, sunlight, atmospheric pressure, other people. But in view of all we have done you swiftly recognize that ultimately intellectual honesty demands that you posit an uncaused necessary being in order to explain why you exist. This uncaused being causes you to be. Link this chain of reasoning to the "something absolute and eternal" experienced in your love and you will become more stunned at how blind you have been. There's more!

Only meager knowledge of what this uncaused being is is ever reached but you can know that the uncaused being exists and that it has whatever is necessary in order to cause contingent beings, including you. But you are intelligent, you are able to love, you are a person. Can the uncaused entity be less than what it causes? Could I teach you mathematics, could I cause you to know mathematics if I do not have knowledge of mathematics? Surely this uncaused being, cause of your being, must also be intelligent, capable of love, personal.

But what does intelligent, capable of love, and personal mean when affirmed of the uncaused being? Once again, remember how little we can know about this being. Anything we predicate of the uncaused necessary being simply has to go through a threefold predication. I know that the uncaused being is intelligent since I am intelligent and am caused by the uncaused cause. But I must immediately deny that the uncaused being is intelligent, for my understanding of "intelligent" derives from the intelligent beings I know and the only intelligent beings I know are contingent and limited. Thus in saying that the uncaused being is intelligent I do not mean intelligent like any contingent intelligent being. So the uncaused being is not intelligent in that way. I cannot, however, stop there, for the reason I deny the perfection or characteristic of the uncaused being is not because somehow the uncaused being is deficient, but because it must possess the characteristic, in this case intelligence, in a superior and unimaginable way. The same must be said about "capable of love" and "personal" as predicated of the uncaused being. The uncaused being always remains shrouded in the darkest mystery. But what little we "see" orients us toward a personal being.

It seems reasonable, then, to interpret my relationship of utter dependence on the uncaused being as a personal relationship, for I now see that the uncaused being is characterized as intelligent and capable of loving, clearly marks of a person. I am related somehow to something personal, something that knows me in a way superior to any other knower, something that loves me in a way superior to any other lover. And, therefore, in religious experience and in loving another human person, it is a "someone" whom I experience.

GOD REALLY LOVES

I hear someone say,

> Wait a minute. How do I know this uncaused being is capable of love, that the uncaused being loves me? I catch a glimmer of your claim that the uncaused being knows me, for this personal cause must know what it is causing. But love? I can't imagine what it would mean to speak of the uncaused being loving.

Not only is this person baffled by what love could mean when said of the uncaused being, but he or she is, I believe, touching the nerve of ultimate human desire. We are made for love and every atom of our being, every aspect of our person is ordered to the union, the communion, of love with God. The only satisfying means to overcome the dread of aloneness is love. All other means provide but temporary relief or serve as ways of escape. But the human heart can never be fully satisfied except by eternal union with the perfect lover. Nothing short of that, not even an ideal love of a human person, can be enough. So beneath the intellectual search to understand why anything can happen or be, pulses the drive for union. No wonder abstract, dessicated proofs can leave a person unmoved.

This profound need and desire is experienced, but not conceptualized. So people may be blocked from responding in love partially because they are caught by a false image of love--which prevents them from perceiving that the uncaused being could love them. The false image supposes warm bodily response. The "do-gooder" who wants to be charitable and help others but who doesn't *care* about them personally, turns people off. And they may fear that a disembodied uncaused being could only be "charitable" and not really care.

It is true that the uncaused being simply cannot respond with a bodily, chemical warmth. The uncaused being as unconditional and pure act is not material, is not "bodily." This is part of what must be denied of its love, for I must not only say the uncaused being loves each person, but also I must deny the uncaused being loves them - that way. But examine your image of love. Does genuine human love in its essence consist of bodily, chemical responses? The exhausted mother, cleaning up after her child has been sick, is acting out of love. Rather than any warm bodily response of love she probably experiences bodily disgust at the mess she's cleaning up. The husband or wife sitting exhausted by the bedside of a comatose spouse is acting from and expressing love, but it's unlikely that there will be warm, chemical response. The heart of love is wanting good for the one loved.

Anyone who wants to assess his love for another should not ask, "Does she make me feel good?" or "How warmly do I respond to her?" Yes, I'm sure she makes you feel wonderful and that you frequently glow with warmth both in her presence and in doing things for her. The core question is, "Do I want her to be happy? to be fulfilled?" Surely it is clear that an affirmative answer could well involve losing the "feeling good" and warmth. Wanting her fulfillment might require sending her away for graduate studies, might even lead you to leave her if that would be better for her.

Well, the uncaused being, wanting only your good, brought you into being. As unconditioned and absolute the uncaused being needs nothing. So motivation for acting, for causing you to be, can only be for your good. A Christian might find John's definition of God flashing to mind. "For God is love." Substituting that definition, look what we get: Love caused you to be. And if we reflect that the uncaused being, God, is absolutely simple, (God's act of causing you or of doing anything is identically God's being), then the causing is identically the "love." And so we get, " Love loved you into being." The uncaused being really can and does love you. Has anyone else given you as much, your very life and continued existence?

We can make it more striking. Four characteristics are found in genuine human love. Love involves *caring* and a sense of *being responsible* for the beloved. But since these two characteristics, caring and feeling responsible for, can lead to smothering the other, there must be *respect*, a readiness to stand back and let the other make decisions and do for him/herself. And to do this one has to *know* the other as fully as possible.

What about the "love" of the uncaused being for you? Is there personal *caring* and taking *responsibility* for you? Look back on our discussion of your being caused. It is both your coming into being and your *continued* being which depends on the personal uncaused being. Could there be greater caring or assumption of greater responsibility for you? As for *respect*, your freedom of will says it all. Although you may, like so many, avoid exercising your freedom, what you are to be is totally in your creative hands. Yes, many things are outside your choice, but how you will respond, even to the inevitable, is in your hands. And the uncaused being made you as you are, free. This personal uncaused being *knows* you in a mysterious, supreme way of knowing. Your very being is the result of God's willing you as known, and so known in the most intimate aspects of your being.

If you can accept the truth about the relation of the uncaused being and yourselves, you can recognize how reasonable it is to interpret your relationship with the uncaused being as a personal relationship of love. Knowing this love is personally for you evokes a responding love for this transcendent something within your own experience of the precious human love you have for one another.

It gets embarrassing, even painful, to realize that for so long one has ignored this personal relationship, this loving God.

EXPERIENCING THE PRESENCE OF GOD

If then I am able to experience this personal, loving, uncaused being in loving, I know that God must be near. It seems reasonable to look for other indications of this mysterious presence. Is it only in loving that I encounter God? Once I have interpreted the experience of loving as involving encounter with this uncaused, loving being, I can recognize the mysterious presence in other experiences. The stab of consciousness I feel when I meet exquisite beauty in nature, painting, or music, the awe that comes over me when I see majestic beauty; the sense of the sacred in dealing with others; the awareness of personal responsibility in face of this personal being inviting me in my conscience to do what is right; the peaceful sense that wells up when I contemplate the sea, its waves, and currents - all of these experiences can be interpreted as encounters with the uncaused, personal, loving being.

A skeptic can challenge the interpretation of these as experiences of God. But once God's existence has been rigorously established and linked with the experience of love, it is reasonable to interpret these other experiences in that way as well. They can at the very least be reminders that God is real and present. Certainly they intimate something beyond the sensible and the ordinary.

Surely not all we experience is beautiful. But this is not the place to open up the problem of evil, the moral evil of human sinful choices with the resulting human suffering or the physical evil of disease or the seeming viciousness of a nature involving large scale killing and death of some things for the survival of others. The problems involved are profound. Some people find evil so overwhelming that they feel there can be no God. It is essential that the question be asked only after one has discovered the need to affirm God's existence. In fact it makes little sense to try to solve the problem of evil before one recognizes that reason leads to the affirmation of an infinite, good being.

Volumes have been written on this *problem*, which is more aptly looked upon as a mystery. Let me just mention three insights I find helpful. Evil is not just negation, but privation of good. Lack of sight in a rock is negation, in a person it is privation, the absence of a good which *ought* to be present. Privation occurs then in something existing. Only if there is something can privation occur. We have argued in great detail that for anything to be there is need of an uncaused being. Therefore only if there is an uncaused being can there be privation! For only if there is an uncaused being can there be anything in which privation could occur.

On the other hand to claim there could be a better way to have created this universe seems laughable. Does anyone imagine he understands so well what is involved in creating a universe that he knows how the uncaused being could have created a better one?

Finally, as I see it, I have sufficient evidence that God is and that God is good and loving that I trust God cares and will work good out of the evil. And that in heaven I'll understand this mystery.

I find it reasonable and I prefer to bracket the mystery of evil and to concentrate on the positive reminders that God is and is near and caring.

THE RELIGIOUS DIMENSION OF THE PERSON

All of this intellectualizing can mislead. To enter into personal relationship with the transcendent is a matter of holistic response, a matter of religion, not of philosophy. In fact your relation to this transcendent something grows out of a response different from any evoked so far. The heart of the response so far has been intellectual - seeking an answer to the question, "Why do contingent beings exist?" Linking the answer, the uncaused necessary being, with your experience of love and the other experiences mentioned can transform the response because you can realize that you have already been knowing and meeting this uncaused being in these experiences. But it remains a "knowing" - of the head rather than the heart.

Furthermore, if you feel delighted with the firm foundation given your love by the rigorous reasoning process, the feeling will not last! Why? Because the reasoning to the uncaused entity is highly abstract and before long its force will fade. So you need to nurture your conviction in the reality of this being and in the relation it has to your love.

To encourage a personal relationship with the uncaused being, examine other deep needs you surely experience. At times you must experience a dread of aloneness, of being alone, for actually you are alone, separate, cut off from everyone and everything. One of the great joys in your love for one another, the sense that you will "never be alone again," is an illusion. He or she will die some day and you will be even more alone than ever. It's also common to repress the very idea of dying. You yourself will die and what then? Will you simply be no more or will you face a terrifying unknown alone?

So you experience these other deep questions. I say you "experience" but normally you are affected through repression of them. The deepest you nonetheless thirsts for answers and solutions. Am I totally alone? Is this life all there is? Does everything happen by chance? Is there no thing, no one, who cares for this universe and who ensures that ultimately everything makes sense and works out for good; that good, not evil triumphs? These are the questions that the religious dimension of the human person poses, if one is courageous enough to articulate them and one's culture permits entertaining them.

These are concerns for which, through experience and reflection, the centuries have provided answers, negations, corrections, and reaffirmations. I hope only to open up the central avenues of these solutions. If the suggested answers beckon, you can stroll down those avenues, since answers have been discovered and communities around you do live out the answers.

The way the God issue has been developing is the exact reverse of the way religion developed historically. Babies are born atheists. The human race began as atheists. I mean this in the sense that people had to discover God. Youngsters have to learn about God. Deep within the human person, however, pulsates a religious sense. Once people became self-conscious through the emergence of language, this religious sense became articulated, providing the mythical and cultic answers to deeply experienced problems about death, about suffering, about chance, about being alone, about the very meaning of life.

In the early chapters I described the development of religion as response to human needs once people became self-conscious. Religion was purified and elevated in the unique election of Abraham and the Jewish people; it culminated in Christianity.

Errors, aberrations, harmful practices happened of course. Judaic religion, especially when it flowered in Christianity, leavened the religious world. Belief in one God spread and with it superstitions were overcome and inhuman practices ceased; at least the ideal was set. Development of theology through application of Greek theoretical thinking allowed reflective control of meaning and truth within religion. Actually it was theoretical thinking as philosophy that enabled individuals to establish the reasonableness of interpreting religious experience as genuine encounter with God. Communities could move with confidence in the reasonableness of such interpretation even as they do in the reasonableness of medicine and science in general, because *some* individuals of the community understand.

God was discovered historically through religious response. Only later did we acquire intellectual justification of belief in God and intellectual refinements to insure reasonableness of human responses. Excessive emphasis on theoretical thinking, as it developed into the sciences and technology, led to rationalism and secularism. Belief in God eventually came to be repressed.

Because of this recent state of our history, I find myself developing the God-issue in exactly the reverse order. I start with a theoretical, reasoning justification of belief in the existence of God as the foundation of religion. Only then do I try to make people aware of the religious dimension of the human person: the experienced needs for which religion provides solutions.

It was not by design that I developed the God issue this way. It seemed the most natural thing to appeal first to people's intelligence. Our culture not only greatly esteems intelligence but also has had much experience with religious fraud. People deeply immersed in contemporary consciousness tend to assume there are no rational grounds for belief in God; often they see no difference among religions, lumping sound religious church communities with fads, cults, and bizarre practices. It was essential to establish that belief in God is intellectually responsible and respectable. Only after a rigorous intellectual process can the typically modern person respond to the deep human yearning for God.

Yet intellectual conviction is only the beginning. If people are to open the religious dimension of their "selves," a gift of faith is required. How can they respond religiously to the "necessary being" who personally loves them? If the conviction really counts they will integrate it with their every-day living and their choices will agree with what their reason has established. Tragically, some people intellectually recognize the cogency of the reasoning, and walk away. Has the gift of faith not been proffered? Have they refused the gift? Have other human goods been preferred?

Suppose, then, that readers do open themselves to their religious dimension. They have reasoned to an uncaused being which they identify with the absolute and eternal experienced in their love. Philosophical unfolding of the implications of this uncaused being has made them aware that this encounter with the absolute and eternal establishes a personal relationship with a transcendent person, knowing and loving them. They have at least started to recognize this personal presence in experiences of beauty and majesty, in conscience, and so forth. They are ready for a vital religious union with God.

RELIGIOUS RESPONSE AND HUMAN FULFILLMENT

Why do I hope that the relationship with God will be vital in their lives? For God's benefit? By no means. God is self-sufficient and whatever God does is done for our benefit, not for God's. Well, how is it beneficial? First of all doesn't it seem intelligent that a person live as consciously as possible within all that is real? If it is true that there is a God, doesn't it seem only sensible to live with great awareness of this most important being?

This is not the place to develop what could or should be one's relationship with God, but just consider some ways this awareness can enrich one's life. First of all, belief in God enriches love. Love becomes sacred and definitely forever.

Again, a person can become aware that he is never alone. Nurturing God's presence in prayer can mitigate dreaded loneliness. Since God is always near that means never being alone again. The conviction that someone wonderful and loving is near can dispel the pain of *feeling* absolutely alone.

Aloneness and death are our deepest dreads. Religion has always offered some explanation of death as a means of defusing this dread of dying. In order to establish rigorously that the human person passes to another way of life in dying would require an extended treatment of the spiritual nature of human intelligence and so of the human soul.

Here are listed some aspects of experience which point to that truth, "intimations of immortality": the amazing impossibility to imagine not being, the sacredness of love, the intention that love be forever, the sense that the world cannot be so absurd that the brilliant intelligence, the creative art, the goodness of people I know can simply cease to be.

Christian faith, of course, was launched on belief in the resurrection of Jesus, and on this as the promise of resurrection for all. All this and more prompt me to affirm life, to affirm that somehow those I love will live on beyond death, that I shall live on beyond death. If this uncaused being, intelligent and personal, can love me into being and sustain me here, why wouldn't life with my beloved be possible after the body dies? Especially within a Christian context, the terror of dying is allayed.

Different religions propose different reasons for suffering and change in life. Philosophy can, I submit, establish a providential care for us. Christians believe that not a hair of our heads falls without God, our Father, knowing and caring for us.

In the conflict of choosing between the morally right and the popularly approved, conviction in the existence of God provides strength to persevere in doing what is right. Thus people have the means of standing tall in choices made in the face of social pressure. Confidence that nothing happens without God can generate a profound peace in the face of life's vicissitudes.

PRAYER

Prayer is fundamental in cultivating religious experience. Not *saying* prayers, but prayer. To pray is to turn to God, to enter into communion with God. Recalling that God is ever present, place yourself in God's presence. How do you do that? It is not bizarre, but very similar to the way you can make a loved one present in your mind. You think about her and perhaps imagine being with her; in any event you become very conscious that she is real. This interior presence makes all relationships very precious. Generally we are not really present to each other in this way even when physically present! Normally to establish this sense of the presence of God you have to quiet your body, still your emotions, quiet your imagination, stop your racing thoughts - and gradually come to "feel" the presence of the Lord.

You won't always be able to quiet yourself completely, but your very attempt will be a "successful" prayer. Still I think you can see what I am suggesting. Just think or feel or say what is in your heart. Talk to God. But how do I converse when I do not see anyone or hear any response? You know God is present and frequently you will sense a distinctive presence. So, act as though you are in God's presence. Does God speak in turn? He does, if you let him. What does that mean, "if you let him"? First of all, I'm not saying you will hear voices or any audible response. Any response normally will be interpretative. Often we talk so much in prayer that we do not even try to listen. It is not unlike the garrulous person who just pours out words, draws his conclusions, states them as your advice, thanks you, and leaves--hearing scarcely a word from you. So in prayer you may need to *start* by talking or thinking but then you have to silence both your talking and thinking. Sometimes this leads to emotional, affective response which helps for union. But sometimes there is no affective response and you need to remain silent, even with no affection.

If you do continue silent, not infrequently there is reply from God. Reply in the form of insight that occurs so you understand something about God, about yourself, or about what you should do - something you may never have realized before. The truth aspect of the insight is, I submit, a sign that God is communing with you. Sometimes what comes to mind goes counter to what you usually think or want to do. I believe you can interpret this as God's response. Anyone who enters prayer in this way will understand what I am saying and know satisfying communion with God.

This is not the place for a developed treatment on prayer. If a person recognizes the value and need for prayer at this point, I suggest consulting a spiritual director, since the best way to learn is from a live teacher. At the very least one should consult some books and articles on prayer. God

REVELATION

I would like to open a window on a very profound challenge. Once people have grasped the reality of the uncaused being and the fact that they have met this being and perhaps been united through personal prayer, I suggest they inquire whether this God has ever "spoken" to, ever made contact in a special way, communicated in unmistakable ways, with people. Has God revealed the God-self to people, letting them know who and what God is? Has God given direction for human fulfillment?

Each person must face this challenge for himself. I can only witness that I have lived as a Christian and a Roman Catholic all my life and found the beliefs, practices, and community most satisfying and enriching. These experiences of satisfaction and enrichment cannot logically be grounds for belief, but they do confirm the truth and values of my belief. So I am convinced that Jesus Christ is God become human and that he established a community, a church, on his apostles and that church is found subsistently in the Roman Catholic Church. Since the Second Vatican Council I have been taught to rejoice at how much other Christian churches, other religions share with me.

Within my Christian faith I consider that people are called to be fulfilled both as individuals and in community. They cannot be fulfilled without Jesus Christ. Now to possess Jesus Christ one needs the church to communicate and nurture new life through the sacraments and to inspire and direct through the Scriptures.

I say this not to offer a defence for my life nor to proselytize. Rather I want to show the full picture of the life that is possible. So I ask, "What do you think of Jesus Christ? Who do you say he is?"

Grounding this question about "revelation" is the spontaneous desire to try to understand who this God is that I am now convinced I meet in religious experience or in the experience of love. Here reason can provide only little. Which leads me to the next point.

RELIGIOUS COMMUNITY

The response to an encounter with the transcendent has always been not only prayer but also worship. Normally one worships within a community. So I urge people to examine various religious communities and discover whether any of them appeal as true and responsive to their needs. Not only do they need a community for worship, they need the support of believing, prayerful friends in order to keep their relationship with God vibrant and growing.

Traditional religious communities, fundamentalist groups, fringe groups, and cults abound, so discretion is needed. Keep in mind that although a person can with reason abandon the demand for scientific evidence in religious matters, one ought never to be <u>un</u>reasonable. Common sense can weed out certain groups.

In assessing different religious groups observe certain priorities and orientations. The human person is primarily ordered, it seems clear, to be fulfilled as a human person. This involves physical development, development of the intellect as well as acquisition of knowledge, growth in self control and expansion of the heart in love, not to mention aesthetic appreciation. Religion is a human development aimed at helping in all these directions.

Religion as a human development, of course, is not some arbitrary technique created by people. Particular *forms* of religious lifestyles and particular activities common to all religions were selected and developed by people. But the *foundations* of religions are realities *discovered* by people, not created by them. I have in mind the reality of a transcendent uncaused being and the corresponding validity of worship and prayer. I have in mind the experienced need to understand the meaning of life and death, of suffering and chance, the way to cope with aloneness. I also have in mind revelation accepted reasonably, but, of course, with the gift of faith.

With these preliminaries limned, I advise people to be sure that the religious group they choose does contribute to their growth as intelligent, free, and loving human beings. Communities that, no matter how subtly, impose a leadership cult where the individual abandons his/her intelligence, are simply in error. As a Catholic I submit to Pope and bishops to be guided in my beliefs and practices. But I do so with reflected conviction that God has given them supernatural guidance. All the time I remain attentive to the consistency of their teaching with the entire tradition of the church and I *remain free* to request explanation and even to leave the church if I were to find I couldn't retain personal integrity.

Granted they have embraced what they know by reason, people must find a believing community to nurture their union with God.

Believing Community and Human Needs

Will this believing community isolate one from the broad civic, economic, international community, the human family? Possibly; *de facto* it has and can again. But *de jure* it ought not. In this country Catholics, at least, tended for long time to live a ghetto existence. Even so they built hospitals, orphanages, welfare support systems, schools, colleges, and universities. As a matter of fact, for a long time

Secular Humanists and Marxists have been disconcerted by Christians' involvement in coping with human, this-worldly needs.

Speaking as a Catholic I call attention to the Second Vatican Council's commitment of the Church to this world's needs in *The Pastoral Constitution on the Church in the Modern World* (*Gaudium et Spes*). Clearly the Church proclaims that her people stand shoulder to shoulder with all people as they struggle to develop this world economically, socially, and politically. Sharing the same human nature and thrust-to-fulfillment, they join all others in mutual effort to discover how to build a world of justice and peace and prosperity. They bring the message and empowerment of Christ to shed light on our problems, to achieve mutual goals.

In fact as I synthesize Christian belief, in my commitment in faith to Jesus Christ I become united with Jesus and in that union am united with the Blessed Trinity. I am then missioned not to the Church but to the family of humankind. God's love embraces all people and wants to lead all to human and eternal fulfillment. I, and all Christians, are God's way of being present to empower individuals and societies in achieving human and eternal fulfillment. I retain and need communion with the Church for continued nurturing by gospel and sacraments.

Current concern about overpopulation and pollution remind Christians that God committed the material universe to human beings when Adam and Eve were directed in the initial covenant to "be fruitful and multiply, and fill the earth subdue it; and have dominion over the fish of the sea...and over every living thing..." "Subdue" of course involves responsibility for the flourishing of all things. We do not compete with God when we take responsibility for the future of our universe. But we do try to look upon the universe as God does, who freely and lovingly brought all things into being. Likewise we are open to all that human development and science have uncovered about biological interdependence and the effect of pollution on various forms of life.

An emphatic "No!" then to fear that involvement with a believing community will isolate a person from broader human concerns.

REPLY TO THE TWO INITIAL QUESTIONS

Since the uncaused entity is indeed God and since now it is reasonable to interpret religious experiences and experience of truth and love as encountering God, a resounding "Yes!" to our first question. An intelligent person can and ought to acknowledge there is a God.

Intellectual reflection can apply the reasoning process from a contingent event (Someone will read a sentence...) to one's love (which, though it wondrously is, need not be), and to one's very self. God loves me into existence; God ultimately causes my love. "The world is full of the grandeur of God," Hopkins sang. Once convinced that God exists, a person is sensitive to other signs of God's presence.

It is unlikely that intellectual speculation can generate such intimate response. But men and women are more than intellects and people depend on lifestyle more than intelligence. Centuries before theoretical thinking emerged people discovered religion as the means to accept chance and suffering, to face dying, and to find meaning for life itself. False beliefs and excesses penetrated religions, causing terrible human harm. Judaism with its rigid monotheism and faith, a blend of assent to God speaking, trust in God promising and obedience to God commanding, especially as transformed by Christianity, purified religion - at least so I believe. With the polytheistic deities banished and the intelligibility of the universe accepted, science could rise and flourish. Reason came to be esteemed and superstition was substantially muted if not eliminated. Excess once again, this time in esteem of reason, particularly scientific reason, generated secular humanism, banishing religion to the realm of imagination. But granted that belief in God is reasonable, then it is also reasonable to cultivate relationship with God and accept the benefits of religion into our lives. Religious people will of course be more critical than in earlier days. Truth will be checked and demanded in every area. Values will be assessed in terms of human fulfillment.

The resounding "Yes" to our initial question echoes in answering the second one. It seems only logical to recognize that knowing and relating to God is a basic part of human nature.

SUMMARY AND CONCLUSION

And so in summary - if you have accepted each step as valid, then your intellectual integrity demanded that you acknowledge there is an uncaused being. If you accepted my interpretation of your experience in your love, namely that somehow you encounter something absolute and eternal in your love, then you can see it is reasonable to interpret that experience and, all the more, religious experiences as encountering this uncaused being. If you accepted as valid my unraveling the implications of the uncaused being, you know you have a relationship with a personal, intelligent, loving being. If you have perceived the connection of your other experiences,--such as beauty, majesty, sacredness, conscience--with this personal being, that relationship has been enriched. If you have allowed yourself to face your experienced needs for an answer to your aloneness, to your awareness of death as inevitable, to the meaning of suffering, chance, of life itself, then you will also have allowed your own religious dimension to be expressed. If you have entered into prayer and investigated religious communities, especially after inquiring whether God has ever revealed himself, then you have established a religious lifestyle, capable of nurturing your relationship with God. You have agreed to embrace the world view and lifestyle of the community. You are well on your way to a life of love and the richest form of sharing, -- on your way to the greatest happiness this world has to offer. And this life of love, sharing, and happiness will have you facing out to all the world, joining with all, believers and nonbelievers, to correct the abuses of our material universe and the gross economic imbalances - ready to build a new world of justice and peace.

APPENDIX I

GLOSSARY

ACT AND POTENCY

> **ACT**: the correlate of potency which expresses the fully present realization or completion of potency.
> **POTENCY**: the capacity or aptitude in a being to receive some perfection or perform some action.
> [Matter is potency; form is act. Essence is potency; existence is act.]
> Potency and act defy identification, conceptually and ontologically
> **N.B.** Cf. Chapter 12 for explanation of Matter and Form, Essence and Existence, Potency and Act.
> Potency and act are not things but principles and as such are essentially incomplete and naturally corroborative.

AWARENESS: This author's preferred term for what is generally referred to as consciousness.
> Awareness is always awareness of something (e.g. color, pain) and simultaneously awareness of being aware. Awareness is always of *being aware*, of having been aware, and of going to be aware. Likewise, awareness is awareness of being now, of having been, and of going to be. As listed in Chapter 6 we find eleven forms of awareness, only one of which is awareness of knowing. However, knowing seems to infuse all other forms of awareness and to monitor all other awarenesses. It is the ultimate arbiter of truth in all awarenesses.

CAUSE: A state of affairs which obtains (occurs or exists), an extrapropositional condition not included in another state of affairs, one which must be satisfied in order that the latter state of affairs may obtain (occur or exist).

CONTINGENT: A state of affairs which might or might not obtain
> A proposition which picks out a contingent state of affairs.

ESSENCE AND EXISTENCE

> Essence and existence are co-principles of being whence the existent thing is constituted.

ESSENCE: as a principle of an actual existing thing, it is the element that provides a full explanation of the whatness of the existent as being, i.e. as susceptible of the formal act of "esse" or existence.

EXISTENCE: (makes not the smallest addition to that whatness) It is the primary component of actuality. It is not a form, but an act, the act whereby a thing is present in nature, whereby a thing is different from nothing and outside the causes of its becoming. Existence is the act that effects the release of essence from a most remote hold on actuality; prior to this release, essence's only claim to actuality is its susceptibility to receive it.

EXTRAPROPOSITIONAL: Pertains to the state of affairs or fact. To be not only in the proposition in the mind, but also outside the proposition or outside the mind.

MATTER AND FORM

MATTER: the subject of change, that which is capable of taking on new forms.

Primary Matter: the subject of substantial change (as in generation and corruption)
Generation: from non-being to being - e.g., nondog to dog
Corruption: change from being to non-being - e.g. from dog to cadaver or non-dog

Secondary Matter: the subject of accidental change (as in a dog undergoing growth)

NATURALISM: The philosophical and (a)theological world-view that this material universe is all there is. The fundamental form of atheism.

NECESSARY: A state of affairs or a being which cannot not be. Pertains to God as the uncaused entity.
A proposition which picks out a necessary state of affairs or a necessary being.

OBTAIN: The "state of affairs" or "fact" "exists."
The state of affairs picked out by the proposition by that very fact is in the mind. That state of affairs also is outside of the mind, outside of the proposition if it obtains. It is *extra*propositional. A

state of affairs obtains when the proposition which picks out that state of affairs is true. In most contexts "occur" or "exist" is a synonym for "obtain."

PICKS OUT: The function of a proposition
The understanding presents a delimited content.
The proposition presents, pro-poses to the mind this delimited content to be assessed and subsequently to be either affirmed or denied.

POSIT: Declare something exists. E.g. "to posit an uncaused cause" is to declare an uncaused cause exists.

POTENCY: See Act and Potency - p. 255

PROPOSITION: The interior act of knowing, which is expressed by a (declarative) sentence.

Parts: Its parts are "name," which identifies the referent, that to which the knowing refers, and "predicable," which determines the sense, that which is being entertained by the mind about the referent. E.g., In "John is tall" the "name" is John; the "predicable" is, is tall.

Name and predicable together pick out or present or propose a state of affairs for the mind to assess and then to affirm or deny. E.g., "Vacation is over."

Truth: **True Proposition**: A proposition is true when the state of affairs it picks out obtains or exists. E.g., Bluejays fly.

False Proposition: A proposition is false when the state of affairs it picks out does not obtain or exist. E.g., Horses fly.

True Affirmation: One affirms a proposition which is true.

False Affirmation: One affirms a proposition which is false.

True Denial: One denies a proposition which is false.

False Denial: One denies a proposition which is true.

N.B. One has truth, one knows what is real, when one affirms a true proposition or when one denies a false proposition.

SELF-SUFFICIENT: A state of affairs or a being which has within itself the reason or grounds for being what it is and for obtaining or existing.

STATE OF AFFAIRS: The content of a proposition
The "fact" the mind proposes for assessment and affirmation or denial
That which corresponds in reality to what the mind proposes for assessment, etc.

That which is real if the proposition is true
> **N.B.** This use of "fact" permits that what is considered a fact may not be a fact, may be an error.
> The proposition is in the mind, the state of affairs is what corresponds in reality, if the proposition is true.
> Thus propositions are true or false. States of affairs obtain or do not obtain, exist or do not exist.

THEORETICAL STATE OF AFFAIRS OR BEING: A state of affairs or a being which reason leads us to posit or to declare exists. A person reaches knowledge of such a state of affairs or being because he knows his proposition about it is true even without any new awareness of it. "Theoretical," however, is not the same as "hypothetical."

UNCAUSED CAUSE: A cause which exists and causes without dependence on anything other than itself for its being or causing.

UNCAUSED ENTITY: A being which exists but has no cause of its existence. It exists because of what it is.

VIRTUALLY UNCONDITIONED: The unconditioned is that which cannot not be. It has no conditions. The virtually unconditioned is something conditioned, something which is, *only* if certain conditions are fulfilled and the conditions *are* actually fulfilled. Thus it is called virtually unconditioned because, granted the conditions are fulfilled, it cannot not be.

To know what is real is to grasp the virtually unconditioned. Once a question arises within some awareness, a proposition is formed to be assessed, then affirmed or denied. When a person understands what must be the case for the proposition to be true, under what conditions it would be true, and recognizes that such is the case, that those conditions obtain, he grasps the virtually unconditioned. Then a person experiences the need to affirm the proposition.

APPENDIX II

REFINEMENT BETWEEN UNCAUSED CAUSE AND UNCAUSED ENTITY

I have not denied the traditional understanding of God as uncaused cause. The refined distinction between uncaused cause and uncaused entity required for the quasi-empirical proof used to be discussed from a different perspective in traditional metaphysics.

Consider the subtle problem this perspective raises and its solution.

Traditional theistic metaphysics explains the distinction between uncaused cause and uncaused entity by holding that God creates freely. This freedom in creation alerts us to God's love for us. Love prompts God to communicate being to us. Satisfying as this may be emotionally, it poses one of the greatest mysteries in the human effort to understand God. If creation is not free then God creates necessarily and it becomes difficult to avoid pantheism, difficult to see how we can reason to a transcendent being at all.

Metaphysics can show that God is infinite and immutable. But the decision to create freely would seem to demand that something be added to the infinite God and that the immutable God must be affected. We cannot positively explain how God is not affected by a free decision to create. Furthermore, to deny that creation brings about change in God would, in human terms, seem to suggest that "It doesn't matter" to God whether God creates or not, whether we exist or not!

Change in God is contradictory. Far more satisfying is the mystery of free creation not affecting the infinite, immutable God. As Thomas insists, human knowledge of God ends in darkness and mystery, for while we can know *that* God exists, we can not know *what* God is.

SOURCES AND ENRICHMENT

Part I
Chapter 1

Besides the references in the text such as the plays, Freud, Jung, and Lepp, consider:

Casey, Joseph H. *From Why to Yes.* Washington, D.C.: University Press of America, Inc., 1982
Fowler, James W. *Stages of Faith.* San Francisco: Harper & Row Publishers, 1981.
———. *Faith Development and Pastoral Care.* Philadelphia: Fortress Press, 1987.
Stokes, Kenneth. *Faith Is a Verb.* Mystic, Connecticut: Twenty-third Publications, 1989.

Chapters 2, 3, and 4

Data on the origin, growth, and likely growth of Atheism I take from Buckley's work.

Buckley, Michael, S.J. *At the Origins of Modern Atheism.* New Haven: Yale University Press, 1990.

Contemporary Consciousness

I insist that contemporary consciousness blocks out consideration of God, certainly a strange claim since so many people profess and practice Christian, Jewish, Muslim, and Hindu religions. And since the media cover events in the respective religious communities, reference to God, to services of prayer and worship, is not everybody exposed to the media conscious of God? It was therefore critical to establish that there is a "historically distinctive dominant mainstream consciousness" influencing the many consciousnesses proper to distinctive communities. I am indebted to Professor Paul G. Schervish of the Sociology Department of Boston College for invaluable suggestions on the necessary distinctions. The following works provided the light.

Abercrombie, N., S. Hill, B. Turner. *The Dominant Ideology Thesis.* London: George Allen & Unwin, 1980.
Bellah, Robert N. *Beyond Belief.* New York: Harper & Row, Publishers, Inc., 1970.

Bellah, Robert, Richard Madsen, William M. Sullivan, Ann Swidler, and Steven M. Tipton. *Habits of the Heart.* New York: Harper and Row, 1985.
Herberg, Will. *Protestant-Catholic-Jew.* Garden City, New York: Doubleday & Co., 1960.

Characteristics of Contemporary Consciousness

I relied largely on Gilkey and Tyrrell.
Gilkey, Langdon. *Naming the Whirlwind: The Renewal of God-Language.* Indianapolis: Bobbs-Merrill, 1969.
Tyrrell, Francis M. *Bernard Lonergan's Philosophy of God.* Notre Dame, Indiana: University of Notre Dame Press, 1974.

The following books may prove helpful. Bloom, Allan. *The Closing of the American Mind.* New York: Simon and Schuster, Inc., 1987.
Curtis, Charles, Gerald Kreyche, and Helmut Loiskandl. *Perspectives on God: Sociological, Theological and Philosophical.* Washington, D.C.: University Press of America, 1978.
Dunne, John S. *A Search for God in Time and Memory.* Notre Dame, Indiana: University of Notre Dame Press, 1977.
Robinson, John A. *Honest to God.* Phildelphia: Westminster Press, 1963.

Elsewhere I have reported on the way contemporary theater portrays the consciousness of people today. I found the same reflected in movies and especially on television. I shall just mention some playwrights and their plays and a few helpful books.
Sam Shepard, *Buried Child, Fool for Love, A Lie of the Mind*
David Rabe, *Streamers, Sticks and Bones, Hurlyburly*
Christopher Durang, *Sister Mary Ignatius Explains It All for You, Beyond Therapy*
August Wilson, *Fences*
Alfred Uhrey, *Driving Miss Daisy*
Lanford Wilson, *Burn This*
David Mamet, *Edmond, Speed the Plow*
Daving Henry Wang, *M. Butterfly*
Wendy Wasserstein, *The Heidi Chronicles, Isn't It Romantic?*

Compare the presence or absence of God in such contemporary plays and the great Greek tragedies, the mystery plays of the Middle

Ages, Shakespeare, or Graham Greene's *The Potting Shed* or Peter Shaeffer's *Amadeus* or *Equus*.

The following works broaden understanding of contemporary playwrights.

Mamet, David. *Writing in Restaurants.* Viking Penguin Inc., 1986.
Marranca, Bonnie. ed. *American Dreams.* New York: Performing Arts Journal Publications, 1981).
Mottram, Ron. *Inner Landscapes.* Columbia: University of Missouri Press, 1984)
Savran, David. *In Their Own Words: Contemporary American Playwrights.* New York: Theatre Communications Group, 1988.
Shewey, Don. *Sam Shepard.* New York: Dell Publishing Co., 1985.
Oumano, Ellen. *Sam Shepard.* New York: St. Martin's Press, 1986.

I found these four books helpful for covering the movies.

Butler, Ivan. *Religion in the Cinema.* New York: A. S. Barnes & Co., 1969.
Campbell, Richard H. and Michael R. Pitts. *The Bible on Film.* Metuchen: The Scarecrow Press, 1981.
Keyser, Les and Barbara. *Hollywood and the Catholic Church.* Chicago: Loyola University Press, 1984.
May, John R. and Michael Bird, eds. *Religion in Film.* Knoxville: The University of Tennessee Press, 1982.

I just mention the following for television and sociology.

Fink, Conrad C. *Media Ethics.* New York: McGraw-Hill Book Company, 1988.
Fore, William F. *Television and Religion.* Minneapolis: Augsburg Publishing House, 1987.

Chapter 3

The idea of and framework for the development of Contemporary Consciousness through options is found in John Courtney Murray's *Problem of God*, the series of lectures he delivered at Yale.

Foundational to the treatment of the historical development was *The Legitimacy of the Modern Age.* Crombie and Dampier fill out the data. Barbour addresses the limited area of science.

Barbour, Ian G. *Issues in Science and Religion.* Englewood Cliffs, New Jersey: Prentice-Hall, Inc., 1966.
Blumenberg, Hans. *The Legitimacy of the Modern Age.* translated by Robert M. Wallace, Cambridge, Mass.: MIT Press, 1983.

Crombie, A. C. *Augustine to Galileo.* Cambridge, Mass.: Harvard University Press, 1953.
Dampier, Sir William Cecil. *A Shorter History of Science.* New York: Meridian Books, 1959.
Murray, John Courtney, S.J. *The Problem of God.* New Haven: Yale University Press, 1964.

Copleston has a remarkable gift for simplifying and synthesizing. So I recommend appropriate sections in Vol. III for the period preparing for Galileo, in Vol. V for Hume's philosophy, Vol. VI for Kant, and Vol. VII for Nietzsche.

Copleston, Frederick S.J. *A History of Philosophy.* Vol. III: Ockham to Suarez. Vol. V: Hobbes to Hume. Vol. VI: Wolff to Kant. Vol. VII: Fichte to Nietzsche. London: Burns and Oates Limited, 1963.

More serious challenge and analysis of Hume and Kant can be found in these works:

Donceel, J, ed. *A Maréchal Reader.* New York: Herder and Herder, 1970.
Grisez, Germain. *Beyond the New Theism.* Chapters 6-9. Notre Dame, Indiana: University of Notre Dame Press, 1975.
Shine, D. J. ed. *An Interior Metaphysics: The Philosophical Synthesis of Pierre Scheuer, S.J.* Weston, Mass.: Weston College Press, 1966.

Multiple currents of influence emerged in the 19th and 20th centuries. Ellul uncovers the spread of "technique" into all areas of life. Murray again brilliantly etches the characteristics of Marxist Communism and despairing Existentialism. But selected readings in Kierkegaard and Nietzsche themselves are invaluable.

Bretall, Robert. ed. *A Kierkegaard Anthology.* New York: Random House, 1946. [especially "Either/Or" and "Fear and Trembling"]
Ellul, Jacques. *The Technological Society.* translated by John Wilkinson. New York: Random House, 1964.
Jaspers, Karl. *Nietzsche.* translated by Charles F. Wallraff and Frederick J. Schmitz. Tucson, Arizona: The University of Arizona Press, 1965.
Manthey-Zorn, Otto. ed. *Nietzsche: An Anthology of His Works.* translated by Otto Manthey-Zorn. New York: Washington Square

Press, 1964. [especially "Thus Spoke Zarathustra," "The Birth of Tragedy," and "Will to Power"]
Murray, John Courtney, S.J. op. cit.

The work on Communism and Existentialism is so vast I limit myself to a few suggestions.
Cochrane, Arthur C. *The Existentialists and God.* Philadelphia: The Westminster Press, 1956.
Lescoe, Francis J. *Existentialism.* New York: Alba House, 1974.
Marcel, Gabriel. *Problematic Man.* translated by Brian Thompson. New York: Herder and Herder, 1967.
Marx, Karl and Frederick Engels. *Manifesto of the Communist Party.* Moscow: Foreign Languages Publishing House, 1957.
Sartre, Jean-Paul. *Existentialism.* translated by Bernard Frechtman. New York: Philosophical Library, Inc., 1947.
_____. *Being and Nothingness.* translated by Hazel E. Barnes. New York: Washington Square Press, 1973.
Wetter, Gustav A. *Dialectical Materialism.* translated by Peter Heath. New York: Frederick A. Praeger, Inc., 1958.

The understanding of the counterculture is basically my own. But these few references capture the meaning and the spirit of the movement. Nietzsche's *The Birth of Tragedy* provides the distinction of the Apollonian, Dionysian, and Socratic elements in all of us.

Reich, Charles A. *The Greening of America.* New York: Random House, 1970.
Winter, Gibson. *Being Free.* New York: Macmillan Company, 1970.

For the significant section on apologetics leading to atheism at the hands of Diderot and d'Holback I have "pirated" the brilliant study by Michael Buckley, S.J.
Buckley, Michael, S.J. *At the Origin of Modern Atheism* [data given in Chapter 2]

Chapter 5

Throughout this work I inveigh against "scientism" but no one can get a hearing today who does not respect "science." The collaborative effort between religion and science is recorded in the two volumes referred to: *On Science and Religion and Physics, Philosophy and Theology.* The latter is referred to under "Dispositive Arguments" as well.

The challenge to fideists is derived from J. C. Murray's *Problem of God*. My references to Thomas might profitably be checked, especially since I appeal often to our ignorance of what God is and the threefold way of predicating anything of God.

Aquinas, St. Thomas. *Summa Theologiae*, Blackfriars Edition. New York: McGraw-Hill, 1964. Part I, Question 1, Article 1; Question 2, Article 1; Question 3, Introduction; Question 12, Article 12; Question 13, Article1.

Murray, John Courtney, S.J. op. cit.

In order to ensure that readers approach the question of God's existence as a serious question I expose the "dispositive arguments" in Van Steenberghen's book.

Van Steenberghen, Fernand. *Hidden God*. translated by Theodore Crowley, O.F.M. St. Louis, Missouri: B. Herder Book Co., 1966.

For readers desiring more information about primitive religions I suggest these works:

Dawson, Christopher. *Religion and the Rise of Western Culture*. New York: Doubleday & Company, Inc., 1958.
_____. *Progress and Religion*. New York: Sheed and Ward, 1938.
Eliade, Mircea. *Myth and Reality*. translated by Willard Trask, New York: Harper and Row, 1963.
_____. *Myths, Dreams and Mysteries*. translated by Philip Mairet, New York: Harper and Brothers, 1960.
Radin, Paul. *Primitive Man as Philosopher*. New York: Dover Publications, Inc., 1957.
Schmidt, W. *The Origin and Growth of Religion*. translated by H. J. Rose, London: Methuen & Co. , 1931.

Part II
Chapter 6
The steps taken to reach agreement on the meaning of God are my own, influenced however by Linguistic Analysts like Wittgenstein, Ramsey, and Flew.

Flew, Antony and Alasdair MacIntyre. *New Essays in Philosophical Theology*. New York: Macmillan Company, 1955.
Ramsey, Ian T. *Religious Language*. London: SCM Press Ltd., 1957.
Wittgenstein, Ludwig. *Philosophical Investigations*. translated by G. E. M. Anscombe. Oxford, England: Basil Blackwell and Mott, Ltd., 1953.

Chapters 7 and 8

The second point of necessary agreement, the method of reasoning, prompts a brief exposition of the theory of knowledge. Some years ago I worked out an explanation of "awareness," one form of which is "knowing." I incorporate Grisez's theory of knowledge within my analysis of the awareness of knowing. My approach is phenomenological and closely dependent upon Aristotelian-Thomistic theory of knowledge.

Grisez, Germain. *Beyond the New Theism.* Notre Dame, Indiana: University of Notre Dame Press, 1975.
Hoenen, Peter, H. *Reality and Judgment according to St. Thomas.* translated by Henry F. Tiblier. Chicago: Henry Regnery Co., 1952.

Background for rejection of scientism has already been given, see especially Copleston, Shine, Donceel and Grisez.

I did not attempt a thorough, technical treatment of knowing or/and reasoning. Nor do I intend a scholarly set of references. But it is essential to explain what is involved in, and the need for, an intellectual conversion. What I have in mind is Lonergan's "virtually unconditioned." His *Insight* and *Method in Theology* are fundamental. Tyrrell's summary may prove more manageable.

What is most worthy of concentration is the "virtually unconditioned" and intellectual conversion.
Lonergan, Bernard J. F., S.J. *Insight.* New York: Philosophical Library, 1956.
_____.*Method in Theology.* New York: Herder and Herder, 1972.
Tyrrell, Francis M. op. cit.
Finally, the two other conversions, moral and religious: Lonergan for the former; Marcel, DeLubac, and Lonergan for the latter.

DeLubac, Henri. *The Discovery of God.* translated by Alexander Dru. Chicago: Henry Regnery Company, 1967.
Lonergan, Bernard S.J. *Method in Theology.*
Marcel, Gabriel. op.cit.
Tyrrell, Francis M. op. cit.

Part III
Chapters 9 and 10

I have merely simplified and spelled out Grisez's argument in Chapters 4 and 5 of his *Beyond the New Theism*.

Some modern presentations of the traditional metaphysical argument (in order of simplicity):
Purtill, Richard L. *Thinking about Religion*. New Jersey: Prentice-Hall, 1978. Chapters 3 and 4.
Benedetto, Arnold, S.J. *Fundamentals in the Philosophy of God*. New York: The Macmillan Company, 1963.
Maritain, Jacques. *Approaches to God*. translated by Peter O'Reilly. New York: Harper, 1954.
von Balthasar, Hans Urs. *The God Question and Modern Man*. translated by Hilda Graef. New York: The Seabury Press, 1967.
DeLubac, Henri, op.cit.
Clarke, W. Norris, S.J. T*he Philosophical Approach to God*. Winston-Salem, North Carolina: Wake Forest University, 1979.

Contemporary research on the existence and nature of God can be tasted in the following. The first underscores the Catholic Church's openness to science and contemporary thought. Pope John Paul II convoked a meeting of twenty-one eminent researchers at the Papal Residence at Castel Gandolfo to explore topics of common interest for scientists, philosophers, and theologians. The second proffers typical research today on the God-issue.

Russell, Robert J., William R. Stoeger, S.J., George V. Coyne, S.J. eds. *Physics, Philosophy, and Theology*. Notre Dame, Indiana: University of Notre Dame Press, 1988.
Morris, Thomas V. ed. *The Concept of God*. New York: Oxford University Press, 1987.
Davies, Brian. *Thinking about God*. London: Geoffrey Chapman, 1985.
McCabe, Herbert. *God Matters*. London: Geoffrey Chapman, 1987. Part I.

Chapter 11

For experience of the eternal and absolute, the best work on "love" as involving encounter with God is Hassel's. For experience of God in truth I suggest two works by Donceel.

Donceel, J. F., S.J. *Natural Theology.* New York: Sheed and Ward, 1962.

_____.*The Searching Mind.* Notre Dame, Indiana: University of Notre Dame Press, 1979.

Hassel, David, S.J. *Searching the Limits of Love.* Chicago: Loyola University Press, 1985.

Part IV
Chapters 12 through 16

To catch the flavor of humanistic Naturalism I'd suggest two short books, *Common Faith* and *A Short History of Western Atheism.* For the strongest case made against belief in God's existence I recommend Flew. Son of a parson, he understands religion; he also understands traditional arguments. I have studied under him, have taught his book, and feel comfortable about refuting all his arguments.

Dewey, John. *A Common Faith.* New Haven: Yale University Press, 1934.

Thrower,l James. *A Short History of Western Atheism.* London: Pemberton Publishing Co. Ltd., 1971.

Flew, Antony. *God and Philosophy.* New York: Harcourt, Brace and World, Inc., 1966.

Here are works by Naturalists justifying their position.

Huxley, Julian. ed. *The Humanist Frame.* London: George Allen and Unwin, Ltd., 1965.

Lamont, Corliss. *Humanism as a Philosophy.* New York: Philosophical Library, Inc., 1949.

Martin, Michael. *Atheism: A Philosophical Justification.* Philadelphia: Temple University Press, 1990.

Wieman, Henry Nelson. *Man's Ultimate Commitment.* Carbondale, Illinois: Southern Illinois University Press, 1958.

Cohen, Jack J. *The Case for Religious Naturalism.* New York: The Reconstructionist Press, 1958.

Krikorian, Yervant H. *Naturalism and the Human Spirit.* New York: Columbia University Press, 1944.

Another work gives us "A major statement of the case against belief in God." A series of articles by convinced atheists.

Angeles, Peter. ed. *Critiques of God*. Buffalo, New York: Prometheus Books, 1976.

Interestingly, two authors approach the God-question on the basis of probability, with contradictory results: Mackie for atheism while Swinburne finds grounds for belief in God.

Mackie, J.L. *The Miracle of Theism*. Oxford: Clarendon Press, 1982.
Swinburne, Richard. *The Existence of God*. Oxford: Clarendon Press, 1979.

To frame Naturalism historically Hartshorne and Reese and Collins should help.

Hartshorne, Charles and William L. Reese. *Philosophers Speak of God*. Chicago: University of Chicago Press, 1953.
Collins, James. *The Emergence of Philosophy of Religion*. New Haven: Yale University Press, 1967.

Ways of appreciating the issue and the believer's response may be found in the following -- as well as in the works previously listed, such as Grisez, DeLubac, Maritain, von Balthasar, Norris Clarke, and Marcel.

Hebblethwaite, Peter, S.J. *The Council Fathers and Atheism*. New York: Paulist Press, 1966.
Tyrrell, Francis M. *Man: Believer and Unbeliever*. New York: Alba House, 1973.
Masterson, Patrick. *Atheism and Alienation*. Notre Dame, Indiana: University of Notre Dame Press, 1971.
Bertocci, Peter. *Introduction to the Philosophy of Religion*. New York: Prentice-Hall, Inc., 1955.
Thompson, Samuel. *A Modern Philosophy of Religion*. Chicago: Henry Regnery Company, 1955.

As for my rejection of the first supposition, the idea that the logic of explanation ultimately demands the acceptance of matter of fact is in Flew (*God and Philosophy*). Lonergan's tour de force argument I took from *Insight* (XIX, 8). Grisez's *Beyond the New Theism*, Chapter 5, employs the rationality norms.

The treatment of Naturalism's second supposition derives from Grisez's *Beyond the New Theism,* Chapter 5, but developed considerably. I outline a proof of freedom of self-determination based upon Free Choice and intimate the direction to argue the immortality of the soul. For the latter you would find Reichmann helpful. To get to the heart of the challenge of Naturalism I had to introduce Aristotelian-Thomistic metaphysics. For further probing of those insights I suggest Wallace and Sweeney. M. Clark's Aquinas Reader will give you Thomas's argument for the identity of essence and existence in God.

Grisez, Germain. op. cit. Chapter 5.
Boyle, Joseph, Jr., Germain Grisez, and Olaf Tollefsen. *Free Choice.* Notre Dame, Indiana: University of Notre Dame Press, 1976.
Clark, Mary T. ed. *An Aquinas Reader.* I. Uncreated Being: God, 1. His Existence. Garden City, New York: Doubleday & Company, Inc., 1972.
Reichmann, James B., S.J. *Philosophy of the Human Person.* Chicago: Loyola University Press, 1985.
Sweeney, Leo, S.J. *A Metaphysics of Authentic Existentialism.* Englewood Cliffs, New Jersey: Prentice-Hall, Inc., 1965.
Wallace, William A., O.P. *The Elements of Philosophy.* New York: Alba House, 1977.

Chapter 17

The final chapter attempts to lead the reader, assuming she has been convinced by the reasoning to the uncaused being, to incorporate that truth into her life. Erich Fromm offers the four characteristics of love I suggest pondering. Becker uncovers the universal dread of dying. Adler opens the door to revelation and Reiser's book on *A Spirituality of Revelation* may prove helpful. The following works on prayer may open horizons to new dimensions of living. If one enters a life of prayer he may want to get Father William Menninger's tapes on Centering Prayer.

Adler, Mortimer. *How to Think about God. A Guide for the 20th Century Pagan.* New York: Macmillan Publishing Co., Inc., 1980.
Becker, Ernest. *The Denial of Death.* New York: Macmillan Publishing Co., Inc., 1975.
Bloom, Anthony. *Courage to Pray.* New York: Paulist Press, 1973.
Catechism of the Catholic Church. Liguori, MO: Liguori Publications, 1994

de Mello, Anthony, S.J. Sadhana: *A Way to God.* St. Louis: The Institute of Jesuit Sources, 1978.
Fromm, Erich. *The Art of Loving.* New York: Bantam Books, 1967.
Green, Thomas H., S.J. *Opening to God.* Notre Dame, Indiana: Ave Maria Press, 1977.
Grisez, Germain. op. cit. Chapter 15 (on Revelation).
John Paul II. *Crossing the Threshold of Hope.* New York: Alfred A. Knopf, 1994.
Kreeft, Peter and Ronald Tacelli. *Handbook of Christian Apologetics.* Downer's Grove, IL 60515: Intervarsity Press, 1994
Lewis, C. S. *Letters to Malcolm:* Chiefly on Prayer. New York: Harcourt, Brace & World, 1964.
Menninger, William. *Centering Prayer.* Snowmass, CO 81654: Cistercian Abbey, 3 audio cassettes.
Pennington, M. Basil, O.C.S.O. *Daily We Touch Him.* Garden City, New York: Doubleday and Company, Inc., 1977.
Reiser, William E., S.J. *Drawn to the Divine.* Notre Dame, Indiana: Ave Maria Press, 1987.
Wijngaards, John, M.H.M. *Experiencing Jesus.* Notre Dame, Indiana: Ave Maria Press, 1981.